Praise

In a fast-changing culture that seems alien to many Christians (just as Christians seem alien to many in the culture!), it is easy for Christians to throw up their hands in despair and adopt a purely defensive mode. In this important book, Tim Keller unpacks the gospel and gently but firmly reminds us that it is nonnegotiable. At the same time, he enables us to think through how we can responsibly interact with the culture, how we can—indeed, must—appreciate good things within it, and how we can firmly and faithfully apply the gospel to it. But this is not a mechanical how-to book; rather, it is a reflective meditation on some hugely important themes in Scripture written by someone who has exercised faithful pastoral ministry in a major city for two decades.

> D. A. CARSON, research professor of
> New Testament, Trinity Evangelical Divinity School

No one has listened more closely to the harmonies of city, culture, church, and Scripture than Tim Keller. In *Center Church*, he not only describes the different strains of music but also tells us how he has orchestrated the results for the sake of ministry outreach and renewal. Now it's our turn to listen, as Tim practically yet powerfully prepares us to participate in this great symphony of the gospel.

> BRYAN CHAPELL, president, Covenant Theological Seminary

Center Church is an immensely helpful resource for the next generation of church leaders. It is theologically profound, thought provoking, and energizing, and it will make you uncomfortable in measure. Once again, Tim Keller has hit the bull's-eye!

> ALISTAIR BEGG, senior pastor,
> Parkside Church, Cleveland, Ohio

We don't need another "do ministry like my church does ministry" book. Nor do we need another book that critiques other church models. We need a book that helps us think critically and biblically as we structure our churches. *Center Church* is packed with Tim Keller's experience, humility, and wisdom. This book will help you if you are serious about seeing your city transformed by the gospel of grace.

DARRIN PATRICK, lead pastor,
The Journey, St. Louis, Missouri

Church leaders abandon their unique calling if they merely think theologically to the exclusion of seeing the world in light of the gospel and helping their churches live in the world with gospel wisdom. No one makes this case more clearly today than Tim Keller. He resists the all-too-easy pattern of selling a simple model of what it means to be the church that fits every setting. Instead he brings to life the myriad ways churches are called to be faithful and fruitful in their own unique cultural context. Read this book if you want to learn how to ask the really important (and difficult) questions by which the gospel confronts our ecclesial identity.

RICHARD LINTS, Andrew Mutch distinguished professor
of theology, Gordon-Conwell Theological Seminary

Cities are challenging and complex but also important and strategic. And those who are called to minister in cities need encouragement and resources that fuel hope and effectiveness. That's why I'm so glad that Tim Keller has written this book. His passion for the gospel, heart for the city, and vision of a movement of the Holy Spirit that will transform lives and bring hope and peace to our cities has compelled him to share his insights and thinking with us. What's more, the church he serves speaks to the integrity of his heart and the possibility of the reality of this vision. Be prepared. Your thinking will be sharpened, and your heart will be moved.

DR. CRAWFORD W. LORITTS JR., senior pastor,
Fellowship Bible Church, Roswell, Georgia

This outstanding book, like the Manhattan ministry out of which it has come, shows how Reformed theological acumen and wise pastoral intelligence may combine to achieve spiritual fruitfulness in urban contexts everywhere. Every page illuminates. Keller is a huge gift to today's church.

J. I. PACKER, professor emeritus, Regent College

Most of us observe and see the obvious. Tim Keller observes and sees that which is unseen by others — especially when it comes to the truth of God's Word and the culture of the day. Once again, he has given us deeper insights — this time regarding the church and how she can experience her healthiest potential. How foolish to know of this book and not read it!

RANDY POPE, pastor, Perimeter Church, Atlanta, Georgia

Tim Keller has given us the must-read book on gospel-shaped ministry. Robustly theological and profoundly practical, it is a top-to-bottom survey of gospel implications for the life and ministry of the church. The gap between biblical and practical theology is masterfully bridged. Having worked with Tim and Redeemer City to City, I have benefited from the content of this book and can also attest to its profound influence on ministers and churches throughout the world. This is not simply curriculum content; it is exactly the kind of life-giving, generative gospel theology our churches need. No thoughtful Christian's bookshelf should be without it.

STEPHEN T. UM, senior minister,
Citylife Presbyterian Church, Boston, Massachusetts

In *Center Church*, one of the great missionary statesmen of our times lays out a vision of the church vigorous enough to transform entire cities through its agency of the gospel. Tim Keller is a gifted teacher, an outstanding leader, and an exemplary disciple of Jesus. A worthy read!

ALAN HIRSCH, founder of 100Movements
and the Forge Mission Training Network

We live in a day of remarkable church leaders and wonderful Christian thinkers, but I'm not sure there's a more thoughtful church leader in our day than Tim Keller. *Center Church* is his call for church ministry formed by deep theological reflection and sensitive cultural exegesis executed by courageous leaders so that the city may once more flourish under the gospel.

JOHN ORTBERG, senior pastor,
Menlo Park Presbyterian Church, Menlo Park, California

Tim Keller's church in New York City serves as one of the world's best models for gospel-centered ministry that wisely, biblically, and fruitfully connects with its community. This is mainly due to Dr. Keller's deep understanding of the gospel and his exceptional gift for interpreting culture. His latest book will be immensely helpful to anyone doing ministry anywhere. *Center Church* is not a manual for replicating Keller's ministry, but something much more important: a theological vision for how the gospel of Jesus Christ relates to culture, ministry, and the Christian life.

PHILIP RYKEN, president, Wheaton College

I'm not exaggerating when I say that *Center Church* is my favorite book Tim Keller has written thus far. Perhaps this book simply represents the distillation of Tim's wisdom — the synthesis of years of marinating in the gospel, exegeting the text of Scripture, and engaging the soul of our culture; his willingness to dialogue without diatribe; his ongoing commitment to think through the radical implications of God's grace; his great love for Jesus' bride, God's kingdom, and the history of redemption. It's all refreshingly here. What an awesome and practical read! I cannot wait to use this book with emerging leaders and churches willing to dream.

SCOTTY SMITH, founding pastor,
Christ Community Church, Franklin, Tennessee

SERVING A MOVEMENT

DOING BALANCED, GOSPEL-CENTERED MINISTRY IN YOUR CITY

A New Edition of
Section Three
of Center Church

TIMOTHY KELLER

WITH NEW CONTRIBUTIONS FROM TIM CHESTER, DANIEL MONTGOMERY, MIKE COSPER, AND ALAN HIRSCH

ZONDERVAN

Serving a Movement
Copyright © 2016 by Redeemer City to City, Timothy J. Keller, Alan Hirsch, and Zondervan

This title is also available as a Zondervan ebook. Visit www.zondervan.com/ebooks.

Requests for information should be addressed to:

Zondervan, 3900 *Sparks Dr. SE, Grand Rapids, Michigan* 49546

ISBN 978-0-310-52057-3

Cover design: Lucas Art and Design
Interior design: Kait Lamphere

Printed in the United States of America

16 17 18 19 20 21 /DHV/ 20 19 18 17 16 15 14 13 12 11 10 9 8 7 6 5 4 3 2 1

CONTENTS

Part 3: Movement Dynamics

SERIES
INTRODUCTION

Two kinds of books are ordinarily written for pastors and church leaders. One kind lays out general biblical principles for all churches. These books start with scriptural exegesis and biblical theology and list the characteristics and functions of a true biblical church. The most important characteristic is that a ministry be faithful to the Word and sound in doctrine, but these books also rightly call for biblical standards of evangelism, church leadership, community and membership, worship, and service.

Another category of book operates at the opposite end of the spectrum. These books do not spend much time laying biblical theological foundations, though virtually all of them cite biblical passages. Instead, they are practical "how-to" books that describe specific mind-sets, programs, and ways to do church. This genre of book exploded onto the scene during the church growth movement of the 1970s and 1980s through the writing of authors such as C. Peter Wagner and Robert Schuller. A second generation of books in a similar vein appeared with personal accounts of successful churches, authored by senior pastors, distilling practical principles for others to use. A third generation of practical church books began more than ten years ago. These are volumes that directly criticize the church growth how-to books. Nevertheless, they also consist largely of case studies and pictures of what a good church looks like on the ground, with practical advice on how to organize and conduct ministry.

From these latter volumes I have almost always profited, coming away from each book with at least one good idea I could use. But by and large, I found the books less helpful than I hoped they would be. Implicitly or explicitly, they made near-absolutes out of techniques and models that had worked in a certain place at a certain time. I was fairly certain that many of these methods would not work in my context in New York and were not as universally applicable as the authors implied. In particular, church leaders outside of the United States found these books irritating because the authors assumed that what worked in a suburb of a U.S. city would work almost anywhere.

As people pressed me to speak and write about our experience at Redeemer, I realized that most were urging me to write my own version of the second type of book. Pastors did not want me to recapitulate biblical doctrine and principles of church life they had gotten in seminary. Instead, they were looking for a "secrets of success" book. They wanted instructions for specific programs and techniques that appealed to urban people. One pastor said, "I've tried the Willow Creek model. Now I'm ready to try the Redeemer model." People came to us because they knew we were thriving in one of the least churched, most secular cities in the U.S. But when visitors first started coming to Redeemer in the early and mid-1990s, they were disappointed because they did not discern a new "model" —at least not in the form of unique, new programs. That's because the real "secret" of Redeemer's fruitfulness does not lie in its ministry programs but in something that functions at a deeper level.

Hardware, Middleware, Software

What was this deeper level, exactly? As time went on, I began to realize it was a middle space between these two more obvious dimensions of ministry. All of us have a *doctrinal foundation* —a set of theological beliefs—and all of us conduct particular *forms of ministry*. But many ministers take up programs and practices of ministry that fit well with neither their doctrinal beliefs nor their cultural context. They adopt popular methods that are essentially "glued on" from the outside—alien to the church's theology or setting (sometimes both!). And when this happens, we find a lack of fruitfulness. These ministers don't change people's lives within the church and don't reach people in their city.

Why not? Because the programs do not grow naturally out of reflection on both the gospel and the distinctness of their surrounding culture.

If you think of your doctrinal foundation as "hardware" and of ministry programs as "software," it is important to understand the existence of something called "middleware." I am no computer expert, but my computer-savvy friends tell me that middleware is a software layer that lies between the hardware and the operating system and the various software applications being deployed by the computer's user. In the same way, between one's doctrinal beliefs and ministry practices should be a well-conceived vision for how to bring the gospel to bear on the particular cultural setting and historical moment. This is something more practical than just doctrinal beliefs but much more theological than how-to steps for carrying out a particular ministry. Once this vision is in place, with its emphases and values, it leads church leaders to make good decisions on how to worship, disciple, evangelize, serve, and engage culture in their field of ministry—whether in a city, suburb, or small town.

Theological Vision

This middleware is similar to what Richard Lints, professor of theology at Gordon-Conwell Theological Seminary, calls a "theological vision."[1] According to Lints, our doctrinal foundation, drawn from Scripture, is the starting point for everything:

> Theology must first be about a conversation with God ... God speaks and we listen ... The Christian theological framework is primarily about listening—listening to God. One of the great dangers we face in doing theology is our desire to do all the talking ... We most often capitulate to this temptation by placing alien conceptual boundaries on what God can and has said in the Word ... We force the message of redemption into a cultural package that distorts its actual intentions. Or we attempt to view the gospel solely from the perspective of a tradition that has little living connection to the redemptive work of Christ on the cross. Or we place rational restrictions on the very notion of God instead of allowing God to define the notions of rationality.[2]

However, the doctrinal foundation is not enough. Before you choose specific ministry methods, you must first ask how your doctrinal beliefs "might relate to the modern world." The result of that question "thereby form[s] a theological vision."[3] In other words, a theological vision is a vision for what you are going to *do* with your doctrine in a particular time and place. And what does a theological vision develop from? Lints shows that it comes, of course, from deep reflection on the Bible itself, but it also depends a great deal on what you think of the culture around you. Lints offers this important observation:

> A theological vision allows [people] to see their culture in a way different than they had ever been able to see it before ... Those who are empowered by the theological vision do not simply stand against the mainstream impulses of the culture but take the initiative both to understand and speak to that culture from the framework of the Scriptures ... The modern theological vision must seek to bring the entire counsel of God into the world of its time in order that its time might be transformed.[4]

In light of this, I propose a set of questions that can guide us in the development of a theological vision. As we answer questions like these, a theological vision will emerge:

- What is the gospel, and how do we bring it to bear on the hearts of people today?
- What is this culture like, and how can we both connect to it and challenge it in our communication?
- Where are we located — city, suburb, town, rural area — and how does this affect our ministry?
- To what degree and how should Christians be involved in civic life and cultural production?
- How do the various ministries in a church — word and deed, community and instruction — relate to one another?
- How innovative will our church be and how traditional?
- How will our church relate to other churches in our city and region?

- How will we make our case to the culture about the truth of Christianity?

Our theological vision, growing out of our doctrinal foundation but including implicit or explicit readings of culture, is the most immediate cause of our decisions and choices regarding ministry expression. It is a faithful restatement of the gospel with rich implications for life, ministry, and mission in a type of culture at a moment in history. Perhaps we can diagram it like this (see figure).

Center Church

This book was originally published in 2012 as one of three sections of a longer work called *Center Church*. In that book, I presented the theological vision that has guided our ministry at Redeemer. But what did we mean by the term *center church*? We chose this term for several reasons.

1. The gospel is at its center. It is one thing to have a ministry that is gospel-believing and even gospel-proclaiming but quite another to have one that is gospel-centered.

WHAT TO DO

How the gospel is expressed in a particular church in one community at a point in time

- *Local cultural adaptation*
- *Worship style & programming*
- *Discipleship & outreach processes*
- *Church governance & management*

↑

HOW TO SEE

A faithful restatement of the gospel with rich implications for life, ministry, and mission in a type of culture at a moment in history

- *Vision and values*
- *Ministry "DNA"*
- *Emphases, stances*
- *Philosophy of ministry*

THEOLOGICAL VISION

↑

WHAT TO BELIEVE

Timeless truths from the Bible about God, our relationship to him, and his purposes in the world

- *Theological tradition*
- *Denominational affiliation*
- *Systematic & biblical theology*

2. The center is the place of balance. We need to strike balances as Scripture does: of word *and* deed ministries; of challenging *and* affirming human culture; of cultural engagement *and* countercultural distinctiveness; of commitment to truth *and* generosity to others who don't share the same beliefs; of tradition *and* innovation in practice.

3. Our theological vision must be shaped by and for urban and cultural centers. Ministry in the center of global cities is the highest priority for the church in the twenty-first century. While our theological vision is widely applicable, it must be distinctly flavored by the urban experience.

4. The theological vision is at the center of ministry. A theological vision creates a bridge between doctrine and expression. It is central to how all ministry happens. Two churches can have different doctrinal frameworks and ministry expressions but the same theological vision — and they will feel like sister ministries. On the other hand, two churches can have similar doctrinal frameworks and ministry expressions but different theological visions — and they will feel distinct.

The Center Church theological vision can be expressed most simply in three basic commitments: Gospel, City, and Movement.[5] Each book in the Center Church series covers one of these three commitments.

Gospel. Both the Bible and church history show us that it is possible to hold all the correct individual biblical doctrines and yet functionally lose our grasp on the gospel. It is critical, therefore, in every new generation and setting to find ways to *communicate the gospel clearly and strikingly*, distinguishing it from its opposites and counterfeits.

City. All churches must understand, love, and identify with their local community and social setting, and yet at the same time be able and willing to critique and challenge it. Every church, whether located in a city, suburb, or rural area (and there are many permutations and combinations of these settings), must become wise about and conversant with the distinctives of human life in those places. But we must also think about how Christianity and the church engage and interact with culture in general. This has become an acute issue as Western culture has become increasingly post-Christian.

Movement. The last area of theological vision has to do with your church's *relationships*—with its community, with its recent and deeper past, and with other churches and ministries. Some churches are highly institutional, with a strong emphasis on their own past, while others are anti-institutional, fluid, and marked by constant innovation and change. Some churches see themselves as being loyal to a particular ecclesiastical tradition—and so they cherish historical and traditional liturgy and ministry practices. Those that identify very strongly with a particular denomination or newer tradition often resist change. At the other end of the spectrum are churches with little sense of a theological and ecclesiastical past that tend to relate easily to a wide variety of other churches and ministries. All of these different perspectives have an enormous impact on how we actually do ministry.

The Balance of Three Axes

One of the simplest ways to convey the need for wisdom and balance in formulating principles of theological vision is to think of three axes.

1. **The Gospel axis.** At one end of the axis is legalism, the teaching that asserts or the spirit that implies we can save ourselves by how we live. At the other end is antinomianism or, in popular parlance, relativism—the view that it doesn't matter how we live; that God, if he exists, loves everyone the same. But the gospel is neither legalism nor relativism. We are saved by faith and grace alone, but not by a faith that remains alone. True grace always results in changed lives of holiness and justice. It is, of course, possible to lose the gospel because of heterodoxy. That is, if we no longer believe in the deity of Christ or the doctrine of justification, we will necessarily slide toward relativism. But it is also possible to hold sound doctrine and yet be marked by dead orthodoxy (a spirit of self-righteousness), imbalanced orthodoxy

(overemphasis on some doctrines that obscure the gospel call), or even "clueless orthodoxy," which results when doctrines are expounded as in a theology class but aren't brought together to penetrate people's hearts so they experience conviction of sin and the beauty of grace. Our communication and practices must not tend toward either law or license. To the degree that they do, they lose life-changing power.[6]

underadapted
only challenge

CITY

overadapted
only appreciate

2. The City axis (which could also be called a Culture axis). We will show that to reach people we must appreciate and adapt to their culture, but we must also challenge and confront it. This is based on the biblical teaching that all cultures have God's grace and natural revelation in them, yet they are also in rebellious idolatry. If we overadapt to a culture, we have accepted the culture's idols. If, however, we underadapt to a culture, we may have turned our own culture into an idol, an absolute. If we overadapt to a culture, we aren't able to change people because we are not calling them to change. If we underadapt to a culture, no one will be changed because no one will listen to us; we will be confusing, offensive, or simply unpersuasive. To the degree a ministry is overadapted or underadapted to a culture, it loses life-changing power.

structured organization
tradition and authority

MOVEMENT

fluid organism
cooperation and unity

3. The Movement axis. Some churches identify so strongly with their own theological tradition that they cannot make common cause with other evangelical churches or other institutions to reach a city or work for the common good. They also tend to cling strongly to forms of ministry from the past and are highly structured and institutional. Other churches are strongly anti-institutional. They have almost no identification with a particular heritage or denomination, nor do they have much of a relationship to a Christian past. Sometimes they have virtually no institutional character, being completely fluid and informal. A church at either extreme will stifle the development of leadership and strangle the health of the church as a corporate body, as a community. To the degree that it commits either of these errors, it loses its life-giving power.

The more that ministry comes "from the center" of all the axes, the more dynamism and fruitfulness it will have. Ministry that is toward the end of any of the spectrums or axes will drain a ministry of life-changing power with the people in and around it.

As with the original publication of *Center Church*, my hope is that each of these smaller volumes will be useful and provoke discussion. The three volumes of the paperback series each correspond to one of the three axes.

Shaped by the Gospel looks at the need to recover a biblical view of the gospel. Our churches must be characterized by our gospel-theological depth rather than by our doctrinal shallowness, pragmatism, nonreflectiveness, and method-driven philosophy. In addition, we need to experience renewal so that a constant note of grace is applied to everything and our ministry is not marked by legalism or cold intellectualism.

Loving the City highlights the need to be sensitive to culture rather than choosing to ignore our cultural moment or being oblivious to cultural differences among groups. It looks at how we can develop a vision for our city by adopting city-loving ways of ministry rather than approaches that are hostile or indifferent to the city. We also look at how to engage the culture in such a way that we avoid being either too triumphalistic or too withdrawn and subcultural in our attitude.

Serving a Movement shows why every ministry of the church should be outward facing, expecting the presence of nonbelievers and supporting laypeople in their ministry in the world. We also look at the need for integrative ministry where we minister in word *and* deed, helping to meet the spiritual and physical needs of the poor as well as those who live and work in cultural centers. Finally, we look at the need for a mind-set of willing cooperation with other believers, not being turf con-scious and suspicious but eagerly promoting a vision for the whole city.

The purpose of these three volumes, then, is not to lay out a "Redeemer model." This is not a "church in a box." Instead, we are lay-ing out a particular theological vision for ministry that we believe will enable many churches to reach people in our day and time, particularly where late-modern Western globalization is influencing the culture. This is especially true in the great cities of the world, but these cultural shifts are being felt everywhere, and so we trust that this book will be found useful to church leaders in a great variety of social settings. We will be recommending a vision for using the gospel in the lives of contemporary people, doing contextualization, understanding cities, doing cultural engagement, discipling for mission, integrating various ministries, and fostering movement dynamics in your congregation and in the world. This set of emphases and values—a Center Church theo-logical vision—can empower all kinds of church models and methods in all kinds of settings. We believe that if you embrace the process of making your theological vision visible, you will make far better choices of model and method.

A NOTE FROM TIMOTHY KELLER

C*enter Church* is a textbook for church leaders working at ministry today, especially for those in urban or urbanized areas. The volume in your hands is the third in a series (along with *Shaped by the Gospel* and *Loving the City*). It consists of material from the last three parts of *Center Church*, namely, Missional Community, Integrative Ministry, and Movement Dynamics, together with three essays by other authors giving their reflections on the content, followed by my responses to their reflections. The first essay reflecting on Missional Community is by pastor-theologian Tim Chester. The second essay on Integrative Ministry is by Daniel Montgomery and Mike Cosper, pastors at Sojourn Church in Louisville, Kentucky. Alan Hirsch, a missional church writer and thought leader, writes the third essay on Movement Dynamics.

As you can see from the titles, these parts of *Center Church* have to do with practical questions about how the church reaches out in a post-Christian culture. They wrestle with the issues of the "missional church" movement of the past twenty years, in which older forms of doing church, even the recently successful approaches of the seeker church, were perceived as ineffective in reaching an increasing secularized, global, late-modern culture.

Many people say the missional/emerging church movement is over. But the problem it tried to address is still with us, namely, finding an answer to Lesslie Newbigin's question, "How does the church here have a missionary encounter with secular, post-Christian culture?" A missionary encounter implies neither being co-opted and assimilated by the culture (such that there is no "mission") nor being withdrawn into hermetically sealed enclaves (so no "encounter"). This question, I believe, is the origin of the very term *missional church*. Now that the Western church is further out of sync with its surrounding societies for the first time in centuries, how does it become like churches in the rest of the world that have learned to be in missionary encounters with their cultures? Maybe it is true that energy around earlier efforts to answer Newbigin's question has been spent. But is the question dated or less relevant today? Hardly. Several developments in the past few years have left many Christians in the West feeling dazed, disoriented, and like exiles in their countries. So the issues being treated in this volume are more relevant and urgent than ever.

The essayists here are well equipped to offer perspectives and experiences that help us greatly. A quick glance shows the global perspective they bring. Tim Chester is a British pastor and theologian, while Alan Hirsch was born and raised in South Africa and studied, ministered, and taught in Australia. Alan has traveled widely and has observed ministry "at the edges" in an enormous number and variety of places around the world. Daniel Montgomery and Mike Cosper, by contrast, are younger ministers in the United States who provide an instructive account and case study of one new church seeking to discover practical ways to have Newbigin's missionary encounter in their city. Their church's name—Sojourn—speaks to, among other things, how they have migrated through a number of ways of understanding their mission, vision, and ministry.

One of the key lessons I've been learning throughout the interactions with all the essayists in this series is germane to the readers of this one. *Center Church* looks quite long—intimidatingly long, even—yet it does not purport to be a complete "practical theology" of church ministry. For example, there is little in *Center Church* about preaching, despite some indications about its importance. It would be important to read *Preaching: Communicating Faith in an Age of Skepticism* to get a clearer picture of what I believe ministry in our late-modern culture should look like. Also, while I've done some reflecting in *Center Church* on the biblical theology of the gospel and of the city, in most chapters I could not take the time to provide a strong underpinning. So, for example, when I discuss worship, community formation, mercy and justice, and evangelism, I do not provide a full theological foundation. Ordinarily I refer to other books that do this well. So, for example, the content in Integrative Ministry (part 2 in *Serving a Movement*) assumes the ecclesiology and doctrine in books like the ones written by Edmund Clowney. The material in the chapters on justice and on how faith shapes our work (chapters 7 and 8 in *Serving a Movement*) refer to my own books, *Generous Justice* and *Every Good Endeavor*, where I do more theological grounding than I do in *Center Church*. Please bear that in mind.

The essays woven throughout the three volumes in this series enhance the value of *Center Church*, to say the least. The experiences, accounts, and critiques of the authors provide richness to the pattern of teaching here. My mind has been stretched, and I am better equipped now to do my ministry than before I plunged into these great conversations. I believe you will discover this to be true for you as well.

Part 1

MISSIONAL COMMUNITY

Chapter 1

THE SEARCH FOR THE MISSIONAL CHURCH

The word *missional* first became popular after the 1998 publication of the book titled *Missional Church*, and in the years since, it has been adopted and used widely.[1] Many are asking, "How can we really be missional?" An entire generation of younger evangelical leaders has grown up searching for the true missional church as if for the Holy Grail. Seemingly a dozen books come out each year with the word *missional* in their title, but a survey of these books reveals that the word has significantly different meanings and is used in different ways by different authors, organizations, and churches—leading to much confusion about what, exactly, the term *missional* means.

Before the term *missional* exploded throughout the Christian world, it was primarily used in mainline Protestant and ecumenical circles in a manner closely associated with the Latin phrase *missio Dei*. The phrase was originally coined to convey the teaching of Karl Barth about the action of God in the world. According to Lesslie Newbigin, the term *missio Dei* became prominent after the 1952 world mission conference in Willingen, Germany. It was a way of referring to the idea that God is active in the world, working to redeem the entire creation, and that the church's task is to participate in this mission.[2]

In his influential 1991 book *Transforming Mission*, David Bosch explained that the term *missio Dei* was firmly grounded in Trinitarian theology. Bosch noted that in the past, mission was largely viewed as a category of soteriology (as a way to save souls) or as a category of ecclesiology (as a way to expand the church). In contrast, the concept of *missio Dei* implied that mission should be "understood as being derived

25

from the very nature of God ... put in the context of the doctrine of the Trinity, not of ecclesiology or soteriology."[3] The Trinity is, by nature, "sending." The Father sends the Son into the world to save it, and the Father and the Son send the Spirit into the world. And now, said Bosch, the Spirit is sending the church. In short, God does not merely send the church in mission. God already is in mission, and the church must join him. This also means, then, that the church does not simply have a missions department; it should wholly exist to *be* a mission.

At first glance, this seemed to be a strong and sound theology of mission. As time went on, however, it meant the church actually came to be seen as less relevant. Lesslie Newbigin wrote these words in the late 1970s: "If God is indeed the true missionary, it was said, our business is to not promote the mission of the church, but to get out into the world, find out 'what God is doing in the world,' and join forces with him. And 'what God is doing' was generally thought to be in the secular rather than in the religious sectors of human life. The effect, of course, was to look for what seemed to be the rising powers and to identify Christians' missionary responsibility with support for a range of political and cultural developments."[4]

Harvey Cox of Harvard Divinity School wrote, "What God is doing in the world is politics ... Theology today must [therefore] be that reflection-in-action by which the church finds out what this politician-God is up to and moves in to work along with him."[5] In many mainline and ecumenical circles, *mission* came to mean working with secular human rights movements or rising left-wing political organizations. The results, Newbigin wrote, were "sometimes bizarre indeed. Even Chairman Mao's 'little red book' became almost a new Bible."[6] Newbigin, who was one of the key people involved in the forming of the World Council of Churches, became increasingly concerned that the concept of the *missio Dei* left little need for the church. The church could not meet human needs as well as social service agencies could, nor could it change society as well as political parties and organizations could. So in this view, the church became inconsequential.

In *The Open Secret*, Newbigin criticized what he called the "secularization" of mission. He argued that conversions, the growth of the church, and the quality of Christian community were all critical and central to mission. Newbigin looked with favor on the theories of missiologist Donald McGavran, who taught that the purpose of mission was "church growth" in quality and quantity.[7] Nevertheless, Newbigin retained the term *missio Dei* and its original theological concept of a missionary God. He insisted that the church needed to grow through evangelism yet be involved in service and in the struggle for justice in the world as well. Newbigin sought to uphold the basic idea of the *missio Dei*, but he tried to save it from the excesses and distortions of the ecumenical movement.

The Newbigin-Bosch Rescue

Lesslie Newbigin had been a British missionary in India for several decades. When he returned to England in the mid-1970s, he saw the massive decline of the church and Christian influence that had occurred in his absence. At the time he left England, Western society's main cultural institutions still Christianized people, and the churches were easily gathering those who came to their doors through social expectation and custom. Churches in the West had always supported "missions" in overseas non-Christian cultures (such as India). There on the "mission field," churches functioned in a different way than they did in Europe and North America. Churches in India did not merely support missions or even do missions—they *were* missional in every aspect. They could not simply process Christianized people as churches did in the West. Rather, every aspect of their church life—worship, preaching, community life, and discipleship—had to be a form of mission.

For example, on the mission field, visitors to a worship service could not be expected to have any familiarity with Christianity. Therefore the worship and preaching had to address them in ways both comprehensible and challenging. On the mission field, believers lived in a society with radically different values from those they were taught in church. This made "life in the world" very complicated for Christians. Discipleship and training had to equip believers to answer many hostile questions from their neighbors. It also had to spell out Christian personal and corporate behavior patterns that distinguished them and showed society what the kingdom of God was all about. In other words, away from the West, churches did not simply have a missions department; Christians were "in mission" in every aspect of their public and private lives.

When he returned to England, Newbigin discovered that the ground had shifted. The cultural institutions of society were now indifferent or overtly hostile to Christian faith, and the number of people who went to church had plummeted. Western culture was fast becoming a non-Christian society—a "mission field"—but the churches were making little adjustment. While many Christian leaders were bemoaning the cultural changes, Western churches continued to minister as before—creating an environment in which only traditional and conservative people would feel comfortable. They continued to disciple people by focusing on individual skills for their private lives (Bible study and prayer) but failed to train them to live distinctively Christian lives in a secular world—in the public arenas of politics, art, and business. All they preached and practiced assumed they were still in the Christian West, but the Christian West was vanishing.

This was a disastrous tactic. Western churches, Newbigin argued, had to put the same kind of thought and effort into reaching their alien, non-Christian culture as the churches in India, China, and the rest of the world did. Over the last twenty-four years of his life, Newbigin argued tirelessly and trenchantly that the church had to come to grips with the fact that it was no longer functioning in "Christendom." Rejecting the common view that the West was becoming a *secular* society without God, Newbigin viewed it as a *pagan* society filled with idols and false gods.[8] He especially criticized the ideology of the European Enlightenment and its idolatrous commitment to the autonomy of human reason that had led to the illusion of neutral, value-free, objective knowledge. This commitment to reason had seduced Western cultural leaders into believing we did not need God or any particular religious faith in order to have a well-ordered, just, and moral society. Critical to the church's mission in the West, he said, was the unmasking of this false god by showing the futility of the "Enlightenment project"—the fruitless effort to find consensus on morality, right and wrong, justice, and human flourishing on the basis of secular reason.

In his books *The Open Secret, Foolishness to the Greeks,* and *The Gospel in a Pluralist Society,* Newbigin fleshed out what mission to Western society could look like.[9] It included a public apologetic against the autonomy of human reason that was overtly indebted to Alasdair MacIntyre and Michael Polanyi but that incorporated the approach of Abraham Kuyper and Herman Bavinck as well. It also emphasized equipping believers to integrate their faith and work, changing society as they moved out into their vocations in the world, as well as emphasizing the importance of the Christian church as a "hermeneutic of the gospel." Newbigin believed that the love, justice, and peace that ought to characterize the Christian counterculture were primary ways of bearing witness to God in a pluralistic society. With these last two emphases—the renewal of society and the church as a "contrast" community—Newbigin combines several of the cultural approaches we looked at earlier.

Most important, Newbigin proposed something of a middle way (though he never used that term) with the *missio Dei.* In his critical review of Konrad Raiser's book defending the approach of the World Council of Churches (*Ecumenism in Transition: A Paradigm Shift for the Ecumenical Movement?*), Newbigin wrote the following:

> Raiser, of course, is absolutely right to protest against an ecclesiocentric concept of mission, as though the church were the author and the goal of mission. But this whole vision is too much shaped by the ideology of the 1960s with its faith in the secular, and in human power to solve problems. The thesis is heavily marked by a model … that interprets all situations in terms of the oppressor and the oppressed and that tends to interpret the struggles of the oppressed as the instrument of redemption. This model owed not a little to Marxist thought, and the collapse of Marxism as a world power has created a new situation with which the WCC has to come to terms.[10]

Newbigin rejected the direct identification of God's redemption with any movement that improves socioeconomic well-being. He rightly said that the idea of defining mission as "what God is doing out in history" too closely draws its origins from the Marxist ideas of class struggle as the meaning of history. But then Newbigin sought to strike a note of balance:

> The (literally) crucial matter is the centrality of Jesus and his aton-ing work on the cross, that work by which he has won lordship over the church and the world ...
>
> It is one of the most pressing tasks for the immediate future to rediscover a doctrine of redemption that sees the cross not as the banner of the oppressed against the oppressor but as the action of God that brings both judgment and redemption for all who will accept it, yet does not subvert the proper struggle for the measure of justice that is possible in a world of sinful human beings.[11]

Here Newbigin takes the struggle for justice in the world out from the center of the meaning of redemption. Redemption is first of all the action of God in Christ, and this action calls for a decision. It must be accepted, not rejected.[12] And yet there is still a place for us to struggle for the "measure of justice" in this world.

In *Transforming Mission*, David Bosch further develops Newbigin's idea of the *missio Dei*. In Bosch's examination of Luke's theology of mission, he sees a charge to proclaim Christ and the call for conversion, as well as to show God's concern for justice for the poor. In his *Believing in the Future*, Bosch goes further in spelling out a vision for mission in a post-Christian West. He restates the core idea of the *missio Dei*—that God's mission is to restore creation, and the church is called to partici-pate in this mission. Bosch says that mission is not just "recruitment to our brand of religion; it is alerting people to the universal reign of God."[13] Then he suggests how this may be done. First, he says, we must avoid two opposing errors: (1) trying to re-create a Christian society (the mistake of medieval Christendom) and (2) withdrawal from society into the "spiritual realm" (the mistake of modernity).[14] Second, we must learn how to publicly and prophetically challenge the idol of autono-mous reason and its results.[15] Third, we must take pains to make our churches into contrast societies, countercultures that show society what human life looks like free from the idols of race, wealth, sex, power, and individual autonomy.[16] So we contextualize our message in ways that avoid syncretism on the one extreme and irrelevance on the other; we better equip the laity for their public callings; and we cultivate vital, life-shaping worship as the dynamic heart of mission. These steps show the world a countercultural model of society and shape people so that the gospel influences how they live in the world.[17] Finally, we must model to the world as much unity between churches as is practically possible.

An insight animating all of this work is the idea of *the cultural captivity of the church* in the West. Bosch, like Newbigin, is especially critical of Enlightenment rationalism and its various effects in Western culture — materialism, consumerism, individualism, and the breakdown of community. He maintains that the church is too deeply shaped by the spirit of the age, in *both* its conservative and liberal forms. In its liberal form, it has bought uncritically into a secular account of things, de-supernaturalizing the gospel so that the Spirit's work is seen mainly in secular movements of liberation, thus turning the liberal mainline churches into little more than social service centers where the language of secular rights activists reigns. In its conservative form, it has bought uncritically into the idea of religion as the fulfillment of individual consumer needs, thus turning the conservative church into something like felt-need shopping centers where the language of modern therapy and marketing reigns. People see Christ as a way to self-fulfillment and prosperity, not as a model for radical service to others. Both wings of the Christian church are, then, captive to the reigning idols of Western culture.[18] They are failing to challenge these idols in their preaching and practice.

Because of the influential writings of Newbigin and Bosch, a new, more fully realized understanding of the *missio Dei* was developing by the mid-1990s. It sought to avoid the secularization of mission found in the liberal churches. The overarching narrative was still that God is in mission to renew the whole creation, but the new view stressed the public proclamation of Christ as Lord and Hope of the world and therefore the necessity of both conversion and the growth of the church. This new, rehabilitated view of the *missio Dei* began to capture the attention of many Christians outside of the liberal mainline who were struggling with the question of how to relate to an increasingly post-Christian culture.

The Missional Church Movement Today

When *Missional Church* (edited by Darrell Guder) first appeared in 1998, it built on this new understanding of *missio Dei* that had been previously developed by Lesslie Newbigin and David Bosch. The book laid out the same dilemma: the culture was no longer Christianized and now the church was "on the mission field to the modern world," yet the church was captive to the culture of modernity and thus had no real alternative to offer. The church must therefore reform itself and discover new ways to engage culture. But how was this to be done? Again, the answers sounded many of the same themes as Newbigin and Bosch: the church as a contrast community, contextualization of the message, concern not only for church growth but also for justice. The book's theological commitments were firmly based on the concept of the mission as participation in the purpose of the triune God to redeem creation.[19]

The time for these ideas was ripe, and the term *missional church* became popular in evangelical circles. The evangelical church as a whole was becoming aware of the cultural shift happening around them and the growing ineffectiveness of much of the traditional ministry approach. Some in the mainline church were becoming disenchanted with the emptiness of ecumenical theology, but they were either unable to or not interested in joining the evangelical movement. Many of these church leaders picked up the basic vision for the missional church in Western culture found in Guder's book.

But many people picked up the ideas of the *missio Dei* and the missional church and supplemented them with other theological and cultural content, which has led to a dizzying variety of different and sometimes contradictory definitions of the term *missional*. Craig Van Gelder has written an entire volume just trying to categorize the different approaches and definitions around the idea. He and his colleague Dwight Zscheile have discerned four broad, overlapping "streams" of the missional conversation:

1. Being missional is being *evangelistic*. Some churches (and authors) have simply adopted *missional* as a synonym for being highly committed to evangelism and foreign missions. Like all expressions of being missional, the starting point is how our culture has changed, how outreach requires more ingenuity and diligence than ever, and the assertion that every Christian is a missionary. Those in this category also usually embrace a somewhat more holistic approach to outreach, encouraging various forms of community service. However, the underlying theology is quite traditional. Mission is largely conceived as bringing people into individual salvation through the church. The distinctive ideas of the *missio Dei* — the work of God's Spirit in the world to restore all creation and the cultural captivity of the Western church — are missing.[20]

2. Being missional is being *incarnational*. Another set of voices criticizes the Christendom model of church as "attractional." The attractional model is based on non-Christians coming or being invited into the programs and ministries of the church. They come in to hear the preaching, to participate in programs that minister to their felt needs, or to attend baptisms, weddings, and funerals. This, it is said, is now an obsolete model (though it still works in more traditional parts of the West and with the shrinking body of "Christianized" non-Christians).

In place of the attractional model, they recommend an incarnational model, where Christians live geographically close to each other, create a thick and rich community among themselves, and then become deeply involved in the civic and corporate life of their neighborhood or city. Church planting in this paradigm does not need to begin with a full-time minister, a core group, and a worship service. Instead, a few Christian families move into a neighborhood and fully participate in its life, discover the needs of the citizens, and begin to meet them in Christ's name. Christian community grows organically, gradually coming to include many of the nonbelievers who labor for peace and justice in the neighborhood. In general, the adoption of this view leads to the proliferation of informal house churches.[21]

3. Being missional is being *contextual*. Some thinkers put more emphasis on the shifts in late-modern and postmodern culture, the cultural captivity of the church, and therefore the need to contextualize every part of the church's ministry so it engages this post-Christendom reality. This approach includes aspects of the first two views, as thinkers in this category emphasize being ingeniously evangelistic and incarnational in the community—but they go further. In this view it is possible to deepen Christian community and be involved in community service and yet still be a subculture that does not really engage post-Christian Western society. To be a truly missional church involves deep reflection on culture and discovering creative ways of communication and church practice that both adapt to culture and challenge it. Those who fall into this category appreciate the incarnational house church model but see it as one good and possible ministry form among many others.

Van Gelder and Zscheile list authors who advance this view, and many of them seem to assume a more traditional evangelical theology than those in the final category.[22] Still, they all accept that the basic measures proposed by Newbigin for a "missionary encounter with Western culture"—a new apologetic, the church as contrast community, holistic outreach, engaging culture through vocations—are correct. In their own works, they seek to flesh out what Newbigin's measures might look like.

4. Being missional is being *reciprocal* and *communal*. This group of thinkers applauds the emphases of the other three. They are glad to affirm that every Christian is in mission. They support the idea of the church as far more incarnationally involved in the life of its community, and they believe firmly in the importance of contextualization and cultural engagement. They do not, however, believe the others have taken the implications of the *missio Dei* far enough. They believe *missio Dei* calls us to a careful reworking of both our theology and practice.

Those who adopt this approach have arrived at two conclusions. First, if God already has a mission, then a church should not do mission by designing methods to draw people into their services. It must be responsive to what God is already doing in the world. Alan Roxburgh, one of the original essayists in *Missional Church*, writes that the one question missional churches ask over and over is this: "What is God up to in this neighborhood?" The missional church listens to people in the community and "becomes open to being surprised by God's purposes."[23] Rather than simply announcing to the world what it needs to know, the church listens and learns what God is doing and then gets involved.

Second, in order to overcome the Enlightenment's individualism, the church must redefine sin, mission, and salvation in corporate and communal terms. Rather than speaking of sin primarily as an offense against a holy God, sin is seen, in horizontal terms, as the violation of God's shalom in the world through selfishness, violence, injustice, and pride.[24] Rather than speaking of the cross as primarily the place where Jesus satisfied the wrath of God on our sin, Jesus' death is seen as the occasion when the powers of this world fell on Jesus and were defeated.[25] Mission, then, is ultimately not about getting individuals right with God but about incorporating them into a new community that partners with God in redeeming social structures and healing the world.[26]

What Do These Approaches Have in Common?

Many conservative evangelicals reject the term *missional* because of its association with emerging church thinkers such as Brian McLaren, because of its connection to the ecumenical movement and the theology of Karl Barth, or simply because it is such a hard word to define.[27]

I sympathize. But the fact remains that a large number of Christian believers today are on an earnest search for the missional church, regardless of whether or not they use the term. Those who hold to conservative doctrines often inhabit the first category — "missional as evangelistic" — and are now beginning to populate the second and third categories — "missional as incarnational" and "missional as contextual." Those with liberal and mainline church beliefs are also found in the second and third categories but are especially attracted to the fourth category ("missional as reciprocal and communal").[28]

Despite very real and important differences among these four missional streams, I believe they have important things in common. In the remainder of the chapter, I'll summarize the primary areas of consensus and strength in the missional conversation.

The Post-Christendom Age

First, we have entered a post-Christian or post-Christendom age. For centuries in the Western world, the Christian church had a privileged place, but this is no longer true. Rather than being a force at the center of culture, Christianity has moved to the margins. There is broad recognition that the church had allowed cultural institutions to do a lot of its heavy lifting, infusing people with a broadly Christian way of thinking about things—respect for the Bible, allegiance to the Ten Commandments, commitment to the ethical teachings of the Gospels; belief in a personal God, an afterlife, a judgment day, and moral absolutes. But no longer can we expect people who already have these basic beliefs to simply come to church through social pressure and out of custom. The times have changed.

Cultural Captivity of the Church

Second, those in the incarnational, contextual, and communal/reciprocal streams further recognize the cultural captivity of the church and the need to contextualize the gospel message so it is both comprehensible and challenging for those in a pluralistic, late-modern society. Many call for a gospel that escapes cultural captivity by challenging the Enlightenment individualism of both secular people and certain members of evangelical churches. Alan Roxburgh and Scott Boren write, "Modernity replaces mission with self-actualization of the expressive, autonomous individual,"[29] and it is this individualism that must be challenged and confronted. Newbigin argues that the church must also unmask the autonomy of human reason. Remember that contextualization means showing how only in Christ can the baseline narratives of a culture be resolved. To the self-absorbed culture we say, "You must lose yourself—in service to Christ and others—to truly find yourself." To the rationalistic culture we say, "You cannot have the things you want—meaning, dignity, hope, character, shared values, and community—without faith."

Sent Out to Be a Blessing

Third, all those pursuing the missional church also believe that Christian mission is more than just a department of the church, more than just the work of trained professionals. The biblical God is by nature a sending God, a missionary God.[30] The Father sends the Son;

the Son sends the Spirit and his disciples into the world. Therefore the whole church is in mission; every Christian is in mission. God never calls you in to bless you without also sending you out to be a blessing (Gen 12:1 – 3; cf. 1 Pet 2:9). So a Christian is not a spiritual consumer, coming in to get his or her emotional needs met and then going home. A missional church, then, is one that trains and encourages its people to be in mission as individuals and as a body. All of the voices in the missional conversation agree that the church must not be *only* attractional; it also must equip and send the laity into the world to minister.

One implication of this view is that missional churches must equip laypeople both for evangelistic witness and for public life and vocation. In Christendom, you could afford to train people solely in prayer, Bible study, and evangelism—skills for their private lives—because they were not facing radically non-Christian values in their public lives. In a missional church, all people need theological education to "think Christianly" about everything and to act with Christian distinctiveness. They need to know which cultural practices reflect common grace and should be embraced, which are antithetical to the gospel and must be rejected, and which practices can be adapted or revised.[31]

A Contrast Community

Finally, most missional thinkers agree that in our Western culture, we must be *a contrast community, a counterculture.* The quality, distinctiveness, and beauty of our communal life must be a major part of our witness and mission to the world. Jesus stated that the quality and visibility of Christians' love for each other will show the world that the Father *sent* him (John 17:20 – 21). In other words, our mission cannot go forward without Christians being involved not only in calling people to conversion but also in service to the community and in doing justice.[32] This is part of the balance Newbigin struck. While many in the liberal church redefine evangelism as seeking a more just society and many conservative churches see Christians' work in the world as strictly proclamation and conversion, most missional thinkers agree that the witness of Christians must be in both word and deed.

Part of being this kind of counterculture involves loving the city—its culture and people. Often, churches gather around them people who do not like the city or who do not expect to stay there. This inclination can occur among conservative churches that despise the secular, immoral society around them or with churches comprised largely of expatriates or immigrants from other countries. Such churches are often indifferent or hostile to their own locale, and as a result, most of the long-term residents of the community will feel unwelcome in these churches. A missional church enjoys, cares for, and prays for its city.

Another aspect of this contrast community is unity across church communities and denominations. In Christendom, when "everyone was a Christian," it was perhaps useful for a church to define itself primarily in contrast with other churches. Today, however, it is much more illuminating and helpful for a church to define itself in relationship to the values of the secular culture. If we spend our time bashing and criticizing other kinds of churches, we simply play into the common defeater that all Christians are intolerant. While it is right to align ourselves with denominations that share many of our distinctives, at the local level we should cooperate with, reach out to, and support the other congregations and ministries in our local area. To do so will raise many thorny issues, of course, but our bent should be in the direction of cooperation.

I believe these points of common ground in the missional conversation are sound and generally consistent with a Center Church theological vision. I would use the term *missional church* less cautiously and more expansively if these were indeed understood to be the key aspects of the definition.

Still, as fruitful as the search for the missional church has been, it has not always taken the church into friendly or helpful territory. Significant and important differences exist among various groupings in the missional conversation. In the next chapter, I'll look at key dangers and imbalances induced by some of the thinkers and practitioners in the missional conversation and suggest some course corrections.

DISCUSSION QUESTIONS

1. Keller writes, "The word [*missional*] has significantly different meanings and is used in different ways by different authors, organizations, and churches—leading to much confusion about what, exactly, the term *missional* means." How have you used or defined *missional*? How has this chapter changed or contributed to your understanding of this term?

2. The concept of *missio Dei* suggests that "God does not merely send the church in mission. God already is in mission, and the church must join him." What do you believe is the mission of God and what role does the church have in that mission? How would you distinguish between the mission of God and the mission of the church?

3. Of the four understandings of "missional" presented in this chapter, which most closely aligns with your own? What is it about the other understandings that you find objectionable?

4. Four common emphases characterize those who embrace the idea of being missional:

   - acknowledging that we have entered a post-Christian age in the West
   - recognizing the cultural captivity of the church and the need to contextualize the gospel for a pluralistic society
   - affirming that mission is the job of every Christian
   - calling the church to be a contrast community

   What are some of the unique elements of each emphasis that are discussed in this chapter? Which of these resonated most with you as you read about them? Which is the most difficult to persuade others of within your community?

Chapter 2

CENTERING THE MISSIONAL CHURCH

Though a clear and valuable benefit exists in identifying the common ground of the missional church, the range of differences among various definitions and viewpoints is great, and many aspects of the visions for "missional living" contradict each other. Everyone involved in the missional conversation concludes that others are making significant errors, and I am no different in this regard. As I have observed the ongoing conversation about the missional church and tested many of these ideas as a practitioner, I have three primary concerns with the way some segments of the missional conversation are appropriating the core insights outlined at the end of the previous chapter. We need to learn how to discern and avoid each of these problems if we are to be effective in developing a ministry with a Center Church orientation.

Problem #1: Not Comprehensive Enough

First, we examine the branch of the conversation that sees the missional church as simply being evangelistic. I agree that any missional church must be pervasively, intensely evangelistic in the common use of the word—we must call people to personal conversion. However, the typical evangelical gospel presentation is too shallow. It speaks cursorily about a God whom we have sinned against, a Savior who died for our sins, and a call to believe in this Savior. The simplicity of this communication presumes that those listening share the same essential understanding of the words *God* and *sin* as the speaker.

But what if a growing majority of people outside the church live by such a radically different view of life that much of what is now said and done by the Christian community is inexplicable or even deeply offensive to them? What if many listeners hold a profoundly different understanding of the concepts of God, truth, right and wrong, freedom, virtue, and sin? What if their approaches to reality, human nature and destiny, and human community are wholly different from our own?

For decades, this has been the situation facing Christian churches in many areas around the world—places such as India, Iran, and Japan. Evangelism in these environments involves a lengthy process in which nonbelievers have to be invited into a Christian community that bridges the gap between Christian truth and the culture around it. Every part of a church's life—its worship, community, public discourse, preaching, and education—has to assume the presence of nonbelievers from the surrounding culture. The aesthetics of its worship have to reflect the sensibilities of the culture and yet show how Christian belief shapes and is expressed through them. Its preaching and teaching have to show how the hopes of this culture's people can find fulfillment only in Christ. Most of all, such a congregation's believers have to reflect the demographic makeup of the surrounding community, thereby giving non-Christian neighbors attractive and challenging glimpses of what they would look like as Christians.

One reason much of the evangelical church in the United States has not yet experienced the same precipitous decline as the Protestant churches of Europe and Canada is that, unlike these places, the U.S. still includes sizable remnants of Christendom. We have places where the informal public culture (though not the formal public institutions) still stigmatizes non-Christian beliefs and behavior. There is, according to journalist Michael Wolff, a "fundamental schism in American cultural, political, and economic life. There's the quicker-growing, economically vibrant ... morally relativist, urban-oriented, culturally adventuresome, sexually polymorphous, and ethnically diverse nation ... And there's the small-town, nuclear-family, religiously oriented, white-centric other America, [with] ... its diminishing cultural and economic force ... two countries."[1]

To reach this growing post-Christendom society in the West will obviously take more than what we ordinarily call an *evangelistic* church; it will take a *missional* church. This church's worship is missional in that it makes sense to nonbelievers in that culture, even while it challenges and shapes Christians with the gospel.[2] Its people are missional in that they are so outwardly focused, so involved in addressing the needs of the local community, that the church is well-known for its compassion. The members of a missional church also know how to contextualize the gospel, carefully challenging yet also appealing to the baseline cultural narratives of the society around them.[3] Finally, because of the attractiveness of its people's character and lives, a missional church will always have some outsiders who are drawn into its community to incubate and explore the Christian faith in its midst.

So the idea that "to be missional is to be evangelistic" is too narrow. A missional church is not *less* than an evangelistic church, but it is much more.

Problem #2: Too Tied to a Particular Form

A second major problem is the tendency to put too much emphasis on a particular church form. Many who participate in missional church discussions insist that the church should be incarnational rather than attractional.[4] If taken as a broad principle, this is a correct statement. That is, if an attractional church is understood as tribal, as showing little concern for the broader community, drawing people in from the world and absorbing them into internal church programs that only meet their felt needs rather than equipping them to serve — then a missional church should not be attractional.[5] And if *incarnational* can be defined as a church that listens to its community to learn what its needs are, speaks and interacts with its community with respect, equips and sends its people out to love and serve — then all missional churches should be incarnational.

However, many argue that any church that bases its ministry on bringing people in to a large weekly meeting cannot be missional. David Fitch, a pastor in the missional community Life on the Vine, writes the following about megachurches:

Mega-church ... packages a service to speak a message that they assume can make sense to anonymous guests. Missional assumes the opposite—that people have no language or history by which to understand the words "Jesus is Lord." Therefore we must incarnate/embody the gospel for it to make sense. A packaged entertaining speaker/program every Sunday simply cannot do the job of communicating the gospel in post-Christendom.[6]

Fitch asserts that non-Christians in a post-Christian society will be so completely unable to understand the gospel that any mere verbal presentation of it will not be compelling or understood. In addition, he argues that any church that focuses on a large weekly gathering will by necessity require too much time and money for the church to be missional. For Fitch, to be missional is "to spend most of one's time and ministry outside the four walls of a church building, inhabiting a neighborhood learning who they are, what they do, and where the spiritual/holistic needs are. Its rhythm contradicts the rhythm of an attractional church."[7]

Many believe, along with Fitch, that a missional church cannot take the form of a large church or even of a small traditional church that is centered on a weekly worship and preaching service. Those who hold this view organize either as small house churches (ten to fifty people) with bivocational pastors and leaders or as a network of midsize house churches that gather for larger "attractional" meetings occasionally.

Michael Frost and Alan Hirsch address this model:

Most of the emerging churches we have been able to uncover are quite intentional about developing smaller communities ... It is also much closer to New Testament ecclesiology and missions practice. The household church unit was the primary unit of missional community in the New Testament. Today whether they meet in homes like the contemporary house church movement or not is irrelevant. What is important is that they tend to be smaller, more diverse, less organized, life-oriented, missional, relational, faith communities, not requiring their own specialized churchy buildings.[8]

I believe this view presents too rigid an understanding of the missional church. I pastored a small church in a small, working-class town for nearly ten years. My church naturally had the kind of characteristics that house churches are seeking to create through intentional planning. Missional communities seek to re-create the *oikos*—the large, extended family of children, grandchildren, relatives, business associates, and neighbors that constituted most churches in the New Testament—and insist that ministry should be informal, relational, and organic.[9]

However, the midsized groups that are gathered into missional communities are not truly *oikoi*. They are usually not related to each other by a variety of blood ties, do not work in the same shops and plants, have not gone to the same schools, and have not belonged to the same clubs and civic organizations—which is how people in a small town know one another. The Christians in my church did not have to find ways to know their geographic neighbors; they were already deeply enmeshed with them. All the believers lived within a few miles of one another and rarely moved out of the area. We ate together, spent lots of time in one another's homes, and were deeply involved in one another's lives apart from Sunday services. And because of these durable and multivalent relationships, a great deal of outreach, pastoral care, fellowship, and community service did indeed happen organically through relationships. In short, small churches in small towns have, in general, the kind of relationships with each other and the surrounding community that missional communities seek to forge.

For more than twenty years, I've led a very large church in Manhattan in which we have significant mobility and turnover and in which people learn, do ministry, and are cared for mainly through large-scale programs. My conclusion? Both churches had seasons of evangelistic fruitfulness. In many cases, the traditional gathered church does tend to draw people "inside the walls" instead of sending and supporting Christians out to minister in their networks of relationships. However, in my own experience, my large urban congregation—particularly in its first decade—was, by and large, far more effective than the small church I served in reaching unchurched and non-Christian people. In the final analysis, I don't believe any single *form* of church (small or large, cell group based or midsize community based) is intrinsically better at growing spiritual fruit, reaching nonbelievers, caring for people, and producing Christ-shaped lives. I say "in the final analysis" because each approach to church—the small, organic, simple incarnational church, and the large, organizational, complex attractional church—has vastly different strengths and weaknesses, limitations and capabilities.

Alan Roxburgh, in his role as a consultant, finds that one of the first questions people ask him is this: "Can you show me a missional church model?"[10] They want a specific way of doing church, with a concrete pattern they can emulate. He rejects the very question, and so should we. Look again at the outline of the features of an effective missional church (pp. 32–35). Those features can be present or absent within any church model and size. Nearly any type of church may embrace or resist these features, though in different ways. All kinds are thriving, and all kinds are failing.

So the idea that "the missional church is the smaller house church" is shortsighted.

Problem #3: Loss of a Clear Understanding of the Gospel

My third and greatest concern is that while all missional church books use the term *gospel* constantly, it is obvious they do not mean the same thing by the term. This is a very serious problem. It is especially true of those who see being missional primarily in communal/reciprocal terms (though it occurs in the other categories as well).

The final result of God's redeeming work in Christ will be a completely renewed cosmos—a new heaven and a new earth. Therefore we can say that God is out not only to pardon and save our souls but also to heal all the ways sin has ruined the creation. However, some stress this aspect of God's saving program to the virtual exclusion of any attention to individual conversion. The reason is, as we have seen, that many redefine sin and salvation in completely corporate or horizontal terms. In their view, sin is mainly the selfishness, pride, greed, and violence that destroy community and God's creation. Accordingly, Christ's redemption is primarily the defeat of the forces of evil in the world that cause the harm, and the Spirit's application of this redemption is by means of tearing down barriers and moving toward a human society of sharing, egalitarianism, and mutuality. Finally, becoming a Christian is not about being reconciled to God through repentance and faith but about joining the new community that is at work to bring about a world of peace and justice. The classic doctrines regarding sin — as an offense against God's holiness that incurs his righteous wrath, as Christ propitiating God's wrath and taking our punishment as our substitute, and as the "great exchange" of our sin being placed on Jesus and his righteousness being placed on us — are rejected as too individualistic and as a contributing reason for the church's failure to become missional. Of course, sin has a devastating effect on our corporate life, and Christ's redemption surely will eventually restore creation, but when these traditional doctrines of sin and atonement are discarded, the corporate dimension virtually eliminates the call for individual repentance, faith, and conversion.

It should be acknowledged that the writers in this category continually speak of individual and corporate redemption in such phrases as "not only individual salvation but also" or "more than individual salvation" as a way of indicating that they are not denying or changing traditional evangelism but rather adding to it. But upon reflection, I find that the individual and corporate aspects of salvation, mission, and Christian living are often pitted against one another, and the individual aspect nearly eliminated. These doctrinal shifts result in a very different way of understanding a local church's mission. Using the concept of sphere sovereignty, it is best to think of the organized church's primary function as evangelizing and equipping people to be disciples and then sending the "organic church" — Christians at work in the world — to engage culture, do justice, and restore God's shalom. In many expositions of the missional church, this distinction virtually disappears.[11]

Most important, this overly corporate definition of sin and salvation results in a very different way of doing evangelism. Let me give one example. This way of reconceiving sin and redemption (as corporate and horizontal rather than as individual and vertical) was given popular-level expression by Dieter Zander, a pioneer of the emerging church.

In an article titled "Abducted by an Alien Gospel," he relates how his aunt shared the gospel with him when he was a child. She said, "If you are lying, you are committing a sin. If you die tonight without having your sins forgiven, you will go to hell." That night, Zander asked Jesus to forgive all his sins and come into his life, and he went to bed sure of eternal life.

After moving as an adult to the San Francisco area, Zander tried talking to a Jewish neighbor about Christianity. What he shared was essentially what he had known of the gospel since childhood: "God loves us, but we've all sinned. God sent Jesus to pay for our sins, and if we trust in Jesus' payment, God will forgive our sins and give us eternal life." But as he spoke, he not only found his gospel presentation ineffective; he found himself thinking, "This just doesn't sound like good *news*."

Going back to Scripture, he came to realize that the heart of Jesus' gospel was "the kingdom of God." And what was this? "The arrival of a different kind of life, under the reign of a present and powerful God who, according to another version of Jesus' good news in Luke 4, was intent upon restoring, healing, redeeming, and reconciling all of creation." Here Zander follows the basic contours of the *missio Dei*. With his new understanding of the kingdom of God as a "different kind of life" and the restoration of all creation, he redesigned his gospel presentation and returned to his Jewish friend:

> I no longer believe that being a Christian is just a matter of having my sins forgiven ... The good news that Jesus announced is that we can live our lives with God—which is the best kind of life that is humanly possible. We don't have to live life alone—taking care of ourselves, being afraid that we don't have what we'll need, being intimidated and controlled by things in our life that we can't seem to change, wondering if there's anything or anyone who can make sense of the whole thing.
>
> Jesus' message is, simply, "Turn around and step into a life with God, the kind of life I lived and invite you to live with me."
>
> When we accept Jesus' invitation, believe that what he is saying is true, and follow him with our whole life, we experience freedom

from past sins and future fears, along with contentment, joy, love, and power today.[12]

Zander reports that his neighbor responded more positively this time. He concludes his article by saying that we must "bring to people the same message that Jesus brought: the offer of life with God and the invitation to be his coworker in what he is doing in the world."

This article vividly captures how our conception of *missio Dei* will play a significant role in what we actually share with people as the gospel. The gospel of Zander's childhood (let's call it the AG for "alien gospel") was indeed inadequate. First, the AG offers an extremely thin concept of sin. Sin is seen as merely breaking the rules, for which you need forgiveness. There is no hint of sin as the deep and settled bent of the heart toward self-salvation and idolatry. Because the AG's account of sin is so shallow, listeners do not get the sense either that their sin is deeply unfair, wrong, and offensive to God or that it is profoundly destructive of their own lives. Instead, this view of sin as "rule breaking" leads listeners to see that their only problem is the legal consequences of the sin they face from the Divine Enforcer. Nothing in this presentation shows sin as intrinsically wrong, hateful, destructive, and shameful in itself.

As a result of this thin view of sin, the AG does not really clarify the classic gospel distinction between grace and works, between faith in Christ's saving work and faith in our own saving work. The average hearer of the AG will see themselves as saved, not primarily because of Jesus' death on the cross, but because they are sincerely submitting to God and begging for mercy and resolving to live a better life. Essentially, they do not see themselves as moving from faith in their own moral efforts (whether as secular or religious persons) to faith and rest in Christ's saving work. Rather, they see themselves as moving from living bad lives to living better ones. Their sins are forgiven, and God accepts them *because* they are now living for Jesus — not the other way around.

When we look at Zander's redesign of the gospel (let's call it the KG for "kingdom gospel"), we find that it doesn't actually change this pattern at all. First, there is still no mention of the cross or why it was necessary for Jesus to die. In fact, there is no mention of Jesus' saving work at all. The emphasis is not on Jesus as substitute but on Jesus as a model of living a particular kind of courageous and loving life ("step into … the kind of life I lived and invite you to live with me"). Second, in order to receive both forgiveness of sins and power within, we must "believe that what he is saying is true, and follow him with our whole life." Instead of being invited to believe and rest in the saving work of Christ, there is an invitation to stop living in one way and start living in another. The listener to Zander's gospel can easily conclude the same thing they did when they heard the AG: "If I live in the right way, then I'll be forgiven and accepted."

In the end, the AG and the KG are not much different. Both of them tell you that Jesus died for your sins and that you need to receive that forgiveness. So far, so good. But both messages fail to present the offensiveness, depth, and destructiveness of sin, and therefore they miss the "sharp point" of the gospel's spear — the distinction between grace and works, between embracing Jesus as your Savior and merely using him to be your own savior. It is understanding and applying this distinction that creates the power for life change. People who believe they are accepted by God because they are leading a traditionally moral, chaste, and good life or because they are living a life of sacrificial service for the needs of the world will be equally insecure, unable to take criticism, prone to look down on people who are not "getting it right," and unsure of God's love or of their identity in Christ. Both are still essentially enslaved to the bonds of works-righteousness. It doesn't matter if it takes a traditional, conservative, moralistic form or a culturally progressive, justice-oriented, kingdom-restoration form.

Evangelicals who describe the gospel as Dieter Zander does will almost always, when asked, profess belief in a traditional understanding of justification by faith. But many others — proponents of the missional church who are outside of the evangelical tradition — have rejected its traditional views of justification and substitutionary atonement. Many will say that talking about the wrath of God and the need for justification simply doesn't work today. Postmodern people, they say, won't find the doctrine of justification by grace compelling because they perceive God, if he exists at all, as someone who accepts them as they are without any need for atonement or radical grace. In the KG presentation, people are called, not to be reconciled to God, but to step out of a life of fear and self-absorption into a life of reliance on God and service to others. You are left with the impression that God has no problem with you—you are just shortchanging yourself by failing to belong to his movement. There is no real barrier to be overcome between you and God other than your reluctance to join his work. I struggle to see how this approach differs in essence from the AG—the classic "salvation by works" way of understanding salvation. It is salvation by a different kind of works. Instead of offering a contextually sensitive starting place for a gospel presentation, it gives us an entirely different definition of salvation altogether, one that is by works rather than by grace.

It naturally follows that this understanding of sin leads to a different understanding of conversion. Traditional Protestantism believed that conversion was more than simply the adoption of a new set of values; it was seen as a radical change in inner identity. The driving motivation of your life was now rooted in grateful wonder and in love for the One who did so much for you. The old motivations of fear and pride were swept away by God's radical grace. But all of this is muted in the kingdom presentation. When someone hears the KG gospel of submitting to Jesus as Lord and joining his kingdom community, how can they sing Charles Wesley's cathartic refrain from "And Can It Be That I Should Gain"?

> My chains fell off, my heart was free,
> I rose, went forth, and followed Thee.

What chains? Set free from what, exactly? The biblical gospel brings people to see their peril in light of God's holiness while simultaneously becoming aware of the costly and amazing sacrifice of Jesus, who took on himself the punishment we deserve. If this is muted in our gospel presentations, we also mute that sense of wonder at the astonishing love of Jesus, the one who has rescued us.

D. A. Carson, in a lengthy review article of various authors who share many similarities with the views of Lesslie Newbigin, David Bosch, and Darrell Guder, wrote the following:

We have repeatedly seen how the "story" of God's advancing kingdom is cast in terms of rescuing human beings and completing creation, or perhaps in terms of defeating the powers of darkness. Not for a moment do I want to reduce or minimize those themes. Yet from what are human beings to be rescued? Their sin, yes; the powers of darkness; yes. But what is striking is the utter absence of any mention of the wrath of God. This is not a minor omission. Section after section of the Bible's story turns on the fact that God's image bearers attract God's righteous wrath. The entire created order is under God's curse because of human sin. Sin is not first and foremost horizontal, social (though of course it is all of that); it is vertical, the defiance of Almighty God. The sin which most consistently is said to bring down God's wrath on the heads of his people or on entire nations is idolatry—the de-godding of God. And it is the overcoming of this most fundamental sin that the cross and resurrection of Jesus achieve. The most urgent need of human beings is to be reconciled to God. That is not to deny that such reconciliation entails reconciliation with other human beings, and transformed living in God's fallen creation, in anticipation of the final transformation at the time of the consummation of all things. But to speak constantly of the advance of the kingdom without tying kingdom themes to the passion narrative, the way the canonical Gospels do, is a terrible reductionism.[13]

Carson's point is vital. There are definitely corporate and horizontal aspects in both sin and redemption. These biblical concepts are deep, comprehensive, and far-reaching. But if in the effort to bring these horizontal aspects out more clearly we deny the classic doctrines of grace, then the result will be a destructive imbalance. The classic Protestant understanding of the gospel includes the notion that God is holy and we are under his wrath and curse, but that Jesus bore in our place that wrath, curse, and punishment. When we repent and believe in him, we are given both pardon and Christ's righteousness. This electrifying experience of God's grace makes a Christian passionate for doing justice—for pursuing the horizontal aspects of the gospel. A Christian's zeal for justice comes from a transformed identity that flows from a grasp of the gospel—a gospel proclaiming that salvation is by faith alone, not by works.

The Marks of a Missional Church

Where does this bring us? I am arguing that a church can robustly preach and teach the classic evangelical doctrines and still be missional. That is, it can still have a missionary encounter with Western culture *and* reach and disciple unchurched, nontraditional nonbelievers in our society. How so?

1. A missional church, if it is to have a missionary encounter with Western culture, will need to confront society's idols and especially address how modernity makes the happiness and self-actualization of the individual into an absolute. One of the manifestations of this idol is materialism—consumerism and greed that lead to injustice. As we have seen, many believe that in order to have this confrontation we must recast the gospel, but as I explained elsewhere at length, the classic messages of substitutionary atonement and forensic justification provide both a strong theological basis and a powerful internal motivation to live more simply and to do justice in the world.[14] Rejecting these doctrines, then, does not aid us in this encounter with Western culture. In fact, nothing challenges and confronts the modern idolization of the "expressive, autonomous individual" like the simple and ancient gospel message that we all are sinners under God's wrath who need to repent and submit to him.

2. A missional church, if it is to reach people in a post-Christian culture, must recognize that most of our more recently formulated and popular gospel presentations will fall on deaf ears because hearers will be viscerally offended or simply unable to understand the basic concepts of God, sin, and redemption. This fact does not, however, require a change in the classic Christian doctrines, but rather skillfulness in contextualizing them so our gospel presentations are compelling even to people who are not (yet) fully persuaded by them. Within Christendom, it was possible to simply exhort Christianized people to do what they knew they should do. Christian communicators now must enter, challenge, and retell the culture's stories with the gospel. And, as I argued there, it is the traditional gospel of salvation by sheer grace that gives us both the internal confidence and the humility to do contextualization.

3. A missional church will affirm that all Christians are people in mission in every area of their lives. We must overcome the clericalism and lay passivity of the Christendom era and recover the Reformation doctrine of "the priesthood of all believers." Again we can see that classic doctrines of salvation do not obscure this critical idea. Its great proponent was Martin Luther, who associated this "ministry egalitarianism" with the doctrine of free justification rather than through works and merit, which can lead to a hierarchical view that ministry is only for the holy and for those removed from the world.[15] To be missional today requires that lay Christians be equipped by their churches to do three things: (1) to be a verbal witness to the gospel in their webs of relationships, (2) to love their neighbors and do justice within their neighborhoods and city, and (3) to integrate their faith with their work in order to engage culture through their vocations. A missional church will be more deeply and practically committed to deeds of compassion and social justice than traditional fundamentalist churches and more deeply and practically committed to evangelism and conversion than traditional liberal churches. This kind of church is profoundly counterintuitive to American observers, who are no longer able to categorize (and dismiss) it as liberal or conservative. Only this kind of church has any chance in the non-Christian West. A church that equips its people in this way will not only be something like a lay seminary in discipleship and training; it will also find ways to strongly support the people in their ministering "outside the walls" of the church.[16] This aspect of missional ministry is so important that I am devoting the next chapter to it.

4. A missional church must understand itself as a servant community—a counterculture for the common good. For centuries in the West, churches could limit themselves to specifically "religious" concerns and function as loose fellowships within a wider semi-Christian culture. Now, however, becoming a Christian involves a much more radical break with the surrounding non-Christian culture. The church can no longer be an association or a club but is a "thick" alternate human society in which relationships are strong and deep—and in which sex and family, wealth and possessions, racial identity and power, are all used and practiced in godly and distinct ways. However, while the Christian church must be distinct, it must be set within, not be separated from, its surroundings. Its neighbors must see it as a servant society, sacrificially pouring out its time and wealth for the common good of the city.

Here again I would argue that this emphasis on deep and counter-cultural community is not undermined by the classic Reformation doctrines of justification and imputation but rather is enhanced by them. No one has argued more compellingly for this than Dietrich Bonhoeffer in his classic *Life Together*.[17] As Bonhoeffer shows, the gospel decenters the ego and clears the way not only for far deeper and more transparent relationships between Christians (helping to make the church a contrast community) but also for humble, servant relationships with people who do not share our beliefs. The sacrificial service of a missional church will show the world, then, a "third way" between the individualistic self-absorption that secularism can breed and the tribal self-righteousness that religion can breed.

5. A missional church must be, in a sense, "porous." That is, it should expect nonbelievers, inquirers, and seekers to be involved in most aspects of the church's life and ministry—in worship, small and midsize groups, and service projects in the neighborhood. A missional church knows how to welcome doubters and graciously include them as much as possible in community so they can see the gospel fleshed out in life and process the gospel message through numerous personal interactions.[18] This will only happen if all of the above ingredients are in place and if believers inside the church are themselves "contextual"—that is, culturally like yet spiritually unlike the people in the surrounding neighborhood and culture.[19] A missional church, then, does not depend on an evangelism program or department to do outreach. Almost all parts of the church's life must be ready to respond to the presence of people who do not yet believe.

6. A missional church should practice Christian unity on the local level as much as possible. In the heyday of Christendom, churches received definition by contrasting themselves with (and constantly criticizing) other denominations and traditions. Today we should define ourselves more by contrasting ourselves with the world and our surrounding culture. The world must see churches avoiding unnecessary divisions.[20]

Six Marks of a Missional Church

1. The church must confront society's idols.
2. The church must contextualize skillfully and communicate in the vernacular.
3. The church must equip people in mission in every area of their lives.
4. The church must be a counterculture for the common good.
5. The church must itself be contextualized and should expect nonbelievers, inquirers, and seekers to be involved in most aspects of the church's life and ministry.
6. The church must practice unity.

These six marks of a missional church can exist in both large and small churches of various forms and are strengthened, not weakened, by a clear grasp of the understanding of the gospel that was recaptured by the Protestant Reformers. There is one mark I think is the most practical single way a church can implement a missional mind-set — *training and equipping the people of the church for ministry*. We will focus our attention on that priority in the next chapter.

DISCUSSION QUESTIONS

1. Do you agree with this chapter's assertion that no "single *form* of church ... is intrinsically better at growing spiritual fruit, reaching nonbelievers, caring for people, and producing Christ-shaped lives"? Be honest about your own biases — which form is most popular in your context? Why? How might this form be adapted to be more missional?

2. Consider Dieter Zander's story in which he compares the "alien gospel" and the "kingdom gospel." How are these two gospels similar to each other? How does the biblical gospel differ from both of them?

3. Keller writes, "The classic Protestant understanding of the gospel includes the notion that God is holy and we are under his wrath and curse, but that Jesus bore in our place that wrath, curse, and punishment. When we repent and believe in him, we are given both pardon and Christ's righteousness. This electrifying experience of God's grace makes a Christian passionate for doing justice—for pursuing the horizontal aspects of the gospel." Which do you tend to emphasize more in your preaching and teaching, the horizontal or the vertical? How are these two aspects of the gospel connected?

4. Six marks of a missional church are presented in this chapter. A missional church should:

   - confront society's idols and address how modernity makes the desires of the individual into an absolute
   - contextualize skillfully and discourse in the vernacular, recognizing that many people are simply unable to understand the basic concepts of God, sin, and redemption
   - recognize that all Christians are people in mission in every area of their lives
   - understand itself as a servant community—a counterculture for the common good
   - be contextualized and expect nonbelievers, inquirers, and seekers to be involved in most aspects of the church's life and ministry
   - practice Christian unity on the local level as much as possible

   For each of these marks, what unique challenges and opportunities does it provide for communicating the gospel? Which of these does your church need to focus on right now?

Chapter 3

EQUIPPING PEOPLE FOR MISSIONAL LIVING

Until now, we've spent most of our time trying to understand the missional conversation, discerning some of its commonalities and strengths, as well as its errors and pitfalls. One recurring theme is the importance of equipping and involving the laity in ministry. Under Christendom, people simply came to the church to receive the ministrations of the professional clergy. We can no longer assume that people will come. This should not be taken to imply that the ordained ministry is obsolete—by no means! It is the responsibility of the ordained leadership to build up the church and its members through the ministry of the Word and sacraments. However, one critical focus of that ministry must now be the discipling of the laity for ministry in the world. This is one of the most practical ways a church can appropriate the insights of the missional conversation, moving toward a centered, balanced approach to ministry.

We find an example of this idea in an interview conducted with Eddie Gibbs and Ryan Bolger of Fuller Seminary. When asked, "What are the marks of churches (people) that live missionally?" Bolger provides a helpful and practical answer: "They no longer see the church service as the primary connecting point with those outside the community. Connecting with those outside happens within the culture, by insiders to that culture who express the gospel through how they live."[1]

The rest of this chapter will propose different ways and means for equipping and encouraging the laity to engage in ministry "within the culture." I give special emphasis to the lay ministry of the Word—the building up of believers and the evangelizing of nonbelievers through preaching and teaching—though in part 2, I will point to some other ways that Christians can do ministry in the world, including the practice of justice and the integration of faith and work.

"Informal Missionaries"

There has always been a strong tendency, as John Stott says, for Christians to "withdraw into a kind of closed, evangelical, monastic community."[2] This is not, of course, how things were in the early church. The Greek word *euangelizō* means "to gospelize," to tell people the good news about what Jesus did for us, and in the book of Acts literally everyone in the early church does it. Not only the apostles (5:42) but every Christian (8:4) did evangelism—and they did so endlessly. Passages such as Romans 15:14; Colossians 3:16; 1 Thessalonians 1:6 – 10; Hebrews 3:13; and 1 John 2:20, 27 indicate that every Christian was expected to evangelize, follow up, nurture, and teach people the Word. This happened relationally—one person bringing the gospel to another within the context of a relationship.

In Michael Green's seminal *Evangelism in the Early Church*, he quotes Adolf von Harnack's conclusion that early Christianity's explosive growth "was in reality accomplished by means of informal missionaries."[3] That is, Christian laypeople—not trained preachers and evangelists—carried on the mission of the church not through formal preaching but informal conversation—"in homes and wine shops, on walks, and around market stalls ... they did it naturally, enthusiastically."[4]

Green quotes pagan writers such as Celsus, who complained with great sarcasm that "we see in private houses ... the most illiterate and bucolic yokels, who would not dare to say anything at all in front of their elders and more intelligent masters. But they get hold of ... any ... who are as ignorant as themselves and say ... 'We know how men ought to live. If your children do as we say, you will be happy yourselves and make your home happy too.'" Green writes, "In fact, of course, it pays the highest compliment to the zeal and dedication of the most ordinary Christians in the subapostolic age. Having found treasure, they meant to share it with others, to the limits of their ability."[5]

Green is careful to point out that not all evangelism in the early church was informal. In his chapter titled "Evangelistic Methods," he speaks of many forms of evangelism that required great training and expertise, including synagogue preaching and open-air preaching, as well as public teaching and "dialogical" evangelism. Early Christian teachers set up academies (schools for instruction in the faith) but also taught science, mathematics, philosophy, and the humanities from a Christian perspective. The great Catechetical School of Alexandria was one, and we know that Justin Martyr started one in Rome. Green shows that many non-Christians came to take classes, listen to lectures, and dialogue with teachers. The original example of this form of evangelism may have been the apostle Paul's lecturing in the public hall of Tyrannus in Ephesus. There he engaged in *dialegomenos*—interactive dialogue with all comers —about the Christian faith daily for two years (Acts 19:9 – 10). Green writes, "The intellectual content of his addresses must have been very stimulating. Here was a man who could hold his own, and presumably make converts, in the course of public debate."[6]

But Green returns to the most important way that Christianity spread—through the extended household (*oikos*) evangelism done informally by Christians. A person's strongest relationships were within the household—with blood relatives, servants, clients, and friends—so when a person became a Christian, it was in the household that he or she would get the most serious hearing.[7] If the head of the household (Greek, *oikos*) became a believer, the entire home became a ministry center in which the gospel was taught to all of the household's members and neighbors. We see this in Acts 16:15, 32 – 34 (Lydia's and the jailer's homes in Philippi); Acts 17:5 (Jason's home in Thessalonica); Acts 18:7 (Titius Justus's home in Corinth); Acts 21:8 (Philip's home in Caesarea); and 1 Corinthians 1:16; 16:15 (Stephanas's home in Corinth).

The home could be used for systematic teaching and instruction (Acts 5:42), planned presentations of the gospel to friends and neighbors (Acts 10:22), prayer meetings (Acts 12:12), impromptu evangelistic gatherings (Acts 16:32), follow-up sessions with inquirers (Acts 18:26), evenings devoted to instruction and prayer (Acts 20:7), and fellowship (Acts 21:7).

If another member of the household became a Christian—the wife, children, or slaves and laborers—then the gospel would spread more indirectly. In his chapter titled "Evangelistic Methods," Green sketches out the different ways the gospel moved through households, depending on who was the first convert.

We also know from the Bible and early historical records that simple friendship was one of the main carriers of the gospel. We see this in John 1 when Philip passes on his knowledge of Jesus to his friend Nathanael. Green relates how Pantaenus led Clement of Alexandria to Christ, Justin led Tatian, and Octavius led Minucius Felix—all through friendship, which was taken very seriously by the ancients.[8]

The Lay Ministry Dynamic

What does this "every-member gospel ministry" look like in today's world? Here are several examples:

- Jerry is asked by his work colleague Bill how his weekend went. Jerry relates that he went on a men's retreat that provided spiritual resources for forgiving people who have wronged us over the years. When Bill raises his eyebrows and says, "That's interesting," Jerry takes a small plunge and mentions that the thing that helped him most was the idea that even though he has not given God his due, God offers him forgiveness through Jesus.
- Dan and Jill help their two sons, ages five and seven, with Scripture memorization and teach them a simple catechism. They field the boys' questions and help them understand the meaning of the texts they are studying.
- Sally gets to know a young woman named Clara at church. Clara confides that she and her husband are having marriage problems and he isn't willing to go to a counselor. Sally and her husband, Jeff, invite Clara and Sam over for a meal. Sam hits it off with Jeff. Afterward, Clara convinces Sam to meet with Jeff and Sally to talk about their marriage issues. They meet together once a month for four months, studying Ephesians 5 and several other biblical texts on marriage.

- John comes to church with his wife, but he isn't sure what he believes or where he stands on faith. The pastor introduces him to an elder named Tom, who begins meeting with John on occasion to read and discuss a book about basic Christianity. After two meetings, John agrees to study the gospel of Mark with Tom every two or three weeks.
- Jenny begins coming to a small group in the church. She was raised in the church but has so many doubts and questions that her group leader, Beth, begins meeting with her one-on-one. They study Bible passages and read books that address each of her questions, one after the other.
- Ted is a young single lawyer. He knows several other lawyers who go to church with him, though they don't work for his firm. He decides to have a Super Bowl party for several of his non-Christian colleagues and invites two Christian lawyers from church and a couple of other believers as well. The men and women from his workplace hit it off with the lawyers from church. About three months later, one of them shows up in church with one of Ted's friends.
- Jessica meets Teresa, a new believer, at church and invites her to work through a series of six Bible studies for new Christians (on issues such as prayer, Bible reading, the role of the church, understanding the gospel better, etc.).
- Fred has been attending a small group for months. At one point he realizes that he assesses the value of the group strictly on what he gets out of it. He then decides to begin preparing well (studying the passage) and praying for the group. When he comes, he looks for every opportunity to help the Bible study leader by making good contributions and for ways to speak the truth in love so others are encouraged and can grow.
- Catherine prays for her friend Megan for months. Megan responds well to two short books on Christian subjects that Catherine has given her. She then invites Megan to an evangelistic event in which Christian truth is presented. On the way home, she fields Megan's questions.

- Joe has a longtime friend from college days named Pete, who is a musician. Pete's performance anxiety is harming his career. Joe has been a sympathetic listener for some time, but finally he bluntly asks Pete to explore the Christian faith with him. "I think maybe it's the only thing that will help you overcome your problem." Pete is taken aback, but after a while, he expresses interest, mainly out of desperation. Joe warns him, "If Christianity is going to be any help, it will only be if you come to the belief that it is not just helpful but *true*." Pete doesn't want to go to any Christian gatherings, so they start studying the Bible together and listening to sermons and lectures and discussing them.

- Kerrie and two other Christian friends are moms who have young kids. They decide to start a daytime moms' group and invite non-Christian friends. For about a year, the group grows to include a similar number of Christians and nonbelievers. The conversations are general and freewheeling—covering spiritual, social, marriage, parenting, and personal issues. As time goes on, several of the nonbelievers begin to go to church with the believers and cross over into faith. After three years, the group is a Christian Bible study but still open and inclusive toward a few nonbelievers who come regularly.

- Jim and Cynthia are both artists who are involved in a citywide Christian artists' fellowship based in their local church. The fellowship typically includes a discussion of the relationship of faith to art that assumes a Christian belief, but the artists have four events a year that will be either a gallery showing or a book event in which a credible working artist talks to a general audience about how their faith relates to their art. Jim and Cynthia are diligent in bringing non-Christian artists or art appreciators to these events.

- Greg comes to faith in Christ through a skeptics/seeker group hosted by a church. When the date for his baptism is set, he invites a number of non-Christian friends to the service and then takes them out for lunch and discusses the whole event. One friend is very moved by the experience, and Greg invites him to come back. Eventually, the friend begins coming to his small group with him.[9]

We can make several observations about these examples. First, it should be clear that we are not just talking about evangelism in the traditional sense here. Some of these examples show instances of encouraging and building up new believers; some point to ways of spurring Christians on to greater growth in Christ; others depict situations of helping believers address particular problems in their lives. And yet the basic form of this every-member gospel ministry is the same:

- **Organic.** It happens spontaneously, outside of the church's organized programs (even though it occasionally makes use of formal programs).
- **Relational.** It is done in the context of informal personal relationships.
- **Word deploying.** It prayerfully brings the Bible and gospel into connection with people's lives.
- **Active, not passive.** Each person assumes personal responsibility for being a producer rather than just a consumer of ministry; for example, even though Fred continues to come to the small group as he always has, his mind-set has changed.

Traditional evangelism is only one piece of this every-member gospel ministry, and it is often not the largest piece. Still, as lay ministry grows in a congregation, so too will the amount of evangelism.

Second, notice we are talking about lay *ministry*, not necessarily lay *leadership*. Often ministers talk about lay ministers and lay leaders as if they are the same thing. But this may betray too much attractional church thinking. By lay leaders, I mean volunteers who lead and run church programs. Being a lay leader can be time-consuming and may even make lay ministry more difficult for a season. Lay leadership usually requires some level of leadership and organizational ability, while lay ministry does not. Lay leaders are extremely important to lay ministry—overworking lay leaders can kill lay ministry in a church—but they are not the same thing. Lay ministers are people who actively bring their Christian example and faith into the lives of their neighbors, friends, colleagues, and community.

My experience has been that when at least 20 to 25 percent of a church's people are engaged in this kind of organic, relational gospel ministry, it creates a powerful dynamism that infuses the whole church and greatly extends the church's ability to edify and evangelize. Lay ministers counsel, encourage, instruct, disciple, and witness with both Christian and non-Christian individuals. They involve themselves in the lives of others so they might come to faith or grow in grace. Then a certain percentage of the people served by these lay ministers come into the lay ministry community as well, and the church grows in quality and quantity. Because they are being equipped and supported by the church's leaders, those involved in lay ministry tend to feel a healthy sense of ownership of the church. They think of it as "our church," not "their church" (referring to the ordained leaders and staff). They freely and generously give of their time, talent, and treasure.

This is the tide that lifts every boat in ministry. Without Christian education and counseling, without formal and informal diaconal work, without the preaching of the Word and administration of the sacraments, without support for family life, without the management and stewardship of resources, without church government and discipline, laypeople will not be built up into lay ministers. But if lay ministry is happening all through and around the church, it grows each of these other functions in quality and quantity. Where do the human resources and even the financial resources come from to do *all* of the work of the church? They come from every-member gospel ministry.

Missional Evangelism through Mini-Decisions

Notice another assumption behind the examples of lay ministry given here: many people process from unbelief to faith through "mini-decisions."

We hold to the classic teaching about the nature of the gospel: to be a Christian is to be united with Christ by faith so that the merits of his saving work become ours and his Spirit enters us and begins to change us into Christ's likeness. You either are a Christian or you are not—you either are united to him by faith or you are not—because being a Christian is, first of all, a "standing" with God. However, we also acknowledge that coming to this point of uniting to Christ by faith often works as a process, not only as an event. It can occur through a series of small decisions or thoughts that bring a person closer and closer to the point of saving faith. In a post-Christendom setting, more often than not, this is the case. People simply do not have the necessary background knowledge to hear a gospel address and immediately understand who God is, what sin is, who Jesus is, and what repentance and faith are in a way that enables them to make an intelligent commitment. They often have far too many objections and beliefs for the gospel to be readily plausible to them.

Therefore, most people in the West need to be welcomed into community long enough for them to hear multiple expressions of the gospel—both formal and informal—from individuals and teachers. As this happens in community, nonbelievers come to understand the character of God, sin, and grace. Many of their objections are answered through this process. Because they are "on the inside" and involved in ongoing relationships with Christians, they can imagine themselves as Christians and see how the faith fleshes out in real life.

The process often looks something like this:

1. Awareness: "I see it." They begin to clear the ground of stereotypes and learn to distinguish the gospel from legalism or liberalism, the core from the peripheral. They make mini-decisions like these:

- "She's religious but surprisingly open-minded."
- "You *can* be a Christian and be intelligent!"
- "The Bible isn't so hard to understand after all."
- "A lot of things the Bible says really fit me."
- "I see the difference between Christianity and just being moral."

2. Relevance: "I need it." They begin to see the slavery of both religion and irreligion and are shown the transforming power of how the gospel works. Examples of mini-decisions here are as follows:

- "There must be some advantages to being a Christian."
- "An awful lot of very normal people really like this church!"
- "It would really help if I could believe like she does."
- "Jesus seems to be the key. I wonder who he was."

3. Credibility: "I need it because it's true." This is a reversal of the modern view that states, "It's true if I need it." If people fail to see the reasonableness of the gospel, they will lack the endurance to persevere when their faith is challenged. Examples of mini-decisions include thoughts like these:

- "I see that the Bible is historically reliable."
- "You can't use science to disprove the supernatural."
- "There really were eyewitnesses to the resurrection."
- "Jesus really *is* God."
- "I see now why Jesus had to die — it is the only way."

4. Trial: "I see what it would be like." They are involved in some form of group life, in some type of service ministry, and are effectively trying Christianity on, often talking like a Christian — even defending the faith at times.

5. Commitment: "I take it." This may be the point of genuine conversion, or sometimes a person will realize that conversion has already happened, and they just didn't grasp it at the time. Examples of mini-decisions include these:

- "I am a sinner."
- "I need a Savior."
- "Though there are a lot of costs, I really must do what Jesus says."
- "I will believe in Jesus and live for him."

6. Reinforcement: "Now I get it." Typically, this is the place where the penny drops and the gospel becomes even clearer and more real.

Creating a Lay Ministry Dynamic

A spiritual dynamic cannot really be created or controlled, but just as we need air, heat, and fuel to have a fire, certain environmental factors must be present for this lay ministry dynamic to occur. At least three factors must be in place: believers with relational integrity, pastoral support, and safe venues.

Believers with Relational Integrity

A message is contextualized if (1) it is adapted into a new language or culture so it is understandable and yet (2) it maintains its character and original meaning in its former language/culture. Here I'm proposing that Christians *themselves* must be contextualized "letters of the gospel" (see 2 Cor 3:1 – 13). In other words, we will have an impact for the gospel if we are *like* those around us yet profoundly different and *unlike* them at the same time, all the while remaining very visible and *engaged*.

So, first of all, Christians must be like their neighbors in the food they eat and clothes they wear, their dialect, general appearance, work life, recreational and cultural activities, and civic engagement. They participate fully in life with their neighbors. Christians should also be like their neighbors with regard to excellence. That is, Christians should be very good at what others want to be good at. They should be skillful, diligent, resourceful, and disciplined. In short, Christians in a particular community should, at first glance, look reassuringly *similar* to the other people in the neighborhood. This opens up nonbelievers to any discussion of faith, because they recognize the believers as people who live in and understand their world. It also, eventually, gives them a glimpse of what they could look like if they became believers. It means it would be good if a nonbelieving young man on Wall Street could meet Christians in the financial world, not only those who are his age but also those who are older and more accomplished, or if an older female artist could meet Christian women who are artists of her own generation as well as others who are not.

Second, Christians must be also unlike their neighbors. In key ways, the early Christians were startlingly different from their neighbors; it should be no different for us today. Christians should be marked by *integrity*. Believers must be known for being scrupulously honest, transparent, and fair. Followers of Christ should also be marked by *generosity*. If employers, they should take less personal profit so customers and employees have more pay. As citizens, they should be philanthropic and generous with their time and with the money they donate for the needy. They should consider living below their potential lifestyle level. Believers should also be known for their *hospitality*, welcoming others into their homes, especially neighbors and people with needs. They should be marked by *sympathy* and avoid being known as self-serving or even ruthless in business or personal dealings. They should be marked by an unusual willingness to *forgive* and seek reconciliation, not by a vengeful or spiteful spirit.

In addition to these character qualities, Christians should be marked by clear countercultural values and practices. Believers should practice *chastity* and live consistently in light of the biblical sexual ethic. Those outside the church know this ethic—no sex outside of marriage—and any inconsistency in this area can destroy a believer's credibility as a Christian. Today, few people apart from those with strong Christian convictions live this way. Outsiders and non-Christians in the community will also notice how you respond to *adversity*. Being calm in the face of failure and disappointment is crucial to your Christian witness. Finally, they will notice if you are seeking *equity*—if you are committed to the common good of the community. Francis Schaeffer gives an example of what these countercultural values look like:

> The Bible does clearly teach the right of property, but both the Old Testament and the New Testament put a tremendous stress on the compassionate use of that property. If at each place where the employer was a Bible-believing Christian the world could see that less profit was being taken so that the workers would have appreciably more than the "going rate" of pay, the gospel would have been better proclaimed throughout the whole world than if the profits were the same as the world took and then large endowments

were given to Christian schools, missions, and other projects. This is not to minimize the centrality of preaching the gospel to the whole world, nor to minimize missions; it is to say that the other is also a way to proclaim the good news.[10]

In addition to being *like* others and *unlike* others, Christians should also be *engaged* with others.[11] Mission for a contextualized believer is a matter of everyday life—of developing nonsuperficial relationships with their neighbors, colleagues, and others in the city.

Here are some practical, simple ways to do this:

Engaging neighbors

- Take regular walks in your neighborhood to meet others who are out and about. Keep a regular schedule. Go to the same places at the same time for groceries, haircuts, coffee, shopping. This is one of the main ways you get to know those who live geographically near.
- Find ways to get to know others in your building or neighborhood—through a common laundry area, at resident meetings, and in numerous other ways.
- Find an avocation or hobby you can do with others in the city. For example, don't form a Christian backpacking club; join an existing one.
- Look for ways to play organized amateur sports in the city.
- Volunteer alongside other neighborhood residents at nonprofits and with other programs.
- If you have children, be involved at the school and get to know other parents.
- Participate in city events—fund-raisers, festivals, cleanups, summer shows, concerts, etc.
- Serve in your neighborhood. Visit the community board meeting. Pick up litter regularly. Get involved in neighborhood associations. Find individual neighbors (especially elderly ones) and find ways to serve them.
- Be hospitable to neighbors—when and where appropriate, invite them over for a meal or a movie, etc.

Engaging colleagues, coworkers, and friends

- Do recreational activities with them—watch sports (live or on TV at home or in a nightspot); go to a theater show, museum exhibit, art gallery exhibit, etc.
- Invite them to join a sports league with you.
- Invite them to work out with you at a gym.
- Put together a movie night.
- Go out of your way to eat with them as often as possible. Invite people over for a meal in your apartment or home or just invite them out to try a new restaurant.
- Plan trips or outings—a trip to a beach, a historical site, etc.
- If the person has a skill or interest, ask them (sincerely!) to educate you.
- Organize a discussion group on something—politics, books, etc., inviting mainly non-Christians.

Part of being engaged is being willing to identify as a believer. Engaging relationally without doing so could be called "the blend-in approach." Many Christians live in a social world of non-Christians but don't think much about their friends' spiritual needs, nor do they identify themselves as believers to their friends. Their basic drive is to be accepted, to avoid being perceived as different—but this approach fails to integrate a person's faith with his or her relationships in the world.

The opposite can be true as well. It is certainly possible for a person to identify as a believer without engaging relationally outside the church. These are Christians who are aware of people's lostness and may get involved in conversations about faith, but their relationships with non-Christians are largely superficial. We could call this "the Christian bubble approach." In this case, believers fill all of their significant relationships outside of work with other Christians and their time with Christian activities. They have not sought opportunities to learn from nonbelievers, appreciate them, affirm them, or serve them—so regardless of what these Christians believe, those outside the church do not know they care about them.

Forty years ago, most of us knew gay people, but we didn't *know* we did because everybody was carefully quiet about it. As a result, it was possible to believe stereotypes about them. Today most young people know someone who is gay, and so it is harder to believe stereotypes or generalizations about them. I suspect most urban skeptics I talk to today do have Christian friends, but they don't know it, because we are more afraid these days of being publicly identified as believers. In this sense, many Christians today are like gay people were forty years ago—so it is quite natural for people to believe caricatures and stereotypes of Christians because the believers they actually know are not identifying themselves. Skeptics need more than an argument in order to believe; they need to observe intelligent, admirable fellow human beings and see that a big part of what makes them this way is their faith. Having a Christian friend you admire makes the faith far more credible.

These three factors—*like*, *unlike*, and *engaged*—make up the foundation of what I call Christian relational integrity. Christians have relational integrity when they are integrated into the relational life of the city and when their faith is integrated into all parts of their lives. Why is Christian relational integrity important for evangelism and mission? Many churches think of evangelism almost strictly in terms of information transmission. But this is a mistake. Christian Smith's book on young adult religion in the United States looks at the important minority of young adults who become much more religious during their twenties. The factors associated with such conversions are primarily significant personal relationships.[12]

Alan Kreider observes that early Christianity grew explosively— 40 percent per decade for nearly three centuries—in a very hostile environment:

> The early Christians did not engage in public preaching; it was too dangerous. There are practically no evangelists or missionaries whose names we know ... The early Christians had no mission boards. They did not write treatises about evangelism ... After Nero's persecution in the mid-first century, the churches in the Roman Empire closed their worship services to visitors. Deacons stood at the churches' doors, serving as bouncers, checking to see that no unbaptized person, no "lying informer," could come in ...

And yet the church was growing. Officially it was a *superstitio*. Prominent people scorned it. Neighbors discriminated against the Christians in countless petty ways. Periodically the church was subjected to pogroms ... It was hard to be a Christian ... And still the church grew. Why?[13]

This striking way of laying out the early church's social situation forces us to realize that the church must have grown because it was *attractive*. Kreider writes, "People were fascinated by it, drawn to it as to a magnet." He goes on to make a strong historical case that Christians' *lives*—their concern for the weak and the poor, their integrity in the face of persecution, their economic sharing, their sacrificial love even for their enemies, and the high quality of their common life together—attracted nonbelievers to the gospel. Once nonbelievers were attracted to the community by the lives of Christians, they became open to talking about the gospel truths that were the source of this kind of life.

Urban people today do not face the same kind of life-threatening dangers that they did in the Greco-Roman world—plagues, social chaos, and violence. In that environment, being in a loving community could literally mean the difference between life and death. But urban residents today still face many things that Christianity can address. They lack the hope in future progress and prosperity that past generations of secular people have had. They face a lonelier and more competitive environment than other generations have faced. The quality of our lives—marked by evident hope, love, poise, and integrity—has always been the necessary precondition for evangelism. But this has never been more necessary than it is today.[14]

Why is there so little relational integrity among believers? The answer is largely—though not wholly—motivational. People who are in the blend-in mode often lack courage. They are (rightly) concerned about losing influence, being persecuted in behind-the-scenes ways, or being penalized professionally. On the other hand, those who are in the bubble mode are unwilling to make the emotional, social, or even financial and physical investment in the people around them. Surprisingly, the Internet contributes to much of this. Technology now makes it possible for a person to move to a city and remain in touch with their Christian friends and family in other places, while unintentionally making it easier to ignore the people who are physically living around us. This can contribute to our reluctance to invest emotionally in people.

But this lack of motivation is not the only reason we fail to see lay-people doing evangelistic outreach. Many are highly motivated but still feel handcuffed by a lack of skill and know-how. They find that the questions their non-Christian friends ask about the faith very quickly stump them or even shake their own faith. They feel they can't talk about the Christian faith with any kind of attractive force. This lack of skill and knowledge accentuates their lack of courage (they are afraid of being stumped) and even affects their compassion for others (they feel as though they won't be of any real help). This leads us to consider the second necessary factor for effective lay ministry.

Pastoral Support

There is a way to pastor that promotes this every-member gospel ministry, just as there is a way to pastor that kills it. Whatever else they do, pastors and other church leaders must be aware of the importance of lay ministry and intentional about preparing people for it. They must be personally involved in the lives of lay ministers. The reasons so many Christians lack relational integrity—lack of motivation, lack of compassion, or lack of ability and knowledge—are often overcome through a strong pastoral connection with the lay ministers.

This connection does not come primarily through formal, content-heavy training sessions on "how to share your faith" (though this is vital and can be very helpful; at Redeemer, we are producing such materials to fit an urban environment). Instead, it is formed through informal teaching and support and ongoing advice from pastors and ministry leaders. Pastors must constantly remember to encourage and push lay-people to use their relationships for the ministry of the Word.[15]

It is important for a pastor to model how to both *talk* to people about faith issues and *pray* for them. In my earlier years at Redeemer, I did this in two ways: through the sermons I preached and in the Q&A

sessions I held after every morning service. I modeled how to pray for people through regular prayer meetings with leaders in which we prayed for our nonbelieving friends. This modeling instills a sense of courage, compassion, and responsibility in people and encourages them to reach out to their friends.

A pastor and his team must be models of Christian relational integrity for the rest of the congregation. David Stroud, a London church planter, shares how his wife, Philippa, became deeply involved in the local public school while he started a neighborhood watch program on their street. These endeavors got them immersed into the life of the city and brought them into many relationships with their neighbors.[16]

In addition to modeling, it is also important that pastors maintain a practical and simple vision for a relational ministry of the gospel. It should be clear that reaching out to friends and colleagues does not necessarily involve sharing a complete gospel presentation in a single encounter. Despite the fact that this was the stated goal of several evangelism training programs a generation ago, only a small number of laypeople (or even clergy!) can do this well. Reaching out to a friend is much more natural. These organic ways of reaching out must be constantly lifted up for people.

I summarize below some ways to do this, listed in order of intensity. Pastors should equip the people in their church to do all of these, pointing out that most of these behaviors require little more than some honesty and courage. Many of these are drawn from the case studies I gave earlier in this chapter.

1. One-on-one—informal

- Let others know of your Christian faith by simply mentioning church attendance or Christian beliefs in casual conversation.
- Ask questions about other people's beliefs and experiences with faith and church and simply listen appreciatively and sympathetically.
- Listen sympathetically to someone's challenges and mention that you will pray regularly for them.
- Share a difficult personal issue that you have and be sure to

mention that your faith helps you by giving you strength and granting you forgiveness, etc.

- Share your spiritual narrative—a brief testimony of your Christian experience.

2. One-on-one—planned/intentional

- Offer someone a book or audio recording about Christian issues and invite them to discuss their reactions.
- Initiate a discussion about a friend's biggest problems with or objections to Christianity. Listen respectfully and give them some things to read and discuss.
- Regularly read a part of the Bible together—preferably one of the Gospels—to discuss the character of Jesus.

3. Provide an experience of Christian community

- Invite friends to situations or activities where they meet believers but where there is no direct Christian event or communication.
- Invite friends to venues where they hear the gospel communicated and discussed—a one-time event, such as an open forum; a fellowship group; a worship service; a group meeting for inquirers, such as a book club, a seeker group, etc.

4. Share your faith

- Share the basics of the Christian faith with your friend, laying out how to become a Christian and inviting them to make a commitment.

It is important for pastors or elders to be readily available to field questions about issues that church members encounter in discussions with their friends. When a non-Christian asks a question such as, "Why does God allow such evil and suffering?" your people need quick turnaround with help on how to respond. A pastor can also provide free or low-cost materials that Christians can share with their friends. For example, if a Christian is sharing how Christianity helped them face a problem, they could give their friend a book or an audio or video selection that conveys the truth they found helpful. Every believer should have access to half a dozen compelling pieces of content on different subjects that they can give to someone after talking about an issue. This, of course, includes the offer to read and study the Bible together. Along the way, a pastor should try to meet regularly with lay ministers to talk about what is happening in their relationships. This has two purposes. On the one hand, it is a time to celebrate and encourage one another; on the other hand, it is a time to hold one another accountable to think about these relationships with a ministry mind-set that commits to reaching out and opening up to people.[17]

Perhaps most important, a pastor must work in a variety of ways to lay a theological motivational groundwork for lay evangelism using the gospel itself. This must be done in all kinds of venues — teaching, preaching, and personal pastoral support. What does this gospel groundwork look like? It means teaching people that the gospel gives you *humility*. As people come to understand the radical gospel analysis — that both "good" and "bad" people are equally lost and can only be saved by grace — it becomes impossible to be proud and condescending toward others without denying the gospel itself. Moralistic Christians do evangelism with the attitude, "I'm right; they're wrong — and I enjoy telling people about it." Nothing could be less attractive or more oblivious to the spirit of the message itself. The gospel, by contrast, leads us to look at non-Christians and know that they may very well be better people than we are. I can look at my Hindu neighbor and realize he may be a much better father to his children than I have ever been. The gospel gives us the foundation of a humble appreciation of others on which winsome relationships can be built.

The pastor can also show people how the gospel gives us hope for non-Christians. It is easy to look at some people and say, "They will never become Christians." But when we grasp the gospel, we know that there is no such thing as a typical Christian. No person is more promising material for Christianity than another. Salvation is an undeserved gift. So there is hope for anyone, no matter how far from God they may seem to be. The attitude of your heart should instead be this: "Me, a Christian? Who would have ever thought that someone like me would be a Christian and a child of God? But that is what I am! It's a wonder and a miracle." This attitude leads us to have expectant hope as we think of anyone else.

Finally, we must explain how the gospel gives us courage for evangelism. One of the reasons we shy away from talking about Jesus and the gospel is that we are afraid. We get our sense of value from what people think of us. We want to appear cool or sophisticated or progressive, or we want to look respectable, so we are careful to mind our own business. Sadly, when we think this way, how God regards us is not important enough to us. But the gospel keeps us from being tied to our reputation. When we know that salvation is by grace alone, we know that people come to faith only if God opens their hearts. No amount of brilliance or overpowering reason will serve to bring someone to faith. Therefore, we don't have to worry about our lack of knowledge. It is God's grace that opens hearts, not our eloquence.

If your lay ministers are ineffective in reaching out to others because they are turned off by certain kinds of people or because they lack the hope or courage to talk to others about Jesus, they may not need another book or a course on evangelism. You may just need to help them get back to the foundation—the gospel—and allow the message of God's gracious, undeserved, merciful love for sinners to work itself into their hearts in new ways. I believe the single most important way for pastors or church leaders to turn passive laypeople into courageous and gracious lay ministers is through their own evident godliness. A pastor should be marked by humility, love, joy, and wisdom that is visible and attracts people to trust and learn from them. As a pastor, you may not be the best preacher, but if you are filled with God's love, joy, and wisdom, you won't be boring! You may not be the most skillful organizer or charismatic leader, but if your holiness is evident, people will follow you. This means, at the very least, that a dynamic, disciplined, and rich prayer life is not only important in the abstract and personal sense; it may be the most practical thing you can do for your ministry.

Safe Venues

It is certainly possible to have an evangelistic dynamic built strictly on relational, informal outreach by laypeople. Nevertheless, laypeople are often encouraged and instructed in their ministry if a church provides a varied set of events, gatherings, and meetings in which nonbelievers are exposed more directly to both Christians and to the gospel. Such settings must avoid two common dangers: *confusing* the newcomer (assuming a particular theological or ecclesiastical background) or *offending* the newcomer (putting unnecessary stumbling blocks in front of them). I daresay that most well-intentioned "outreach" events I witnessed over the years have fallen into one or both of these errors. Use your ingenuity to imagine a variety of meetings and places where people without faith can, through a winsome approach, be stimulated to consider the claims of the Christian gospel.[18] Here are some examples:

- A one-off event, such as an open forum. At Redeemer, these have typically been artistic forums (such as "Excerpts from *Porgy and Bess*," "Coltrane Night," or a Bach Wedding Cantata), followed by a lecture that offers a Christian perspective on the art, with a time for questions and answers.
- A gathering in a small public venue with a brief talk and Q&A on a single topic that addresses problems people have with Christian faith. At Redeemer, we call these "Christianity Uncorked" events.
- A small group that is just beginning to form. When groups are relatively new and the dynamics are still "wet cement," they can better embrace and draw in people who are exploring Christianity.
- A worship service that—through its preaching, music, and liturgy—is comprehensible to non-Christians.
- A group of Christians that meets for four weeks; each week, each member asks one non-Christian friend a question about their religious beliefs for the purpose of listening to (not debating) other religious beliefs and objections to Christianity.
- A group mainly for non-Christians that meets regularly. *Less intense*:

a book club focused on reading fiction books by C. S. Lewis, Flannery O'Connor, J. R. R. Tolkien, G. K. Chesterton, Fyodor Dostoyevsky, etc., that get at Christian themes, or even reading books by non-Christians and talking about the faith perspectives and worldviews they represent. *More intense*: Eight-week "seeker groups" that meet to study a book. Some people may respond well to frank discussions about common "defeaters" of Christianity,[19] while others may prefer to explore the life of Jesus through reading one of the Gospels or using a book such as *Jesus the King*.[20]

- One-time "salons" in which Christians bring non-Christian friends to hear an informal presentation by a Christian speaker on a topic, followed by a discussion.
- Worship "after meetings." Examples include a Q&A session after the church service with the preacher of the day, where any questions are allowed, though usually the topic of the message is covered; an apologetics class (five to seven weeks) that makes a case for the truth of Christianity; or a seven-week class covering basic Christian beliefs and Christian living, oriented to new believers but open to attendance by seekers.
- Affinity-based outreach. Campus ministries, vocational (industry-based) ministries, and men's or women's gatherings can have an evangelistic/apologetics aspect in their regular meetings and may hold outreach events at neutral venues, similar to the ones described above.

Evangelism should be natural, not dictated by a set of bullet points and agenda items that we enter into a conversation hoping to cover. Friends share their hearts with each other and do what's best for each other. Evangelism will come organically in friendship if we don't let our pride, fears, and pessimism cause us to hide our faith and heart. We must help our people naturally talk to their friends about how they see reality. The more these gospel dynamics are present in their lives, the more they will draw in new people like a magnet (Acts 2:47) and help them find faith in the most credible, natural, and fruitful way.

In general, simply bringing nonbelievers into the Christian

community at any point is safe if the whole community is very warm and accepting toward those without faith, if the community is not culturally alien, if the community is shepherded by pastors who make lay ministry a priority, and if the church is doing balanced and integrative ministry. It is to this last subject that we turn our attention in part 2.

DISCUSSION QUESTIONS

1. Read through the various examples of every-member gospel ministry. Which of these situations sound similar to something you have done personally? Which of them spark creative ideas for sharing your faith, as well as for leading others to do so? What could your team do to become more intentional in this type of gospel ministry? Can you add to the list other examples you have seen in your community?

2. What do you think of the idea that people may need to be "welcomed into community long enough for them to hear multiple expressions of the gospel—both formal and informal—from individuals and teachers" before coming to faith? What might keep a nonbeliever from being involved in your community? What are you doing to welcome nonbelievers into your community of faith?

3. This chapter presents the idea of believers having "Christian relational integrity." This means they have an impact for the gospel on the people around them if they are *like* those around them, yet profoundly different and *unlike* them, all the while remaining very visible and *engaged*. What do you think it means to be *like*, *unlike*, and *engaged with* your community? How do you think your team members are doing in each of these areas? How would you rate your church in the area of relational integrity?

4. Which of the various ideas for providing safe venues do you currently practice in your ministry? How "safe" would an unbeliever rate the venues you provide? What single safe venue would you like to prototype?

REFLECTIONS ON MISSIONAL COMMUNITY

Tim Chester, author and pastor of The Crowded House and founder of Porterbrook Seminary

These chapters by Tim Keller are a helpful springboard for exploring what it means to be a missional church and what it looks like in a twenty-first-century Western context. As Keller mentions, the great contribution of Lesslie Newbigin was his recognition that the West is a mission field just as much as what we once called "heathen lands."

I want to interact with Keller's "three primary concerns with ... the missional conversation" (p. 40). As will become clear, I largely share his concerns, but I have some additional emphases and suggestions to make as well.

Don't Assume Evangelism

Keller's first criticism is of those who define *missional* as "simply being evangelistic." The problem with this, he argues, is that "the typical evangelical gospel presentation is too shallow" (p. 40). It assumes the outside world knows what we are talking about when we use words like *God* or *sin*. The Western church needs to contextualize its message, just as missionaries to other parts of the world have learned to do (a task to which Keller himself has contributed much). The value of the word *missional* is that it designates more than simply a church that does a lot of evangelism. It describes a church whose worship makes sense to unbelievers, whose people are known for their compassion, and whose message is contextualized to the culture (see p. 40).

Keller says "any missional church must be pervasively, intensely evangelistic" (p. 40). He makes this claim and goes on to state what else a church needs to be. But I think it is vital to emphasize this point. It is not enough to assert evangelism and move on, when many within the missional movement have become so contextualized or incarnational that the challenge of the gospel is no longer proclaimed. Some have become so good at connecting with the culture that they can no longer confront the culture. They have forgotten how to challenge individuals to faith and repentance.

Earning the Right to Be Heard?

At points in his chapters on missional community, Keller makes it sound as though the church needs to earn the right for the gospel to be heard through our acts of sacrificial service. In a sidebar in *Center Church*, Keller cites Newbigin's claim that we must "[earn] the right to be heard through willingness to serve others sacrificially."[1] But whether or not Keller endorses this, we need to be careful with this idea. Here's why.

I surely recognize the value of serving others sacrificially, but we must reject the idea that we either can or should earn the right to be heard. Our right to be heard is not inherent to ourselves. It comes from the enthronement of Christ by God the Father. When I speak the gospel, I do not speak in my name or in the name of my church; I speak in the name of Christ. And he has a right to be heard. This is one of the implications of the ascension. The Crucified One has been raised from the dead and is enthroned in glory. The One who was silenced by humanity at the cross has been vindicated by the Father through the ascension. He has come, as Daniel 7 predicted, on the clouds into the presence of the Ancient of Days to receive all authority. And it is because he has received all authority that he sends us out in his name to call the nations to obedience.

It is this conviction in the authority of the ascended Christ that drove the mission of the apostles. When the Sanhedrin told the apostles they had no right "to teach in this name," Peter replied, "We must obey God rather than human beings! The God of our ancestors raised Jesus from the dead—whom you killed by hanging him on a cross. God exalted him to his own right hand as Prince and Savior that he might bring Israel to repentance and forgive their sins. We are witnesses of these things, and so is the Holy Spirit, whom God has given to those who obey him" (Acts 5:29–32). The apostle Paul did not arrive in a new town and spend a few months earning the right to speak by doing acts of compassion. He walked into the synagogue and proclaimed the name of Christ.

We can and should seek to gain respect for the message we proclaim. Perhaps that amounts to the very same thing. But I do not want to dissuade Christians from speaking out by making them think there is something they need to *do* before they can *speak* of Christ. We must always be people who proclaim the name of Christ. If at the same time we can serve others sacrificially, so much the better. Our actions will reflect and reinforce our message. But at the heart of mission is evangelism through proclamation.

The Word Must Be Proclaimed

This is because the gospel is a word. It is good news, and news is something you proclaim. It is the declaration of the victory of Christ over sin and death. It is the proclamation of Christ as King. So mission must be word-centered. There is an oft-repeated adage, sometimes attributed to Saint Francis of Assisi: "Preach the gospel; use words if necessary." Like the emperor with no clothes, this needs to be named as the folly that it is. Our actions can illustrate the gospel. But the gospel must still be preached with words. Without words, we are not engaging in mission.

Consider what is communicated if you engage in mercy ministries without any gospel proclamation. You will convey either the impression that salvation equates to socioeconomic betterment or the idea that salvation is attained through good works, since doing good works appears to be your main concern. The message of eternal life given by grace through the finished work of Christ will not be inferred by your actions apart from your words.

I sympathize with Keller's concern that some equate missional church with being "intensely evangelistic." The problem is not that this definition reduces what it means to be missional, but that it is a reductionistic view of what it means to be evangelistic. The problem here is seeing evangelism as a set of timetabled activities or programmed events rather than as a lifestyle. The shift from evangelism as an event to evangelism as a lifestyle is central to being missional. We need in our churches an evangelistic *culture* that shapes the entirety of daily life and the entirety of church life.

What about good works and social involvement?[2] These are important. They are clearly mandated by Scripture and are the natural responses of a Christian to those in need. Those who have received grace naturally extend grace to others. We are called to love our neighbors. But the evangelistic culture that runs through our lives will also run through our social involvement.

Evangelism and social action are, I believe, best thought of in terms of text and context. Every text makes sense in its context. Our text— the message of Christ that we proclaim in our evangelism—makes best sense in the context of lives shaped by that message. We need the context of our lives to help interpret the text of our evangelism. But—and this is important—if a text makes best sense in its proper context, a context makes no sense at all without a text! What Lesslie Newbigin calls a "willingness to serve others sacrificially" and what Keller calls "addressing the needs of the local community" (p. 40) must have at their heart a commitment to proclamation.

This does not mean preaching to the people lined up at the soup kitchen. Often in these discussions the worst practice in evangelism is set up as a straw man to be demolished. Good evangelism is always relational. But so is good social action. And in the context of these relationships, we will look for opportunities to proclaim Christ. After all, we are addressing the greatest need of every person, rich and poor. What counts, then, is gospel intentionality—a commitment to shape our lives around mission and to proclaim Christ when opportunities arise.

Everyday Evangelism

We need to create what Keller, quoting Michael Green, calls "informal missionaries" (p. 56). He cites Green's seminal *Evangelism in the Early Church*, which recognizes the role that evangelistic events played in the spread of the gospel. But Green concludes that the most important way that Christianity spread was through the household (*oikos*) evangelism done informally by Christians (p. 57). Keller traces this through the book of Acts (pp. 57–58). Let me add my own argument from 1 Peter.

Peter writes to a church that finds itself on the margins of the wider culture. These believers are not being persecuted by the state. Instead they face the hostility and slander of their neighbors (2:12, 15; 3:16; 4:4). They find themselves foreigners within their own culture (1:1, 17; 2:11). It is a situation very much like the one in which the church increasingly finds itself in the West. Peter urges his readers not to be surprised by this, "as though something strange were happening to you" (1 Pet 4:12).

How should Christians live in this hostile context? Peter reminds his readers of their missional identity in 2:9: "You are a chosen people, a royal priesthood, a holy nation, God's special possession, that you may declare the praises of him who called you out of darkness into his wonderful light." And he does this using biblical theology. He says the missional identity that Israel received at Mount Sinai in Exodus 19:4–6 is fulfilled in the church. The church is the people chosen to be a kingdom of priests who make God known to the world. The church is the nation that is holy as God is holy so that it displays his character (1 Pet 1:14–15). We are the people who declare the praises of God to the world. This requires us to live distinctive lives (2:11). We should contextualize and connect with people around us. But what will attract people to our message is not what we have in common with them but how we are distinct and different. It is the difference that the gospel makes to our communal life that provokes their questions (3:8–16).

In 2:12, Peter writes, "Live such good lives among the pagans that, though they accuse you of doing wrong, they may see your good deeds and glorify God on the day he visits us." This is his headline call to mission through a distinctive way of life with a declaration of God's praises at its heart. But notice how he works this out in the following verses. In 2:13–17, he talks about life in the civic realm. In 2:18–25, he talks about life in the workplace. In 3:1–7, he talks about life in the home. In each case, his concern is mission. The striking point is that *Peter's mission strategy for the church does not involve evangelistic courses or guest services.* There is nothing wrong with these, and much that is good about them. But the bedrock of Christian mission is ordinary Christians living gospel lives in the context of ordinary life with gospel intentionality. In this regard, Keller provides a helpful list of simple ideas for engaging neighbors, colleagues, coworkers, and friends in this way (pp. 67–68) and a helpful list of simple "organic ways" of sharing the gospel in this relational context (pp. 72–73).

These verses from 1 Peter highlight some key characteristics of an ordinary life lived with gospel intentionality. We are to treat people with respect (2:17; 3:7, 15). Our mission is not to be strident or arrogant. Peter's image of Christians as aliens and foreigners is helpful. Think of an ambassador. An ambassador shows respect to the country to which they have been assigned, but without ever losing their loyalty to their homeland. For the Christian, our homeland is now in heaven (1:3–5), but we engage with the world around us with respect. At the same time, we are to be courageous, for it is God we are to fear, and not people (2:17–18; 3:6, 14–15). This is what will make us bold to speak of Christ.

Above all, our engagement with the culture is to be cruciform, that is, it is to be shaped by the cross and resurrection. The life of those who are in Christ is thereby patterned on the life of Christ. For Christ, suffering was followed by glory (1:11). In the same way, the pattern for those who are in him is suffering followed by glory (4:13; 5:10). So Peter writes that slaves are to follow the example of Christ, who entrusted himself to God when he faced suffering (2:18–25). He then introduces his words to wives and husbands with the words "in the same way" (3:1, 7). In other words, the attitude of wives and husbands is also to be conformed to the cross.

David Bosch identifies two dangers our missional engagement must avoid. In Keller's words, they are "(1) trying to re-create a Christian society (the mistake of medieval Christendom) and (2) withdrawal from society into the 'spiritual realm' (the mistake of modernity)" (p. 28). Evangelicals sometimes succumb to both of these dangers. We try to create a Christian society that allows us to be comfortable within our culture without challenging the underlying idolatries of that culture. This is what we see in "the idea of religion as the fulfillment of individual consumer needs" (p. 29).

Peter navigates us through these dangers. He calls us to engagement by doing good and proclaiming God's praises. But we do this with respect and courage. Above all, our approach is christological. It is patterned on the One in whom we are now hidden. We proclaim the coming kingship of Christ because we know he has been given all authority. One day he will return, and every knee will bow before him. But that day has not yet come. In the meantime, we participate in the sufferings of Christ. Our conformity to the cross takes the form of self-denial, sacrificial love, and service. Christ claims the entire world as Lord, but as the ascended Lord, he rules from heaven. One day he will return, but in the meantime he rules through the cruciform lives of his people as we call people to submit to his lordship through faith and repentance. As Keller puts it, "A missional church must understand itself as a servant community—a counterculture for the common good" (p. 51).

Don't Get Tied to a Particular Form

I was once involved in answering questions about missional church in a Q&A session at a conference for church planters in Europe. It was a frustrating experience both for me and my questioners. The following morning, a participant said to me, "I've realized what was going on last night. You kept talking about what it means to *be* church, and we kept asking you about what it means to *do* church." I think he hit the nail on the head. I was uninterested in the nuts and bolts of church meetings, structures, and processes. More than that, I was reluctant to tell people what we did in our church because I do not think that what we do is what other people should be doing. Every church needs to work out the best way to do things in their own context. What matters to me are the theology and the culture that will drive this outworking.

This concern is reflected when Keller talks about the current missional conversation. He writes, "A second major problem is the tendency to put too much emphasis on a particular church form" (p. 40). He draws attention to those who want to replace what they refer to as "attractional church" with an "incarnational" model.

I agree with Keller's critique. Attractional church can be problematic when it capitulates to a consumerist culture. But attractional church can be done well, allowing unbelievers to observe the church without having first to commit to a small community. Moreover, a church can have a "mixed economy," with an attractive Sunday gathering alongside missional communities. Together these gatherings provide two doors into the church for unbelievers. They may connect through the life of a missional community, or they may be invited to observe a Sunday gathering.

I also think there are problems with the terminology of "incarnational." I am sympathetic with many of the things its advocates want to emphasize. But I believe it is the wrong category to use. The incarnation refers to the act of God becoming man, an act we cannot imitate. Attempts to extend the incarnation into our lives conceive of the church as a replacement for Christ and betray a faulty doctrine of the ascension.

My main concern in this context is the obsession we have with form. The church to which I belong is called The Crowded House, and sometimes people ask us about "The Crowded House model" of church. The reality is that we have changed our structures and our meetings several times in the relatively short life of our church plant. We are constantly adapting to a changing situation, both outside the church as new opportunities arise and within the church as it has grown. It could be that we are simply slow to work out what we should be doing. But I actually think this is how it should be. There is no right model of missional church except perhaps one of constant adaptation.

Ironically, this obsession with form betrays a modernist outlook. A characteristic of modernism is its belief in management, structure, and processes. This is reflected in our age of mass production, where one product could be built for everyone and problems can be solved by improved management or process reengineering. When we take this thinking and apply it to the church, we run into problems. Small may be beautiful for many in the missional community, but they wrongly assume that changing the structure is the solution. And they assume one size fits all. Just as Henry Ford offered us any color of car we wanted as long as it was black, so now we are offered any kind of church we want—as long as it is small.

So what do you do when your small churches grow large?

New life does not come through new structures. That's like putting old wine into new wineskins in the hope that it will somehow renew the wine itself. No, new life comes through the Word and the Spirit. And since we cannot control the work of the Spirit, we might say that new life comes from God in response to the proclamation of the Word and to prayer. When new life comes, you may find you have to create new wineskins for it. But new wineskins do not create new wine. So don't make the mistake of thinking that a new structure will create new missional life in your church.

If missional church cannot be equated with a specific structure, of what does it consist? I think the answer is a missional culture, a culture that is undergirded by a strong biblical theology. In our early days, we often used to say we were nothing but our culture. At that point, we had no building, no staff, and no incorporation. Indeed it was quite a while before we even had a bank account. All we had was our culture. To this day, our culture is something we guard carefully and promote constantly.

Here are some ideas for creating and sustaining a distinctive culture:

Stories. We started by defining our culture according to ten values. Each value had a paragraph that stated what we stood for, as well as what we did *not* do. But we realized that statements like this were not enough to capture people's imaginations. Creating a values statement does not mean you have created a culture. So we created short stories for each value to illustrate what they look like in practice. In the early days, these were fictional. But we have since taken every opportunity we can to tell actual stories that celebrate what people are doing. In sermons, small groups, and now in written communication, we share these real-life stories.

A common question when our missional communities meet is, "How has God been at work in our lives this week?" This provides opportunity to tell stories that put flesh on our values. As a leader, I am always looking for ways to highlight those connections. A community quickly learns to value what is celebrated.

Modeling. Abstract discussions about missional church do very little to create culture. The jargon doesn't help. People need to *see* how it works. So modeling is vital. This means leaders need to have an open life and an open home. There is no substitute for people seeing your life. They need to see how you welcome strangers, nurture your wife, and pastor your children. They need to see what it means for you to bring gospel intentionality to your ordinary life.

Paul writes to Timothy, "You, however, know all about my teaching, my way of life, my purpose, faith, patience, love, endurance, persecutions, sufferings—what kinds of things happened to me in Antioch, Iconium and Lystra, the persecutions I endured. Yet the Lord rescued me from all of them" (2 Tim 3:10–11). It is not enough for people to know "[our] teaching"; they need to know "[our] way of life." If they simply know our teaching, then they will be orthodox. But if we want missional disciples, they need to see how that teaching translates into practice. If we want them to be people who proclaim with courage in the face of hostility, then they need to see "[our] purpose, faith, patience, love, endurance, persecutions, sufferings."

People often ask how they can begin to move a traditional church toward a more missional outlook. My suggestion is to start with one small group. Be part of that group. Model a missional life for them. Give them a mandate to be innovative. Invest heavily in people with the group. And then let that group be a model for others. You cannot simply tell people from the front to be missional. It needs to be modeled. If things go well, then other people will hear the stories the group is telling and start to demand the same permission to be missional.

Core practices. For a long time we have defined our core missional commitments as a commitment to the gospel, community, and mission. These three commitments create three identities: we are disciples, we are family, and we are missionaries. More recently, we have been helped by the work of Todd Engstrom and The Austin Stone Community Church.[3] At The Austin Stone, they speak of three core missional community practices: a family meeting, a life transformation group, and a "third place." We have adapted this to create the following grid:

CORE CONVICTIONS	CORE IDENTITIES	CORE PRACTICES
Community	We are family.	a family meal
Word	We are disciples.	time in the Word
Mission	We are missionaries.	a third space
Mission through community	We are a missional community.	gospel intentionality in everyday life

Time in the word is when our missional communities, either as a whole group or in twos or threes, follow up the Sunday preaching with a view to specific application both in our individual lives and our life together. We also encourage missional application that involves thinking through how we might communicate to our friends and neighbors the truths of the passage we are considering.

A "third space" is a place or event to which people can invite friends to spend time with their Christian community. It is a neutral space where people naturally meet together. It is called a "third space" because it is neither home nor work (the first and second spaces). A group's "third space" could be a common missional project or a place where people naturally gather. If they find it hard to coordinate their schedules, they may identify a couple of "third spaces." A "third space" could be an event held in a home, if this is a natural place for people to hang out. But the danger of choosing a home is that, while it may be a place where we feel comfortable, it may not be a natural place for others to come.

This framework has helped us see how groups can progress from simple Bible study groups to groups committed to serving others to teams of missionaries and then to missional teams.[4] In our final stage, the core practices spill over into a life of gospel intentionality.

The rope model. Another framework we have used from the earliest days of our church is "the rope model." Jesus says, "A new command I give you: Love one another. As I have loved you, so you must love one another. By this everyone will know that you are my disciples, if you love one another" (John 13:34–35). Mission takes place as people see our love for one another. So exposure to the Christian community is a vital part of Christian mission.

This means we need to be communities of love, but we also need to be *seen* to be communities of love. This is the point Jesus is making in Matthew 5:14–16. He has just described his new community as "the light of the world" (v. 14). In the Old Testament, Israel was called to live under the reign of God so they would display the goodness of God's reign to the world. Now the church is to take up this calling to be the light of the world.

But Jesus continues: "Neither do people light a lamp and put it under a bowl. Instead they put it on its stand, and it gives light to everyone in the house" (v. 15). In other words, it is no good displaying the goodness of God in your communal life if no one sees that communal life! So the exhortation of Jesus to his new community is this: "In the same way, let your light shine before others, that they may see your good deeds and glorify your Father in heaven" (v. 16).

The key question then is this: When do people get to see our love for one another? Mission must not only involve contact between unbelievers and individual Christians; it must involve contact between unbelievers and the Christian community as well. Time after time in our experience, people have been attracted to the Christian community before they were attracted to the Christian message. Of course, attraction to the Christian community is not enough. The gospel, as I said earlier, is a word. But in 1 Peter 3:8, it is the life of the Christian community that provokes the questions of verse 15: "Finally, all of you, be like-minded, be sympathetic, love one another, be compassionate and humble … Always be prepared to give an answer to everyone who asks you to give the reason for the hope that you have."

To help people think about what this means in practice, we conceive of mission as a rope with three strands:

- building relationships
- sharing the gospel message
- including people in community

If one strand is missing, then, in God's sovereign plan, the rope may still hold. But it is stronger when all three are present.

We need Christian communities that saturate ordinary life with the gospel. The communities to which we introduce people must be communities in which "God talk" is normal. This means talking about what we are reading in the Bible, praying together when needs arise, delighting together in the gospel, and sharing our spiritual struggles—not only with Christians but with unbelievers as well.

What Do We Mean by the Gospel?

Keller writes, "My third and greatest concern is that, while all missional church books use the term *gospel* constantly, it is obvious they do not mean the same thing by the term. This is a very serious problem" (p. 43). He affirms that "the final result of God's redeeming work in Christ will be a completely renewed cosmos" but adds that "some stress this aspect of God's saving program to the virtual exclusion of any attention to individual conversion."

I agree with this concern, and I agree it is the most serious. It sometimes seems like there are two gospels within evangelicalism—the gospel of the cross and the gospel of the kingdom. The gospel of the cross declares that I have sinned against God and therefore come under his judgment. But God in his mercy sent his Son. Jesus died in my place so my sin could be forgiven and I could receive eternal life. The gospel of the kingdom says Jesus came to restore God's life-giving, liberating rule. He calls us to follow the pattern of his life and model his coming rule as we await his return.

I believe the gospel of the cross can be communicated in a way that is reductionistic. After all, Matthew 4:23 does read, "Jesus went throughout Galilee, teaching in their synagogues, proclaiming the good news of the kingdom." The danger with a reductionistic gospel of the cross is that the scope of repentance is limited. In effect, repentance only affects my sexual and family life, but not my sociopolitical commitments. The reality, however, is that the risen and ascended Christ is Lord of every aspect of my life.

The danger with the gospel of the kingdom (in some of its forms within the missional conversation) is that it misses the call to escape the holy wrath of God by hiding ourselves in Christ, our righteousness, whose substitutionary death atones for the penalty of sin.

It would be pleasing to retain a symmetry in this debate. But it is asymmetrical. Without an emphasis on the kingdom, the gospel of the cross is inadequate. But without an emphasis on the cross, the gospel of the kingdom is not gospel. It becomes a gospel of good works. It may be good works to achieve the kingdom of God rather than good works to achieve personal salvation, but it is still our good works rather than the good work of Christ on our behalf. We are left with a legalistic gospel of self-righteousness through social action.

As Keller notes, many advocates of what I am calling the gospel of the kingdom use the language of "not only individual salvation but also." But Keller concludes, "Upon reflection, I find that the individual and corporate aspects of salvation, mission, and Christian living are often pitted against one another, and the individual aspect nearly eliminated" (p. 44). Sadly, I agree. I suspect many were brought up with reductionistic versions of the gospel of the cross. They have discovered the New Testament's teaching on the kingdom of God. Now they *assume* the need for personal salvation through faith in Christ's work on the cross while they *emphasize* the kingdom of God and the call to social involvement. But the danger is that what is assumed in one generation is lost in the next.

Instead we must connect the kingdom and the cross. The kingdom comes in two stages, firstly secretly in the ministry of Jesus before, secondly, coming in glory at the end of time. The first time around, he does not come in judgment — for that would mean destruction for us all. So there is no judgment at the first coming of Jesus.

Except that this is not quite true. There is a glorious, wonderful twist. There *is* judgment, but that judgment falls at the cross as Jesus cries out under a dark sky, "*'Eloi, Eloi, lema sabachthani?'* (which means, 'My God, my God, why have you forsaken me?'" (Mark 15:34). Here the darkness of judgment hangs over Jesus as he dies, abandoned by his Father, bearing God's wrath against sin. There is judgment, but it is the King who is judged. The kingdom comes in grace as the King dies for his people.

Jesus begins his explanation of the programmatic parable of the sower by saying, "The farmer sows the word" (Mark 4:14). The kingdom grows as God's Word is proclaimed and people respond in faith. We are ambassadors of the King sent into enemy territory to warn of his coming and command people to switch their allegiance to the true King of the world.

This is why the ascension is so important. Jesus reigns in heaven. His reign is real. We are not pretending when we say Jesus is Lord. In heaven he has all authority. There is no doubt about his kingship. But he has not yet come to impose his reign on earth, for that would be judgment on all those who reject him. Instead he first sends his people to proclaim his kingship, to call on the nations to repent and take refuge in him.

● ● ●

As I mentioned at the beginning of my reflections, I am largely in agreement with what Keller has written in these chapters. Though I might add some additional nuance or word things a bit differently at times, I appreciate what he has done in summarizing the history and development of the missional movement and drawing attention to some of its strengths and weaknesses. Clearly the church today needs to be a missional church—a church that is biblically evangelistic and not tied to any particular form, a church that proclaims the gospel by communicating the message of the cross and the kingdom. We serve a risen and ascended Lord who reigns from his throne in heaven and will one day return. Until that day, the future of the church does not lie in developing slick megachurches or cool house churches. It does not lie in creating programs or tinkering with forms. It lies in faithful communities of people shaped by the gospel for the gospel, communities of people who share the gospel in the context of everyday life.

RESPONSE TO
TIM CHESTER

Timothy Keller

Tim Chester's books show up in the endnotes and bibliographies in *Center Church*, and it's great to have his contribution here. It is no surprise to me that he looks at my three "primary concerns" with the missional church movement and chiefly agrees with them. But he agrees with them in extremely helpful ways that provide significant enrichment and supplement to these chapters on missional community.

1. Concern about reductionism. The first concern is that most of the definitions of a missional church are not comprehensive enough. When I surveyed the vast literature of missional church ministry from the last two decades, I discovered no consensus about the definition. A significant cluster of books simply substituted the older word *evangelistic* with the newer *missional*. A larger, more dominant group of thinkers defined the missional church as one that was committed to repairing the world by doing justice and living in more intentional community.

What virtually all the books had in common was how reductionistic they were. The more traditional books defined missional as "numerical church growth." But most defined it almost strictly in terms of what Orlando Costas used to call "incarnational church growth" — doing justice and engagement with culture. Calling people to repentance and conversion essentially disappeared in these volumes. The upshot of my missional community chapters is not that evangelism, service, justice, and community simply need to be added to one another, but that they need to be carefully woven together interdependently through both rich theological understanding and careful practice.

Tim Chester largely affirms this first thesis and offers a helpful discussion of the dangers of the "earn the right to be heard" language. I expressed approval of some who spoke of the second commandment (neighbor love and service) "earning us the right" to speak to the world about the first commandment (loving God). Chester fears this may obscure the true foundation of a Christian's right to proclaim the gospel, which comes from the ascended Christ who sent us out in his name. Chester writes, "When I speak the gospel, I do not speak in my name or in the name of my church; I speak in the name of Christ. And he has a right to be heard. This is one of the implications of the ascension" (p. 80). He worries that if we give Christians the impression that (1) they have to live in a certain way before they can speak out or (2) it is the world that grants them this right rather than Christ himself, then we will be discouraging confident witness.

Chester concedes that the "earning the right" language could be just a way to "gain respect for the message we proclaim"—which is perfectly right. Indeed, later he explicitly encourages this respect gaining when he writes that "we need to be communities of love, but we also need to be *seen* to be communities of love" and cites Jesus' words about our being the light of the world (Matt 5:14). Even so, I found compelling his caution and challenge about grounding witness in the authority of the ascended Christ.

2. Concern about form. The second concern about missional church literature is its overconcern and emphasis on particular forms. Again, the more traditional books that used *missional* as a simple synonym for *evangelistic* gave lip service to the idea of a "culture of evangelism," but in the end they proposed their own round of events and courses designed to attract and process "seekers." Most missional church books, however, were written in strong reaction to megachurches and program-oriented ministries. Sometimes implicitly and sometimes explicitly, these books recommended small, informal, "organic" churches, often called "incarnational," in contrast to large, "attractional" churches. Tim Chester confirms the thesis of *Center Church*, which is that it is a grave mistake to hold that there is a particular form or model of a missional church. His own church, The Crowded House in Sheffield, England, has experienced the same fate as Redeemer in New York City—a stream of visitors coming to learn "how to do your model." He agrees that both large and small churches, both more program-oriented and more informal churches, can be missional. Or not. Being missional does not rest in the form.

Then what is it? Under this heading, Chester dispenses his own wisdom, along with some things he has learned from others by giving an outline of a "missional culture" and how to promote it.

He describes a missional culture as a Christian community that promotes "gospel intentionality" in its members and practices when they are together. Gospel intentionality in daily life is conveyed by the rope image with three strands. First, it is building real friendships—not creating objects for evangelism and ministry, but making true friends and serving others unconditionally with a consciousness of how Christ loves you. Second, it is sharing the gospel message in natural ways. Third, it is welcoming into our believing community our friends who don't believe.

Chester then lists three fundamental missional practices for a missional church. One is the "family gathering" for worship. Everyone in the church must be part of that. The second is some kind of smaller grouping (it can be as small as two or as large as a house church) with other believers to work the Word of God into our lives. The third and most intriguing is to always have a "third space" into which the group can invite its network of unchurched friends with whom they have been living "gospel intentionally." Chester notes that this third space is usually not a home, work space, or church building. It can be a service project in the community, a meeting Christians hold in a public space where people naturally hang out, or a regular "event" that is especially inclusive of both those who believe and those who don't believe.

We have already noted the danger of the modern desire for a technique—for a step-by-step model of a missional church to master and use. Yet in our rightful reaction against this, we can give people almost nothing concrete to go on. And for the person seeking wisdom about this issue, that can be quite frustrating. That is why I find the simplicity and specificity of Chester's outline in his essay to be extremely helpful. It is concrete, yet it generally escapes the trap of dictating a single "form."

As far as I can see, churches of many sizes and shapes can incorporate these elements. Tim Chester, then, succeeds here where many experts on the missional church fail.

Let me accentuate another of Chester's helpful ideas. Since being missional does not reside in a round of programs that can be rolled out, if we're looking at a community-wide set of attitudes, then how do we promote and maintain that missional culture? He says one of the best ways is through using stories — especially stories of things that have taken place in your church's ministry or history that embody the church's vision for what it wants to be (pp. 87–88).

The best example I know of is Bethel Gospel Assembly, an African-American church in Harlem. To convey the mission and vision of the church, its pastor does not point to a set of bullet points or a slogan. Instead, a story is told: In 1916, two young African-American women received Christ and tried to join a church in downtown Manhattan but were denied because of their skin color. A young single woman who was a member of the church, Lillian Kraeger, was distressed at this decision and feared that the two girls would fall away from their profession of faith. She began regularly traveling to Harlem to hold "cottage meeting" Bible study classes for them. Not only did this alienate Lillian from her family and church; her fiancé broke off their engagement. She maintained her commitment to nurture what we today call a small but growing house church. Today this is a thriving church of fifteen hundred people, with an unusually strong commitment to incorporating the poor into its ministry.

This is a terrific story of "exclusion and embrace," which perfectly captures the church's mission today and works on multiple levels. Anglo listeners are both convicted and inspired, since in the story they are both protagonist and antagonist. African-American listeners recognize a story of "life out of death." Lillian Kraeger was willing to join her excluded sisters and be excluded herself, yet doing so bore tremendous fruit. This is an enormous encouragement for those whose entire lives are lived in the shadow of rejection. Bishop Ezra Williams, who was pastor at Bethel for thirty-five years, would tie the story to Isaiah 54:1: "'Shout for joy, you who were never in labor; because more are the children of the desolate woman than of her who has a husband,' says the LORD." The woman forsaken by family and would-be husband ended up having far more children in her faithfulness than she ever would have had if she had not followed the Lord outside the camp.

I admit that few churches have such a dramatic founding story! But true stories of God's work in our midst that also exhibit the church's mission, are told skillfully, and tie well into the themes of the gospel are the best way to form people into a missional community.

3. Concern about the gospel. The last of the primary concerns is the loss of clarity regarding the gospel. Here again Tim Chester confirms the thesis. He restates the issue this way: We must keep the biblical concepts of the cross and the kingdom together in our gospel proclamation. The danger of a "kingdom gospel" only is that it ends up being a "gospel of good works." But a "reductionistic gospel of the cross" means that repentance only deals with private morality and "not my sociopolitical commitments" (pp. 91–92). Keeping these biblical themes together is not easy. But on this subject, I refer readers (and Tim Chester himself) to Andy Crouch's essay "Reflections on Cultural Engagement" in *Loving the City* (book 2 in this series) and especially his material on Image Restoration. Using the image of God in our gospel presentations may help us solve the problem of a gospel reductionism that leaves us with either a withdrawn fundamentalism or a recap of theological liberalism. I believe the missional church movement would do well to learn from the essayists in this *Center Church* trilogy.

Part 2

INTEGRATIVE MINISTRY

Chapter 4

THE BALANCE OF MINISTRY FRONTS

Churches driven by a Center Church theological vision will pursue an integrative, balanced ministry. Because the gospel not only converts nonbelievers but also builds up believers, the church should not have to choose evangelism over discipleship. Because the gospel is presented to the world not only through word but also through deed and community, we should not choose between teaching and carrying out practical ministry to address people's needs. Because the gospel renews not only individuals but also communities and culture, the church should disciple its people to seek personal conversion, deep Christian community, social justice, and cultural renewal in the city. These ministry areas should not be seen as independent or optional but as interdependent and fully biblical.

The reality is that very few churches furnish all of these "ministry fronts" with balanced resources and attention. Many churches are committed to evangelism, church growth, and church planting. Some put all the stress on fellowship and community. Others are radically committed to the poor and issues of social justice. Still others make much of the importance of culture and the arts. But seldom are these traits combined. Indeed, it is normal to find the leaders of these various ministries resisting or even resenting the other ministry emphases. Those working with the poor think "integrating faith and work" is elitist. Those stressing community, discipleship, and holiness often think that emphasizing church growth produces spiritual shallowness.

But engaging on all of these fronts is required by the nature of the gospel. The experience of grace inspires evangelism as well as intimate, glorious worship of the God who saved us. It creates the new transparency and openness that make deep fellowship possible. The grace orientation of the gospel humbles us and gives us a new passion for justice. And the nature of the gospel helps us discern idolatry in ourselves and in our culture that distorts the way we do our work and live our lives in society.

What's more, engaging on all these fronts is required by the nature of our culture. Ministry in which Christians sacrificially serve the common good of the city is not only biblical but a necessary context for any convincing evangelistic call to believe in Jesus. After all, why should the people of the city listen to us if we are perceived to be out simply to increase the size and power of our own tribe? Or consider cultural engagement. In a previous chapter we said that culture cannot be changed simply through people trying to integrate their faith with their work *or* simply through lots of conversions. It must be both. There must be an increasing number of Christians who are shaped by the gospel through a deep experience of Christian community and who are known for their commitment to the poor. It is only as we do all of these ministries at once that any of them will be most effective. Success on any one front depends on success in the other fronts of ministry. The truth is that if we don't make a strong effort to do *all* of these in some way at once, we won't actually do *any* of them well at all. In other words, Center Church ministry must be *integrative*.

Only if we produce thousands of new church communities that regularly win secular people to Christ, seek the common good of the whole city (especially the poor), and disciple thousands of Christians to write plays, advance science, do creative journalism, begin effective and productive new businesses, use their money for others, and produce cutting-edge scholarship and literature will we actually be doing all the things the Bible tells us that Christians should be doing! This is how we will begin to see our cities comprehensively influenced for Christ.

Balancing the Bible's Metaphors for the Church

In an important article, Edmund Clowney demonstrates that there are literally dozens of metaphors used by the Bible to describe the church.[1] The church is called "a chosen people … a holy nation" (1 Pet 2:9) — literally, a distinct ethnic so changed by our encounter with Christ that we are more like one another than like others in our own particular races and societies. The church is also a "family" in which other Christians are my brothers, sisters, mothers, and fathers (Matt 12:49 – 50; 1 Tim 5:1 – 2; 1 John 3:14 – 18). The church is called "the body of Christ" (1 Cor 12:12 – 27), suggesting that all of us, like parts of a human body, have our own different but irreplaceable and interdependent function. These metaphors describe the new connection we have to one another in Christ.

Several metaphors emphasize the unique access we now have to the love and presence of God himself. The church is depicted as the bride of Christ (2 Cor 11:2; Eph 5:32), pointing us to a level of intimacy that goes beyond the deepest of human relationships. It is also referred to as "a royal priesthood" (1 Pet 2:9) and "a holy temple" of God's Spirit, "a spiritual house" (Eph 2:20 – 22; 1 Pet 2:4 – 8).

Other metaphors speak of growth, in both quality and size. The church is "God's field" of crops (1 Cor 3:9), his "harvest" (John 4:35), an "olive tree" (Rom 11:24), and the "branches" on a vine (John 15:5). Along with the references to our role as a priesthood offering sacrifices by sharing and doing good (Heb 13:16) and to our calling to declare God's praises (1 Pet 2:9), these images speak of how we are to serve God as we connect to the world. And these are only a handful of the eighty-some metaphors used by the Bible to describe the church. Clowney rightly warns against focusing too much on any one of them. All of them must inform our practice of church life, and that poses a great challenge.

Our natural tendency is to prioritize one or two particular metaphors in our understanding of the church and its identity in the world and to neglect others. Cardinal Avery Dulles's book *Models of the Church* points out how, at various places in the history of the church and in particular settings across the range of cultures, this has indeed been the case. Various biblical metaphors of the church have come to dominate Christians' thinking and push out other metaphors, and he lists five church models that tend to emphasize one of the metaphors over all others:[2]

1. The *church as institution* model emphasizes doctrine, theology, and ordained ministerial authority.
2. The *church as mystical communion* points to the church as organic community and fellowship.
3. The *church as sacrament* accents corporate worship.
4. The *church as herald* preeminently does evangelism and preaching.
5. The *church as servant* is a radical community committed to social justice.

Church models are in one sense unavoidable. The spiritual gifts and callings of a congregation's leaders, together with their social context (e.g., university town versus inner-city neighborhood) will necessarily mean every church tends to be naturally better at fulfilling some metaphors and doing some kinds of ministry. Some churches will be better at evangelism, others at teaching and discipleship, others at gathered worship and preaching, and others at service to those in need. We know that no one Christian can have all spiritual gifts and carry out all ministries equally well—this is the clear point of 1 Corinthians 12. It can also be argued that no one congregation has all the spiritual gifts (at least not all in proportion) and is therefore unable to do all things equally well. Local churches, just like individual believers, should humbly acknowledge their limitations and recognize that they are just one part of the whole body of Christ in a city, region, or nation.

Four Ministry Fronts

None of the metaphors used to describe the church can be ignored— they are all biblical. Every church must seek to be true to *all* of the rich images in Scripture. Yet no church has a perfectly balanced set of gifts and strengths; nor does it have excess leadership or financial capacity!

What does it mean, practically, to be faithful to these limitations yet true to all the biblical metaphors?

It means a church should strive to supplement its strong ministries by seeking to do *all* the forms of ministry as skillfully as possible in an integrative way. It should recognize and capitalize on its strengths but never give up seeking to shore up its weak areas out of respect for all the things that Scripture says a church is and does. It is not unlike the relationship of individual spiritual gifts to Christian duties. For example, the Bible tells all Christians to evangelize and love their neighbor. Yet some people have gifts of evangelism (Eph 4:11) and others gifts of mercy and service (Rom 12:7 – 8). So Christian individuals should find ample opportunities to use their gifts but must still take care to do what the Bible says are their duties, even those they do not feel they are very good at.

We must admit the difficulty of this task. In fact, it is one of the hardest balances church leaders have to strike. They must recognize that no church can do all things equally well, and yet they cannot let any functions given to the church "fall off the map." And city churches in particular, because of the complexity of metropolitan society, must be especially careful to engage each area of ministry with as much generous commitment and emphasis as they can.

Instead of speaking about metaphors and models of the church, I prefer to talk about distinct "ministry fronts." These are based on the understanding that the various models and metaphors tend to emphasize particular types of ministry and prioritize them over others. Let me propose four "fronts" to ministry:

1. Connecting people to God (through evangelism and worship)
2. Connecting people to one another (through community and discipleship)
3. Connecting people to the city (through mercy and justice)
4. Connecting people to the culture (through the integration of faith and work)

Of course, very few churches actually engage in all four of these fronts with completely balanced focus and attention. The norm, more often than not, is an atmosphere of competition within the church and between churches, with different ministries vying for resources and attention. But engagement of some kind on all four of these fronts is the only way to honor the full range of the biblical metaphors of the church. This is what I am calling *integrative ministry*.

I have not found anyone who has taught the integrative nature of the church's ministry better than Edmund Clowney. In his biblical-theological work on the church, Clowney speaks of the biblical "goals of ministry" as threefold: (1) we are called to minister and serve God through *worship* (Rom 15:8 – 16; 1 Pet 2:9); (2) we are to minister and serve one another through *Christian nurture* (Eph 4:12 – 26); and (3) we are to minister and serve the world through *witness* (Matt 28:18 – 20; Luke 24:48; Acts 5:32). These three goals of ministry show the comprehensive scope of what the church is called to do. We are not called to "specialize" in one of these areas — *only* connecting people to God, to each other, or to the world. We do them all. And Clowney argues that all of these goals are really *one* goal, one fundamental calling and purpose as a church:

> The calling of the church to minister directly to God, to the saints, and to the world is one calling. Paul witnesses to the world of the Gentiles so that they may sing praise to God. Nurture and worship go together too: we sing to God in psalms, hymns, and spiritual songs, but as we do so, we teach and admonish one another (Col 4:16; Eph 5:19). When our hearts are filled with praise to God our very worship becomes a testimony to the world. At Pentecost the disciples praised God in many languages and their praise was a witness to those who heard.[3]

There it is. We have one calling — to sing the praises of God, to declare the excellencies of him who called us out of darkness into his marvelous light (1 Pet 2:9). When we show forth and sing God's praises to the world, we witness. When we show forth and sing God's praises to each other, we build up and disciple. When we show forth and sing God's praises to God in his presence, we worship. We declare and demonstrate the glory and goodness of God in diverse ways to different groups of people. That's why we exist as a church.

The Spheres and Roles of the Church

At this point, it is also helpful to reflect on the distinction Abraham Kuyper made between the spheres of the institutional church and the organic church. The institutional church is the local church under its officers, while the organic church refers to Christians united in a host of formal and informal associations and organizations, or believers simply working as individuals out in the world. The church, both institutional and organic, must be engaged on all four fronts, either directly or indirectly—and the Kuyperian distinction suggests some differences of role and scope between the two spheres.

The ministry fronts of worship/evangelism and community/ discipleship are preeminently the work of the institutional church and its ministers and elders. All individual believers are to be witnesses and to build up other believers. And many parachurch agencies have been very effective in these areas. But the ministry of the local church is the irreplaceable agent for this ministry in the world, for its main task is the ministry of the Word and the sacraments—winning people to faith and building them up as disciples.

When ministering to the economic and material needs of people— the third ministry front of mercy and justice—there is an overlap between the institutional and organic church. The church does the diaconal ministry for people within and immediately around its community. Those in the Reformed tradition believe that the diaconate is a special office within the church dedicated for just this purpose. But there is also the work of economic development and social reform that more systemically tackles the problems of poverty and other societal needs. I believe this type of work is best done by individual Christians or in organizations they form for these specific purposes.[4]

When the institutional church gives attention to cultural engagement—the fourth and final ministry front—it does so primarily by *discipling* a community of believers who work as the church organic. By teaching the Christian doctrine of vocation, the goodness of creation, the importance of culture, and the practice of Sabbath, it should be inspiring and encouraging its members to go into the various channels of culture. It equips its filmmaker members, for example, to be distinctively Christian in their art and work through solid Christian instruction. But in the end, I believe the local church should not form a production company to make feature films.

In the chapters that follow, we will unpack in greater detail what ministry can look like on each of the four fronts, particularly as it integrates with the others. Some of this is merely suggestive, since we obviously cannot set out everything a church should be doing in every area of ministry. Still, I hope it will bring clarity and focus to the mission of the church, along with a much-needed balance in the way we engage in ministry.[5]

DISCUSSION QUESTIONS

1. Which of the metaphors of the church given in Scripture (a holy nation, a family, the body of Christ, the bride of Christ, a royal priesthood, the temple of God's Spirit, God's field and harvest, branches on a vine, etc.) do you naturally tend to prioritize? How do these priorities make your church unique?

2. Which of the five models of church described by Avery Dulles most closely align with your own church's model?

   • the *church as institution* model—emphasizes doctrine, theology, and ordained ministerial authority

   • the *church as mystical communion* model—points to the church as organic community and fellowship

   • the *church as sacrament* model—accents corporate worship

   • the *church as herald* model—preeminently does evangelism and preaching

   • the *church as servant* model—a radical community committed to social justice

   How would you describe your church model to others? What would you emphasize?

3. Keller writes, "When the institutional church gives attention to cultural engagement—the fourth and final ministry front—it does so primarily by *discipling* a community of believers who work as the church organic. By teaching the Christian doctrine of vocation, the goodness of creation, the importance of culture, and the practice of Sabbath, it should be inspiring and encouraging its members to go into the various channels of culture." Do you agree with this premise? What are some of the dangers of the institutional church getting directly involved in this work? What are some of the practical ways your church can disciple believers to engage the culture?

Chapter 5

CONNECTING PEOPLE TO GOD

Two generations ago, almost no one was asking, "How shall we worship?" Every church was solidly encased in a particular theological tradition or denomination, and worship was done in conformity with the tradition. Today, however, there is a dizzying variety of worship approaches and styles being used, not only in churches across the country (as has always been the case) but even in churches within the same denomination. Sadly, this new diversity has been the cause of much strife and confusion.

Probably the single most common fault line in the "worship wars" has been the conflict between contemporary and traditional worship, which I trace in my chapter in *Worship by the Book*.[1] In countless churches during the 1960s, '70s, and '80s, there was a battle between the WWII generation (who favored traditional hymns, choirs, and instrumentation) and baby boomers (who favored praise songs set to contemporary pop music). By the mid-1990s, this struggle was generally won by the boomers. Today, however, things are much more complicated. Not only are there more than two approaches to worship; there are many dedicated efforts to blend some of them.[2]

Because even the most innovative churches cannot completely reinvent their worship service every week, worship traditions are inevitable. See the chart on the next page for a list of the main ones I observe in the American church today.

Some readers may immediately recoil from the question, "How do we choose a worship form?" because they think it reflects an American consumer mentality that designs or chooses ministry strictly to meet

HISTORIC EMPHASIS	CONTEMPORARY EMPHASIS	CONVERGENCE EMPHASIS
LITURGICAL Emphasis on the **physical** and the senses; Eucharist is central *High:* Anglican *Moderate:* Lutheran, Episcopal *Lower:* Continental Reformed, Methodist	**PRAISE AND WORSHIP** Emphasis on the **emotional**; praise music is central *African American:* AME, National Baptist *Classic Pentecostal:* Assemblies of God, Church of God in Christ, Foursquare *Contemporary praise/worship:* Calvary Chapels, Vineyards *Traditional-praise "blend":* 50/50 worship songs and hymns	**FUSIONS OF BOTH FORM AND MUSIC** Emphasis on the **mystical**; story is central *Liturgical contemporary:* Original form was the "folk Mass" of charismatic Catholics and Anglicans. Now we have a variety of specific liturgical traditions (Anglican, Reformed, etc.) or an amalgamated "Great Tradition" using traditional folk, pop/soft rock, indie rock, jazz, rhythm and blues/gospel, hip-hop, eclectic, and others
TRADITIONAL Emphasis on the **mental**; sermon is central *Free church:* Puritan/Reformed, many independent churches *Body life:* Anabaptist, Quaker, smaller churches, Jesus movement *Revivalist:* Baptist, Methodist	**SEEKER-ORIENTED WORSHIP** Emphasis on the **practical**; theme is central *Seeker-driven service:* Willow Creek *Seeker-sensitive worship:* Saddleback	

the felt needs of the customer. But while consumerism can indeed be the force behind such a question, the assumptions behind resistance to the question can be just as suspect. Many shy away from considering different worship forms because they simplistically believe there is only one biblically warranted way to do worship. They wrongly assume their own version of Christianity is ahistorical rather than culturally and socially situated. Or they may avoid the question because of the strength of their own tastes. Some people resonate so strongly with certain forms they insist they simply "cannot worship" any other way. But all human expressions are to some extent culturally embedded, and this applies to worship as well. While the truths we confess and profess transcend culture, no articulation or embodiment of them can be culture transcending.

Earlier we looked at 1 Corinthians 9:19 – 23, where Paul speaks about adapting for various cultures, becoming "all things to all … that by all possible means I might save some." As we observed, this is not a recipe for relativism. Rather, Paul is reminding us that in every culture there are many things that do not directly contradict Scripture and therefore are neither forbidden nor commanded. In charity and humility, such cultural features should generally be adopted to avoid making the gospel unnecessarily foreign. This is true not only for preaching but also for gathered worship.

Each of us has forms of worship that we believe have solid biblical warrant and that we have seen bear much fruit. Yet we should always admit the degree to which any form of worship reflects cultural and temperamental factors, not merely biblical principles. In this I should speak for myself. I find Reformed and Presbyterian worship to be in accord with God's Word and to be richly satisfying. However, this tradition leaves essentially no room for unpredictability or for public displays of emotion. Why? Presbyterians like to cite the Pauline text about doing all things "in a fitting and orderly way" (1 Cor 14:40), even though this text is embedded in a passage that describes a very un-Presbyterian-sounding service. We should admit that, while much of our love for predictability and order comes from a right concern for reverence and decorum in the presence of the King, our particular expression of that reverence is typically strongly northern European and middle-class and often reflects a temperamental bias (maybe even idolatry) regarding control. In short, our preference for a particular way of worship is typically based on a mixture of principle, temperament, and culture.

This gives flexibility, even to those who believe in the "regulative principle" of worship—of whom I am one.[3] That historical view says Christians should not do anything in gathered worship unless there is some warrant for it in the Bible. Yet it makes a distinction between biblical "elements" of worship (e.g., preaching, reading the Word, singing, prayer, and baptism vows) and the "circumstances"—the particular ways in which we do the elements. The Bible does not prescribe or even address innumerable practical considerations. It does not indicate the level of formality and predictability of the service; the length of the service or amount of time devoted to each part; the kinds of harmony, rhythm, or instrumentation of the music; the level of emotional expressiveness; or even the order of worship. There is no equivalent to the book of Leviticus in the New Testament. The Scots Confession of 1560 states, "Not that we think that any policy of order of ceremonies which men have devised can be appointed for all ages, times, and places."[4]

Guiding Principles for Connecting People to God

The Bible, then, leaves us a level of freedom when it comes to many of the practical issues of worship. How do we use this freedom wisely? How can we determine which approach to use? It will be helpful to keep several perspectives in mind as we encourage people to connect to God in worship.

The Normative Perspective: Looking to the Bible and the Past

First, our *biblical theology* of worship shapes the service. Theoretically, our theology of worship should be a fixed, unchanging thing. In reality, however, our sinful hearts and the richness of Scripture mean that our theology of worship is constantly evolving (toward greater fullness and accuracy, we hope!). It is easy to assume we have *the* balanced understanding of worship, but at any given time, we probably don't. Nevertheless, this is where we begin. We must let our best understanding of what the Word says about worship shape the service we design and use every week.

In addition, a *historical tradition* of worship informs the service. Over the years, Christians have developed a number of historical worship traditions. Tradition is valuable because it connects us to the saints and the church of the past, relying on the tested wisdom of the generations. Protestants alone have produced (among others) the Lutheran, Anglican, Continental Reformed, Puritan/Free Church, Anabaptist, Revivalist, Pentecostal, and African-American traditions of worship.

A generation or two ago, most evangelicals conducted nonliturgical traditional worship. Then from the early 1970s on, there was a major move toward nonliturgical contemporary worship. But by the 1990s, many were turning again. Concerned with what was perceived as the overly cognitive nature of traditional evangelical worship and the overly sentimental nature of contemporary evangelical worship, many have turned back to even more liturgical forms than the sermon-oriented traditional worship they had abandoned.[5] Many in this movement do not adopt a service from any particular worship tradition but create a pastiche from diverse historical approaches.

Please exercise great care here. As we have said, each worship tradition is rooted in time, place, and culture, and none of them should be seen as an unchangeable absolute. And it is also true that many now-historical traditions were once innovative revisions of an older approach. Recognize, however, that the different worship and spirituality traditions of the church are also grounded in theological differences. So while we cannot say any one of them is the one and only true way, there are some genuine tensions and even contradictions among them. For example, the difference between more sacrament-centered liturgical worship and more Word- or sermon-centered worship is based in large part on different understandings of how God communicates grace, of how spiritual growth occurs, and of the relationship of doctrine and experience. And, as Michael Allen points out, the difference between more emotionally immediate charismatic worship and classic "Word and sacrament" worship is rooted in different views of the relationship of grace and nature. In the former, grace is seen to work more through immediate experience and interruptions of natural laws, while in the latter, "grace perfects nature, rather than ... doing an end-run around it."[6]

I believe it is best, therefore, to examine the Word, draw our theological conclusions, inhabit or be informed by the historical tradition we think most fits our conclusions, and then (however) be open to cultural adaptations and learning from other traditions.[7]

The Situational Perspective: Cultural and Ecclesial Settings

John Calvin recognized that a worship service is not to be shaped only by theological and historical considerations. He often said that "whatever edifies" should be done: "If we let love be our guide, all will be safe."[8] In other words, it is critical to consider what appeals to the people of our community and our church. Again, let's break this down into two aspects.

First, our *cultural context* shapes the service. Though this idea may be a major source of controversy among some, it is unavoidable nonetheless. We see a strong correlation between approaches to worship and demographic factors such as age, socioeconomic status, and ethnicity. Here are some examples from our own observation in New York City:

- Generally, classical music and liturgy appeal to the educated. "High" cultural forms are those that, by definition, require training to appreciate.
- Generally, contemporary praise/worship approaches are far more likely to bring together a diversity of racial groups.
- Generally, young professional Anglos, especially of the more artistic bent, are highly attracted to the convergence of liturgical/historical with eclectic musical forms.
- Generally, baby boomer families are highly attracted to seeker-sensitive worship and the more ahistorical, sentimental Christian contemporary songs.

As you design your worship, you cannot naively assume you are "just being biblical" about many things that are actually cultural and personal preferences. Think of who is in your community and skew your worship service toward them in all the places where your biblical theology and historical tradition leave you freedom.

Second, keep in mind that our church's *model* and *core values* shape the service. Every church should do worship, evangelism, teaching, community building, and service—but every model relates these elements to one another in different ways. For example, some church models expect to do much of their evangelism in the service; other models do not. Many have pointed out that all worship traditions have slightly different purposes. They are all *worship*—they all aim to honor God by lifting him up, showing everyone his worth, and calling the congregation to give him his due; nevertheless, the different traditions pursue this basic goal in different ways. The traditional/free church approach places more emphasis on *instructing* the worshiper, while the praise/worship approach aims to *exalt and uplift* the worshiper, and the seeker-sensitive approach aims to *uplift* the worshiper while it *evangelizes* the non-Christians present. Our own church model will lead us to either use one of these approaches or mix together various aspects.

The Existential Perspective: Temperament and Affinity

Finally, it is necessary to be aware of our own personal affinities—what we as a pastor or worship leader like or dislike in our own experience of worship. The goal should be to play to our own strengths without privileging ourselves over our congregation. On the one hand, far too many ministers create worship services that delight their own hearts but do not connect at all to people who are less theologically and culturally trained. In reply, the ministers maintain that this is "biblical" or "rich" worship, that in our culture people just want to be entertained, that we have to raise people up to a worthy level, not lower ourselves to their level, and so on. But quite often the problem is simply that the minister has created a service that inspires *him* and few others. The apostle Paul warned us not to please ourselves (Rom 15:1 – 3), a temptation we all face when planning worship.

It is easy to use theological arguments to rationalize our personal preferences and tastes. An example is the objection that popular culture is simply not a worthy medium for worship. Those who raise this objection insist that only high culture music should be used, since it takes much more skill to produce and appreciate. But these same critics don't like the idea of jazz services, even though jazz qualifies as high culture and is far more difficult to master and appreciate than rock, gospel, or pop music. More often than not, this reveals that these critics simply *like* classical music and are looking for some theological justification to universalize their own tastes.

At the same time, we can't lead a worship service well in a style that leaves our own hearts cold. Once we are willing to admit that our preferences and tastes are just that, we are still faced with the fact that we can't lead worship unless we are actually engaged in it ourselves. The music and songs must necessarily touch and stir our own hearts. If we have the personality of the contemplative—one who loves quiet and thoughtful reflection—we may have a lot of trouble concentrating on God in a highly charismatic worship service. Ultimately, our own heart's capacities and experiential temperament *must* be a factor in the worship service we choose, design, and use. One of the reasons I put this existential factor third is so ministers exercise the discipline of consulting the Bible and the people *before* they necessarily consult their own sensibilities.

Seeker-Sensitive versus Evangelistic Worship

In the 1980s, the Willow Creek approach became enormously influential. One of its fundamental premises was the assumption that we cannot reach both Christians and non-Christians in the same gathering. So Willow Creek designed weekend "seeker services." These were not intended to be Christian worship gatherings but were considered outreach events; Christians were encouraged to worship at the midweek services. Ironically, those most hostile to the Willow Creek style of worship usually share the same assumption about worship. They frame the debate like this: "Who is the Sunday service *for*—nonbelievers or God?" Their answer, of course, is that the Sunday worship service is purely for God. They also assume that worship cannot be highly evangelistic. I want to argue that these are false premises.

My thesis is that the weekly worship service can be very effective in evangelism of non-Christians *and* in edification of Christians if it does not aim at either alone but is gospel-centered and in the vernacular. Of course, there will be a need for other, more intense experiences of learning, prayer, and community to help Christians to grow into maturity, just as there will be a need for more specifically evangelistic venues and experiences where non-Christians can have their questions and concerns fully addressed. With an awareness of the need for these additional experiences, I believe it is possible for the weekly worship service to be the core of both evangelism and edification.

The biblical basis for evangelistic worship can be developed by a close examination of two key texts: 1 Corinthians 14:24 – 25 and Acts 2. In the 1 Corinthians passage, Paul is addressing the misuse of the gift of tongues. He complains that if nonbelievers enter a worship service and hear people speaking in tongues, they will think the Christians are out of their minds (v. 23). He insists that the Christians should change their behavior so that the worship service will be comprehensible to nonbelievers. If, however, an unlearned one (an uninitiated "inquirer") comes in and worship is being done unto edification, then the nonbeliever will be "convicted of sin and ... brought under judgment by all" (v. 24). How? "The secrets of their hearts are laid bare" (v. 25). This may mean this person realizes the worshipers around him are finding in God what his heart had been secretly searching for, though in all the wrong ways. It may mean the worship reveals to him how his heart really works. Either way, the result is clear: He "will fall down and worship God, exclaiming, 'God is really among you!'" (v. 25).

This is a rather remarkable passage. Earlier, in verses 15 – 17, Paul insists that God be worshiped in such a way that it leads to edification. Now he tells us worship must also be done in such a way that it leads to evangelism. Many of us get distracted from this fact because we are studying this passage to figure out what tongues and prophecy consisted of and whether they continue today. While all of this is debatable, there is at least one unmistakably clear implication of this passage. Virtually every major commentary tells us that in verses 20 – 25, Paul is urging the Corinthian believers to stress prophecy over tongues for two reasons: (1) prophecy edifies believers, and (2) it convicts and converts nonbelievers.[9] In other words, Paul instructs them to stress prophecy over tongues at least in part because it converts people.[10] Why else would he give a detailed description of how a non-Christian comes to conviction in worship?

In Acts 2, we find further compelling evidence for evangelistic worship. When the Spirit falls on those in the upper room, we read that a crowd gathers because they "hear [the disciples] declaring the wonders of God in our own tongues!" (v. 11). As a result, they are curious and interested: "Amazed and perplexed, they asked one another, 'What does this mean?'" (v. 12). Later, they are deeply convicted: "They were cut to the heart and said ..., 'Brothers, what shall we do?'" (v. 37). Again we find the church's worship attracting the interest of outsiders. This initial curiosity and interest eventually lead to conviction and conversion; in other words, it is evangelistic.

We must acknowledge some obvious differences between the two situations in Acts 2 and 1 Corinthians 14. First Corinthians 14 pictures conversion happening on the spot (which is certainly possible). But in Acts 2, nonbelievers are first shaken out of their indifference (v. 12), with the actual conversions (vv. 37 – 41) occurring after a later encounter in which Peter explained the gospel (vv. 14 – 36) and showed them how to individually receive Christ (vv. 38 – 39). Others have pointed out that the "tongues" referred to in these two situations are different. But again, irrespective of what these passages teach about tongues and prophecy, we should not fail to note what they teach us about the purpose of worship and evangelism more broadly. From our survey, we can conclude at least three things:

1. Nonbelievers are expected to be present in Christian worship. In Acts 2, this happens by word-of-mouth excitement. In 1 Corinthians 14, it is more likely the result of a personal invitation from Christian friends. No matter how they arrive at the service, Paul clearly expects that both "inquirers" (literally, "seekers" or "those who do not understand") and "unbelievers" will be present in worship (1 Cor 14:23).

2. Nonbelievers should find the praise of Christians to be comprehensible. In Acts 2, this understanding happens by miraculous, divine intervention. In 1 Corinthians 14, it happens by human design and effort. But again, regardless of how this understanding occurs, we must not miss the fact that Paul directly tells a local congregation to adapt its worship because nonbelievers will be present. It is a false dichotomy to insist we must choose between seeking to please God and being concerned with how unchurched people feel or what they might be thinking about during our worship services.

3. Nonbelievers can fall under conviction and be converted through comprehensible worship. As I pointed out earlier, in 1 Corinthians 14, this happens during the service, but in Acts 2, it is supplemented by after-meetings and follow-up evangelism. God wants the world to overhear us worshiping him. God directs his people not simply to worship but to sing his praises "before the nations." We are called not simply to communicate the gospel *to* nonbelievers; we must also intentionally celebrate the gospel *before* them.

Three Practical Tasks for Evangelistic Worship

If, as we have seen, it is important to have evangelistic aims in our worship, we are led to a practical question: How do we do it? Let me suggest three practical things churches can do to cultivate evangelistic worship.

2. Get Nonbelievers into Worship

The numbering here is not a mistake. This task actually comes second, but nearly everyone assumes it comes first! It is quite natural to believe we must get non-Christians into worship before we can begin evangelistic worship. But the reverse is actually true. Non-Christians will not be invited into worship unless the worship is *already* evangelistic.

Typically, coming into worship will only happen through personal invitations from Christians. As we read in the Psalms, the "nations" must be directly asked to come (e.g., Ps 96). The main stimuli for these invitations are the comprehensibility and quality of the worship experience.

Almost every Christian, if they pay attention, will be able to sense whether a worship experience will be attractive to their non-Christian friends. They may find a particular service wonderfully edifying for *them* and yet know their nonbelieving neighbors would react negatively, and so they wouldn't even consider bringing them along. They do not think they will be impressed or interested. Because this is their expectation, they do nothing about it, and a vicious cycle begins. Pastors see only Christians present, so they lack incentive to make their worship comprehensible to outsiders. But since they fail to make the necessary changes to adapt and contextualize, outsiders never come. The pastors continue to respond to the exclusively Christian audience that gathers, and the cycle continues. Therefore, the best way to get Christians to bring non-Christians to a worship service is to worship *as if* there are dozens of skeptical onlookers. If we worship *as if* they are there, eventually they will be.

1. Make Worship Comprehensible to Nonbelievers

Contrary to popular belief, our purpose is not to make the nonbeliever "comfortable." After all, in 1 Corinthians 14:24 – 25 and Acts 2:12, 37, nonbelievers are "convicted of sin"; "the secrets of their hearts are laid bare"; they are "amazed and perplexed"; and they are "cut to the heart"! Our aim is to be *intelligible* to them. We must address their *heart secrets* (1 Cor 14:25), and so we must remember what it is like to *not* believe. How do we do that?

a. Seek to worship and preach in the vernacular. It is impossible to overstate how insular and subcultural our preaching can become. We often make statements that are persuasive and compelling to us, but they are based on all sorts of premises that a secular person does not hold. Preachers often use references, terms, and phrases that mean nothing outside of our Christian tribe. So we must intentionally seek to avoid unnecessary theological or evangelical jargon, carefully explaining the basic theological concepts behind confession of sin, praise, thanksgiving, and so on. In your preaching, always be willing to address the questions that the nonbelieving heart will ask. Speak respectfully and sympathetically to people who have difficulty with Christianity. As you prepare the sermon, imagine a particularly skeptical non-Christian sitting in the chair listening to you. Be sure to add the asides, the qualifiers, and the extra explanations that are necessary to communicate in a way that is comprehensible to them. Listen to everything that is said in the worship service with the ears of someone who has doubts or struggles with belief.

b. Explain the service as you go along. Though there is some danger of pastoral verbosity here that distracts from the worship experience, learn to give one-to-two-sentence, nonjargon explanations of each part of the service as it comes. For example, prior to leading a prayer of confession, you might say, "When we confess our sins, we are not groveling in guilt, but we're dealing with our guilt. If we deny our sins, we will never get free from them." It may also be helpful to begin a worship service (as is customary in African-American churches) with a "devotional"—a brief talk that explains the meaning of worship. By doing this, we will continually instruct newcomers in worship.

c. Directly address and welcome nonbelievers. Talk regularly to "those of you who aren't sure you believe this or who aren't sure just what you believe." Give several asides, even trying to express the language of their hearts. Articulate their objections to Christian doctrine and life better than they can do it themselves. Express sincere sympathy for their difficulties, even as you challenge them directly for their selfishness and unbelief. Admonish with tears (literally or figuratively). It is extremely important that the nonbeliever feels we understand them. Always grant whatever degree of merit their objections have.

- "I've tried it before, and it did not work."
- "I don't see how my life could be the result of the plan of a loving God."
- "Christianity is a straitjacket."
- "It can't be wrong if it feels so right."

- "I could never keep it up."
- "I don't feel worthy; I am too bad."
- "I just can't believe."

d. Consider using highly skilled arts in worship. The power of good art draws people to behold it. It enters the soul through the imagination and begins to appeal to the reason. Art makes ideas plausible. The quality of our music, your speech, and even the visual aesthetics in worship will have a marked impact on its evangelistic power, particularly in cultural centers. In many churches, the quality of the music is mediocre or poor, but it does not disturb the faithful. Why? Their faith makes the words of the hymn or the song meaningful, despite its lack of artistic expression; what's more, they usually have a personal relationship with the music presenter. But any outsider who comes in as someone unconvinced of the truth and having no relationship to the presenter will likely be bored or irritated by the expression. In other words, excellent aesthetics *includes* outsiders, while mediocre aesthetics *excludes*. The low level of artistic quality in many churches guarantees that only insiders will continue to come. For the non-Christian, the attraction of good art will play a major role in drawing them in.

e. Celebrate deeds of mercy and justice. We live in a time when public esteem of the church is plummeting. For many outsiders and inquirers, the deeds of the church will be far more important than our words in gaining plausibility (Acts 4:32 – 33). Leaders in most places see "word-only" churches as net costs to their community, organizations of relatively little value. But effective churches will be so involved in deeds of mercy and justice that outsiders will say, "We cannot do without churches like this. This church is channeling so much value into our community that if it were to leave the neighborhood, we would have to raise taxes." Evangelistic worship services should highlight offerings for deed ministry and celebrate by the giving of reports, testimonies, and prayers. It is best that offerings for mercy ministries are received separately from the regular offering; they can be attached (as is traditional) to the celebration of the Lord's Supper. This connection brings before the non-Christian the impact of the gospel on people's hearts (i.e., the gospel makes us generous) and the impact of lives poured out for the world.

f. Present the sacraments so as to make the gospel clear. Baptism, and especially adult baptism, should be given great significance in evangelistic worship. Consider providing an opportunity for the baptized to offer their personal testimony as well as to respond to certain questions. Make the meaning of baptism clear through a moving, joyous, personal charge to the baptized (and to all baptized Christians present). In addition, the Lord's Supper can also become a converting ordinance. If it is explained properly, the nonbeliever will have a specific and visible way to see the difference between walking with Christ and living for oneself. The Lord's Supper confronts every individual with the question, "Are you right with God today? Right now?" There is perhaps no more effective way to help a person take a spiritual inventory. Many seekers in churches in the United States will only realize they are not truly Christians during the "fencing of the table."[11]

g. Preach grace. The one message that both believers and nonbelievers need to hear is that salvation and adoption are by grace alone. If our response to this emphasis on grace-oriented preaching is, "Christians will be bored by all of this," I believe we are revealing a misunderstanding of the gospel. The gospel of free, gracious justification and adoption is not just the way we enter the kingdom; it is also the way we grow into the likeness of Christ. The apostle Paul tells us it is the original, saving message of "grace alone" that leads to sanctified living: "The grace of God has appeared that offers salvation to all people. It teaches us to say 'No' to ungodliness and worldly passions, and to live self-controlled, upright and godly lives in this present age, while we wait for the blessed hope — the appearing of the glory of our great God and Savior, Jesus Christ" (Titus 2:11 – 13).

Many Christians are defeated and stagnant in their growth because they try to be holy for wrong motives. They say no to temptation by telling themselves:

- "God will get me."
- "People will find out."

- "I'll hate myself in the morning."
- "It will hurt my self-esteem."
- "It will hurt other people."
- "It's against the law, and I'll be caught."
- "It's against my principles."
- "I will look bad."

Some or all of these statements may be true, but the Titus passage tells us they are *inadequate*. Only the grace of God expressed through the logic of the gospel will work.

Therefore, there is one basic message that both Christians and nonbelievers need to hear, again and again: *the gospel of grace*. It can be applied to both groups directly and forcefully. Moralistic sermons will only be applicable to one of the two groups—Christians or non-Christians. But Christocentric preaching of the gospel grows believers and challenges nonbelievers. Yes, if our Sunday service and the sermon aim primarily at evangelism, eventually we will bore the saints. And if in our preaching we consistently aim primarily at education, we will eventually bore and confuse nonbelievers. But when our worship and preaching aim at praising the God who saves by grace, we will challenge and instruct both believers and nonbelievers.

3. Lead People to Commitment

We have seen that nonbelievers in worship actually "close with Christ" in two basic ways: some may come to Christ during the service itself (1 Cor 14:24 – 25), while others must be "followed up with" by means of after-service meetings. Let's take a closer look at both ways of leading people to commitment.

It is possible to lead people to a commitment to Christ during the service. One way of inviting people to receive Christ is to make a verbal invitation as the Lord's Supper is being distributed. At our church, we say it this way: "If you are not in a saving relationship with God through Christ today, do not take the bread and the cup, but as they come around, take Christ. Receive him in your heart as those around you receive the food. Then immediately afterward, come up and tell an officer or a pastor about what you've done so we can get you ready to receive the Supper the next time as a child of God." Another way to invite commitment during the service is to give people a time of silence or a period of musical interlude after the sermon. This affords people time to think and process what they have heard and to offer themselves to God in prayer.

In many situations, it is best to invite people to commitment through after-meetings. Acts 2 gives an example. In verses 12 and 13, we are told that some folks mocked the apostles after hearing them praise and preach, but others were disturbed and asked, "What does this mean?" Then we see that Peter very specifically explained the gospel, and in response to the follow-up question "What shall we do?" (v. 37), he explained how to become a Christian. Historically, many preachers have found it effective to offer such meetings to nonbelievers and seekers immediately after evangelistic worship. Convicted seekers have just come from being in the presence of God and are often the most teachable and open at this time. To seek to "get them into a small group" or even to merely return next Sunday is asking a lot. They may also be "amazed and perplexed" (Acts 2:12), and it is best to strike while the iron is hot. This should not be understood as doubting that God is infallibly drawing people to himself (Acts 13:48; 16:14). Knowing the sovereignty of God helps us to relax as we do evangelism, knowing that conversions are not dependent on our eloquence. But it should not lead us to ignore or minimize the truth that God works through secondary causes. The Westminster Confession (5.2 – 3), for example, tells us that God routinely works through normal social and psychological processes. Therefore, inviting people into a follow-up meeting immediately after the worship service can often be more conducive to conserving the fruit of the Word.

After-meetings may take the shape of one or more persons waiting at the front of the auditorium to pray with and talk with seekers who wish to make inquiries right on the spot. Another way is to host a simple Q&A session with the preacher in or near the main auditorium following the postlude. Or offer one or two classes or small group experiences targeted to specific questions non-Christians ask about the content, relevance, and credibility of the Christian faith. Skilled lay evangelists should be present to come alongside newcomers, answer spiritual questions, and provide guidance for their next steps.

"What about Deeper, Meatier Teaching?"

A recurring concern I hear is that evangelistic worship will keep Christians from deeper, meatier types of teaching. Some mean by this that they want theological distinctives spelled out—teaching on how the church's view of certain doctrinal issues differs from that of other churches and denominations. But why should we spend a lot of time preaching about these distinctives when many people present in the service do not believe in (or live as if they do not believe in) the authority of the Bible or the deity of Christ? Don't we want the principal distinctive of the preaching to be the offense and consolation of the gospel to believers and nonbelievers alike? I believe that if we make sure this happens, we will create quite a sharp enough distinction from other churches in our worship.

For example, should a Presbyterian pastor do an extended series of sermons on the case for infant baptism? Apart from the fact that my Baptist friends don't believe that such a case exists (!), this is what I call a Z doctrine, and it is based on X and Y doctrines—such as the authority of the Bible, the truths of the gospel, and the cost of discipleship. We must preach the whole counsel of God, and when preaching expositionally, we cover and teach what the text teaches. But in general we must stress the X and Y doctrines in our services, continually revisiting them and building on them to explain other truths that may be addressed less often.

It is natural to ask whether this approach is being too timid and is just looking to avoid controversy. But consider this list of the doctrines we hit hard and often in our preaching:

- Jesus is the only way to God (a defense of Christian exclusivism)
- the authority and inerrancy of Scripture

- the Trinity
- propitiation and penal substitution
- imputation
- justification by faith alone
- sanctification by faith alone
- last-day judgment and the reality of hell
- the reality of transcendent moral absolutes
- total depravity and inability to meet moral absolutes
- the orientation of the heart to idolatry
- the sinfulness of any sex outside of marriage
- the sovereignty of God over every circumstance, including trouble and suffering

I address each of these topics in sermons regularly. As you can well see, they are not only theologically substantial; they are also controversial. But we are choosing to contend and argue for the basic truths of the faith, of the gospel. I have come to believe that when people clamor for "meaty" teachings, they are not always asking for in-depth treatments of the doctrines that are central to Christian conviction and life; they want to know more about what separates churches and denominations from each other. As the focus of a worship service (not a lecture) and in a setting designed to include nonbelievers, these types of discussions aren't terribly helpful. So our counsel to people asking the questions is, "Go deeper and learn the details and distinctions in classes, small groups, and in individual relationships with pastors and other Christians" (the lay ministry dynamic at work). Again, this is not avoiding the bold proclamation of the truth; rather, it is leading with the offense of the gospel instead of with the truths that are predicated on the gospel. And then, of course, it is our responsibility to teach the issues in those other settings—without perpetuating the error that we can leave the gospel behind as we do.

We must acknowledge that no approach to preaching, by itself, can be fully adequate for all the training necessary for mature discipleship. Every Christian will need to delve into biblical and theological details that are simply less appropriate for a sermon than for another venue—a class, a lecture, small groups, one-on-one relationships. In this respect, almost every preacher will have someone in their congregation who draws the line between "sermon" and "lecture" further toward the lecture than the preacher does. Some of these will eventually leave to find a church where the preacher draws the line further over so sermons are more like lectures. I almost always find that these churches have worship services that feel much more like classrooms. They are highly cognitive and contextualized to a northern European cultural style. In many such cases, education is actually squeezing out worship.

● ● ●

So how do we choose a worship form? How do we connect our people to God? We must find a balance between the consumer mentality that seeks only to meet felt needs and our self-centered tendency to assume our own preferences are the only biblically right way to meet God. Instead, we can humbly learn from what the Bible teaches about worship while recognizing that God gives us great freedom in the particulars. As we fill in the blanks for our own worship, we must take into account what the Bible teaches, our own cultural and ecclesial setting, and our own personal temperament and preferences.

In addition, we should intentionally create services in which both evangelism and edification can occur. The weekly worship service can be very effective in evangelism of non-Christians *and* in edification of Christians if it is gospel-centered and in the vernacular of the community. In the next chapter, we will turn from the ministry front of connecting people to God to examine how missional churches connect people to one another in that community.

DISCUSSION QUESTIONS

1. Which of the five categories of worship traditions most closely matches your own personal style and recent history?

   - *liturgical*—emphasis on the physical
   - *traditional*—emphasis on the mental
   - *praise and worship*—emphasis on the emotional
   - *seeker-oriented*—emphasis on the practical
   - *fusions of both form and music*—emphasis on the mystical

   Have you experienced worship in each of the other traditions? What did you learn from those experiences?

2. Keller writes, "Many now-historic [worship] traditions were once innovative revisions of an older approach." Have you ever researched the history of your tradition's liturgy (or lack thereof)? Against which prior trends was it a reaction? Which beliefs and preferences informed it?

3. Consider the seven suggestions for making worship comprehensible to unbelievers. Which of these are you currently doing? What can you begin to do to make your worship more understandable to outsiders?

4. Do you hear the objection that your church should have "deeper, meatier teaching" in worship? Do you have venues outside the worship service to deal with the "details and distinctions," and do people really hear them there? Can you make your own list of substantial and controversial topics that you "hit hard and often" in your preaching?

Chapter 6

CONNECTING PEOPLE TO ONE ANOTHER

The gospel creates community. Because it points us to the One who died for his enemies, it creates relationships of service rather than selfishness. Because it removes both fear and pride, people get along inside the church who could never get along outside. Because it calls us to holiness, the people of God live in loving bonds of mutual accountability and discipline. Thus the gospel creates a human community radically different from any society around it.

Accordingly, the chief way in which we should disciple people (or, if you prefer, to form them spiritually) is through community. Growth in grace, wisdom, and character does not happen primarily in classes and instruction, through large worship gatherings, or even in solitude. Most often, growth happens through deep relationships and in communities where the implications of the gospel are worked out cognitively and worked in practically—in ways no other setting or venue can afford. The essence of becoming a disciple is, to put it colloquially, becoming like the people we hang out with the most. Just as the single most formative experience in our lives is our membership in a nuclear family, so the main way we grow in grace and holiness is through deep involvement in the family of God. Christian community is more than just a supportive fellowship; it is an alternate society. And it is through this alternate human society that God shapes us into who and what we are.

The Function of Community

It is natural to think of "community" as a category separate from evangelism and outreach or from training and discipleship or from prayer and worship. And of course, we have done this by calling it a distinct ministry front. But to do so can be misleading. Community itself is one of the main ways we *do* outreach and discipleship, and even experience communion with God.

Community and Our Witness

Community shapes the nature of our witness and our engagement in mission. The real secret of fruitful and effective mission in the world is the quality of our community. Exceptional character in individuals cannot prove the reality of Christianity. Atheism, as well as many other religions, can also produce individual heroes of unusual moral greatness. Though such individuals may inspire us, it is all too easy to conclude that these individuals are just that—extraordinary heroes who have set unattainable standards for the rest of us. What atheism and other religions *cannot* produce is the kind of loving community that the gospel produces. In fact, Jesus states that our deep unity is the way the world will know that the Father sent him and has loved us even as the Father has loved him (John 17:23). Jesus says that the main way people will believe that Christians have found the love of God is by seeing the quality of their life together in community.

To be faithful and effective, the church must go beyond "fellowship" to embody a counterculture, giving the world an opportunity to see people united in love who could never have been brought together otherwise, and showing the world how sex, money, and power can be used in life-giving ways:

- **Sex.** We avoid both secular society's idolization of sex and traditional society's fear of sex. We also exhibit love rather than hostility or fear toward those whose sexual life patterns are different from ours.

- **Money.** We promote a radically generous commitment of time, money, relationships, and living space to social justice and the needs of the poor, the immigrant, and the economically and physically weak. We also must practice economic sharing with one another so "there are no needy persons among us."
- **Power.** We are committed to power sharing and relationship building among races and classes that are alienated outside of the body of Christ. One practical evidence of this is that we need to be as multiethnic a body as possible.

Western believers usually think we show Christlikeness through our individual lives as believers. But it is just as important to exhibit Christlikeness through our *corporate* life together.

Community and Our Character

Community shapes the development of our character. In a classroom relationship, students and teachers have contact with one another primarily at the level of the intellect. The teacher and his students do not live together, eat together, or have much additional contact with one another socially, emotionally, or spiritually. We do not find a classroom relationship between Jesus and his students, nor did his students relate this way with one another. Instead, he created a community of learning and practice in which there was plenty of time to work out truth in discussion, dialogue, and application. This example suggests we best learn and apply what we are learning in small groups and among friends, not in academic settings alone.

Our character is mainly shaped by our primary social community— the people with whom we eat, play, converse, counsel, and study. We can apply all of the "one another" passages of the Bible to this aspect of Christian community. We are to honor (Rom 12:10), accept (Rom 15:7), bear with (Eph 4:2; Col 3:13), forgive (Eph 4:32; Col 3:13), pray for, and confess sins to one another (James 5:16). We are to cheer and challenge (Heb 3:13), admonish and confront (Col 3:16; Gal 6:1–6), warn (1 Thess 5:14), and teach one another (Rom 15:14; Col 3:16). We are to stop gossiping and slandering (Gal 5:15) or being fake (Rom 12:9) with one another.

We are to bear burdens (Gal 6:2), share possessions (Acts 4:32), and submit to one another (Eph 5:21). In short, there is no more important means of discipleship—of the formation of Christian character—than deep involvement in the life of the church, the Christian community.

Community and Our Behavior

Community shapes our ethics and the spoken and unspoken rules that guide our behavior. Far more of the biblical ethical prescriptions are addressed to us as a community than as individuals. The Ten Commandments were given to Israel at Mount Sinai to form them into an alternate society that would be a light to the nations. The call of Romans 12:1 – 2 to "offer your bodies as a living sacrifice" is usually interpreted as a call to individual consecration, but it is actually a demand that we commit ourselves to a corporate body and not live as autonomous individuals any longer. All of Romans 12, in fact, should be read as a description of this new society. In the same way, Jesus' call for his followers to be a "town built on a hill" (Matt 5:14) means we must read the entire Sermon on the Mount as a description of this new community, not simply as ethical guidelines for individual believers. Most of the ethical principles or rules in the Bible are not simply codes of behavior for individuals to follow; they are descriptions of a new community that bears the spiritual fruit of love and holiness.

But this should not surprise us. It is really just common sense. Why? Because we all know by experience that it is far harder to live godly lives as individuals. Unless we make ourselves accountable to someone, we will repeatedly slip up and fall away. In addition, many of the ethical prescriptions of the Bible seem maddeningly general—not specific enough to directly address our particular situation. But this is because Jesus expected us to determine how to apply these teachings *as a community*. Take, for example, the numerous warnings against greed in the New Testament writings. Unlike adultery, which is clear and obvious, greed is harder to define. Who is to say when we are spending too much money on ourselves? Greed is so insidious that unless we talk with other Christians about it, we will never see it in ourselves. The battle against these sinful habits and idolatrous affections is best worked out in community. Not only can a body of people, pooling their wisdom and experience, come up with culturally appropriate markers and signs of biblical sins such as greed and ruthlessness in business, but the community can more effectively hold itself to live consistently with its beliefs.

Community and Growing to Know God Better

Community is the key to true spirituality as we grow to know God by learning to know one another in relationships. In a famous passage, C. S. Lewis describes a very close friendship between himself, Charles Williams, and Ronald Tolkien (better known as J. R. R. Tolkien). After Charles Williams died, Lewis made this observation:

> In each of my friends there is something that only some other friend can fully bring out. By myself I am not large enough to call the whole man into activity; I want other lights than my own to show all his facets. Now that Charles is dead, I shall never again see Ronald's reaction to a specifically Caroline joke. Far from having more of Ronald, having him "to myself" now that Charles is away, I have less of Ronald. Hence true Friendship is the least jealous of loves. Two friends delight to be joined by a third, and three by a fourth ... We possess each friend not less but more as the number of those with whom we share him increases. In this, Friendship exhibits a glorious "nearness by resemblance" to Heaven ... For every soul, seeing Him in her own way, communicates that unique vision to all the rest. That, says an old author, is why the Seraphim in Isaiah's vision are crying "Holy, Holy, Holy" to one another (Isa 6:3). The more we thus share the Heavenly Bread between us, the more we shall all have.[1]

Lewis's point is that even a human being is too rich and multifaceted a being to be fully known one-on-one. You think you know someone, but you alone can't bring out all that is in a person. You need to see the person with others. And if this is true with another human being, how much more so with the Lord? You can't really know Jesus by yourself.

Churchly Piety and "Ecclesial Revivalism"

Christian community, then, is perhaps the main way we bear witness to the world, form Christlike character, practice a distinctively Christian style of life, and know God personally. But we must make it clear that we are not speaking merely of informal and individual relationships between Christians but also of membership and participation in the institutional church, gathered under its leaders for the preaching of the Word and the administering of the sacraments of baptism and the Lord's Supper.[2] The preaching of the Word by those gifted, prepared, and authorized by the church to do so, and participation in the Lord's Supper—with all the self-examination and corporate accountability this brings—are critical and irreplaceable ways that Christian community provides witness, spiritual formation, and communion with God.

An old term that summarizes a Christian's life, practice, and spirituality is *piety*. For the past 250 years, there has been a steady move away from a focus on churchly piety toward more individualistic, private piety. Churchly piety puts the emphasis on corporate processes—baptism, submission to the elders and pastors, catechesis in the church's historical confessions, admission to membership, public vows and profession of faith, gathered worship, sitting under the preaching of the Word, regular partaking of the Lord's Supper, and involvement in mission through the church's denominational agencies. Today, however, most evangelical churches stress individualistic piety, which emphasizes private devotions and spiritual disciplines, small group fellowship (with little or no elder oversight), personal witness and service, and participation in many broadly evangelical cooperative ventures.

Historians often trace this shift back to the revivals and awakenings of the eighteenth century and thereafter. As we have said, revivalists believed it was possible for baptized church members to be unconverted and to be relying on their place in the church for their salvation rather than relying on Christ and his finished work. So they (rightly) called people to self-examination, repentance, and conversion. But when revivalists spoke to people in that way, they weakened (in their minds) the necessity of the church. The revivalist insight led to an overemphasis on direct experience and on self-accreditation. "Who needs the church," many thought, "when I am the judge of whether I'm a Christian or not?" For many, the church became an option, an afterthought, rather than the heart of how Christians live their lives.

Earlier I explained that there are indeed real dangers if revivalistic, individual piety becomes excessive. Historian John Coffey notes that revivalism historically encouraged exchanging robust theological confessionalism for a doctrinal minimalism; stressed heart experience over formal churchmanship; de-emphasized sacramental routine for crisis decisions; downgraded the ideal of a learned ministry for populist, simplistic preaching; and shed careful theological exegesis in light of the wisdom of the past for naive biblicism.[3] Out of the revivals of the past has come the individualistic piety of the present day.

This is natural, for it is common to go to the opposite extreme in a well-intentioned effort to make a correction. Nineteenth-century Princeton Reformed theologians such as Archibald Alexander and Charles Hodge took a balanced approach to this issue. On the one hand, they were keenly aware of the dangers of revivalism and stressed the importance of churchly piety. Hodge leveled a sustained critique of Charles Finney's version of revivalism. On the other hand, Hodge was also critical of John Williamson Nevin, who (he believed) overreacted to revivalism in his particular emphasis on the sacraments.[4] As can be seen in Alexander's *Thoughts on Religious Experience* and Hodge's *The Way of Life*, they accepted the basic insights of revivalism, following Jonathan Edwards in his writings on how to discern true spiritual experience; yet they put the church at the center of Christian formation and life.[5]

I have coined the term *ecclesial revivalism* to describe the balance Alexander and Hodge proposed. How can we combine the insights of revivalism with ecclesial practices in the church's ministry today?

1. Preach for conversion yet honor communicant status. One of the ways the Princeton theologians kept the balance can be seen in the way they preached for conversion *and* honored the membership status of believers in the church. Princeton ministers preached that it is possible to mentally subscribe to the doctrines of sin and grace without actually putting heart trust in them and being converted. Conversion, they said, always entails some *heart* conviction of the sin of works-righteousness and some *heart* enjoyment of grace in response to a presentation of the gospel of grace—this is "justifying faith." They directed that Christians should not be admitted to the church, nor baptized children to the Lord's Supper, without an experience of conversion and saving faith. They called existing church members to examine themselves, but they would never declare an individual member unregenerate unless through heresy or moral lapse they came under discipline. If the church had received a person as a member, it was not the place of any individual (other than that person himself) to make a counterdeclaration.

This was an important balance. The Princeton theologians let communicant members know that, under the clear preaching of the gospel, they might come to the conclusion that they had never trusted in Christ savingly but had only been full of "dead works." However, unlike some revivalists, they would never rebaptize a communing member. They would consider such an act too subjective and individualistic. They might say, "You may have a time of spiritual declension and an even greater spiritual renewal sometime in the future. Will you get baptized a third time?" They would direct the person to ground their assurance in both their experience and their participation in the church community and the sacraments. They would say, "You had baptism; now you have an experience of conversion. If you see signs of the fruit of the Spirit growing in you, you can rest assured you are his."

2. Examine candidates for membership. How can we examine people with regard to their Christian experience in such a way that avoids the extremes of formalism and revivalism? Don't insist (1) that everyone has to identify a moment or time in which they were converted, (2) that everyone must have a conversion experience that follows a particular pattern, or (3) that everyone must have a conversion with the same level of experiential and emotional intensity. This is the mistake of overly enthusiastic revivalists. Furthermore, don't look strictly at stated beliefs. Instead, look for gospel beliefs that take "spiritual illumination" to appreciate and grasp. Do they have a view of their sin that goes beyond simply behavior and recognizes idolatry, self-righteousness, and other such sins of heart and motive? Did they have a time in which they realized more clearly that salvation is by Christ's work, not theirs? And be sure to look for spiritual "whole-life effect." There should be something more than mere doctrinal subscription and ethical conformity. There should be some sense in the heart of peace and joy. There should be some growth in love. Nevertheless, we should not preclude people who can thoughtfully profess gospel faith and promise gospel living, even if their temperament shows no great emotion. We also must beware of insisting that people of other cultures conform to our patterns.

This balance is seen in the early Princeton theologians with regard to the way in which they treated baptized children within the church. These theologians understood that baptized children were (1) united to the church through the vows of their parents and therefore accountable to live as Christians and (2) recipients of God's grace in the life of the family through the sacrament. But they exhorted children to put their faith in Christ and counseled them about what conversion looks like. Archibald Alexander taught that children growing up in the church usually had a series of "religious impressions" over the years, and it was hard to tell which ones were spiritual preparation, which one was conversion, and which ones were deeper growth and commitment. But they described to children the conviction of sin and grace that was necessary for being admitted to the Lord's Supper.[6] They looked for a credible profession of faith, rather than simply admitting any child who completed church instruction.

3. Recover catechesis. In the *Apostolic Tradition*, attributed to Hippolytus, we learn that in the early church, conversion was seen as a journey with several stages. First, seekers were admitted to instruction as catechumens. They were given instruction several times a week in basic Christian worldview and ethics. Second, when inquirers became believers, they became baptismal candidates and were admitted to a new course of instruction leading up to public baptism. They were now seen as believers who had not yet been admitted to the community. The baptismal instruction seems to have emphasized orthodox theology and an understanding of the church and its ministry. Third, after baptism, the new member might receive additional instruction in the practical issues of living and working as a believer in a pagan world.

This ecclesial, corporate approach conceives of spiritual formation as a journey with public, communally celebrated milestones that entail water, food and drink, music, and joy. These milestones are baptism, the Lord's Supper, weddings, and funerals. Unlike modern individualistic ministry models that offer short-term events, intensive classes, and programs, catechesis was much different. It was much more communal, participatory, and physically embodied. The seekers met regularly with one another and with Christian instructors. The baptismal candidates met with one another and Christian teachers and sponsors. Memorization and recitation slowed the process and "drilled in" the theology and practice of the church. It brought about greater life change and more solid assimilation into the church than most contemporary seminars and programs can.

In *Grounded in the Gospel*, J. I. Packer and Gary Parrett urge contemporary Christians to restore catechetical instruction to the life of the church.[7] They argue for training people by using three ancient and biblical summaries — the Apostles' Creed (belief), the Ten Commandments (practice), and the Lord's Prayer (experience). They urge that the process be long-term rather than compressed. They make the case for a process that is not merely formal (classroom instruction) but nonformal and informal. That is, it should incorporate practical experience and include many opportunities for developing personal relationships with mature church members. Most important of all, catechesis incorporates instruction and discipleship with the public worship and life of the whole church. In ancient times, seekers, catechumens, candidates for baptism, and new members were all recognized and prayed for in public worship.

4. Recognize that seekers need process. The success of the Alpha course and other similar courses such as Christianity Explored showed the need for a shift from the mid-twentieth-century's prominent modes of evangelism. Crusade evangelism and various personal evangelism methods (e.g., Campus Crusade's LIFE training, using the Four Laws; Evangelism Explosion) were neither communal nor process oriented. They assumed some background knowledge of the Christian faith. The Alpha course was more in the mode of catechesis and began to show that, as the Western world became more pagan, evangelism had to follow the pattern of the early church. Seekers today need to not only get a body of content but also see Christianity embodied in individuals and a community. They need a long time to ask questions and build up their knowledge of the (now very alien) Christian gospel and worldview. As I argued in the previous chapter, it is possible in most cultures today to make the worship service itself part of this process so nonbelievers find the services to be places where their interest and faith can be nursed and grown. Indeed, this is vital to merging the revivalist and the ecclesial. Most ecclesial churches do not think of their corporate worship as evangelistic, while most seeker-oriented churches do not think their seeker services can be theologically rich and spiritually edifying to Christians. We need evangelistic sermons that edify, as well as edifying sermons that evangelize. Supplementing the evangelistic worship must be a great variety of groups, events, and processes by which non-Christians can be introduced to the Christian faith.

5. **Realize that baptism and reception of members can become much more instructive and a bigger part of worship.** Contemporary people will expect brief, intensive procedures they can fit into their fast-changing schedules. Nevertheless, there should at least be a great deal of instruction leading up to any adult baptism. Consider requiring all baptismal candidates to complete a doctrinal course on the Apostles' Creed, the Lord's Prayer, and the Ten Commandments. Also, look for ways that candidates for baptism can be publicly recognized (as in the early church). Seek testimonies of changed lives from new converts who are being instructed and preparing for baptism, even though they haven't yet been baptized. Doing so will highlight to the congregation the importance of the process and also encourage seekers in the congregation to "close with Christ." If your church baptizes infants or has a service of dedication for newborns, consider creating a much more comprehensive process of instructing families in family spiritual formation and discipleship before the rite. In general, we could do a far better job of instructing the congregation on how baptism and membership are milestones in our spiritual journeys.

6. **Use the anticipation of the Lord's Supper as a springboard for a season of preparation.** A pastoral practice used in some churches

that do not have weekly Communion is calling the congregation to brief, focused seasons of preparation. I used to do this at my church in Hopewell, Virginia, where the Lord's Supper was observed only quarterly. For a week or two, as I preached, I asked the church to think about a key area of Christian practice. For example, we might think about our relationships—the need for forgiveness and reconciliation—leading up to Communion Sunday. Everyone was urged to consider whether they should reconcile with anyone in a Matthew 5:23 – 24 or Matthew 18:15 – 17 process. The elders and pastors sometimes would visit the families leading up to the Communion season. Obviously visitation is not always feasible at a large, mobile, urban church, but even this kind of congregation can run classes or have their small groups study a topic and do self-examination regarding specific issues. Sometimes a church can use the period before the Lord's Supper for a time of covenant renewal.

The possibilities are many. But at the end of the day, not many churches combine the power of revivalist preaching and pastoring with ecclesial patterns of church life. Indeed, most people who are strong in one area define themselves over against Christians in the other camp, which makes it harder to incorporate both insights in a healthy way.

The Gospel and Community

Building community is no longer natural or easy under our present cultural conditions. It requires an intentionality greater than that required of our ancestors, and it is uncomfortable for most of us. But our weapon is the gospel itself.

In his classic book *Life Together*, Dietrich Bonhoeffer grounds Christian fellowship solidly in the gospel of justification by faith:

> The Reformers expressed it this way: Our righteousness is an "alien righteousness," a righteousness that comes from outside of us ...
>
> God permits [Christians] to meet together and gives them community. Their fellowship is founded solely upon Jesus Christ and this "alien righteousness." All we can say, therefore, is: the community

of Christians springs solely from the biblical and Reformation message of the justification of man through grace alone; this alone is the basis of the longing of Christians for one another ...

Without Christ we ... would not know our brother, nor could we come to him. The way is blocked by our own ego.[8]

How does this work? Our natural condition under sin is to be "glory empty"—starved for significance, honor, and a sense of worth. Sin makes us feel superior and overconfident (because we are trying to prove to ourselves and others that we are significant) and inferior and underconfident (because at a deep level we feel guilty and insecure). Some people's glory emptiness primarily takes the form of bravado and evident pride; for others, it takes the form of self-deprecation and self-loathing. Most of us are racked by both impulses. Either way, until the gospel changes us, we will use people in relationships. We do not work for the sake of the work; we do not relate for the sake of the person. Rather, we work and relate to bolster our own self-image—to derive it, essentially, from others. Bonhoeffer reminds us that the way to transparency, love, and mutual service is "blocked by our own ego."

But when the gospel changes us, we can begin to relate to others for *their* sakes. It humbles us before anyone, telling us we are sinners saved only by grace. But it also emboldens us before anyone, telling us we are loved and honored by the only eyes in the universe that really count. So we are set free to enjoy people for who they are in themselves, not for how they make us feel about ourselves. Our self-image is no longer based on comparisons with others (Gal 5:26; 6:3 – 5). We do not earn our worth through approval *from* people or through power *over* people. We are not overly dependent on the approval of others; nor, on the other hand, are we afraid of commitment and connection to others. The gospel makes us neither self-confident nor self-disdaining but gives us boldness and humility that can increase together.

Strong community is formed by powerful common experiences, as when people survive a flood or fight together in a battle. When they emerge on the other side, this shared experience becomes the basis for a deep, permanent bond that is stronger than blood. The more intense the experience, the more intense the bond. When we experience Christ's radical grace through repentance and faith, it becomes the most intense, foundational event of our lives. Now, when we meet someone from a different culture, race, or social class who has received the same grace, we see someone who has been through the same life-and-death experience. In Christ, we have both spiritually died and been raised to new life (Rom 6:4 – 6; Eph 2:1 – 6). And because of this common experience of rescue, we now share an identity marker even more indelible than the ties that bind us to our family, our race, or our culture.

Peter writes to the church, "As you come to him, the living Stone — rejected by humans but chosen by God and precious to him — you also, like living stones, are being built into a spiritual house" (1 Pet 2:4 – 5). Like stones that have been perfectly shaped by the mason, the builder lays each block next to the other, and they interlock into a solid, beautiful temple. When we speak to others who know God's grace, we can recognize that their identity is now rooted more in who they are in Christ than in their family or class. As a result, Christ has created a connection that can surmount the formerly insurmountable barriers to our relationships.

● ● ●

We often think of community as simply one more thing we have to follow in the rules of behavior. "OK, I have to read my Bible, pray, stay sexually pure — *and* I need to go to fellowship." But community is best understood as the way we are to do all that Christ told us to do in the world. Community is more than just the result of the preaching of the gospel; it is itself a declaration and expression of the gospel. It is the demonstration of the good news of freedom in Christ through the evident display of our transformed character and our life together. It is itself part of the good news, for the good news is this: This is what Christ has won for you on the cross — a new life together with the people of God. Once you were alienated from others, but now you have been brought near (Eph 2:12 – 13).

DISCUSSION QUESTIONS

1. Keller writes, "The essence of becoming a disciple is, to put it colloquially, becoming like the people we hang out with the most." Does this describe your own experience? How has the community you belong to uniquely shaped and directed your own growth as a Christian? Whom should you hang out with more often?

2. Keller writes, "Exceptional character in individuals cannot prove the reality of Christianity ... What atheism and other religions *cannot* produce is the kind of loving community that the gospel produces." Consider your Christian witness as a community. What are some of the ways your church community lives and relates to one another in distinctly Christian ways? How are you a witness to the surrounding culture?

3. Keller writes, "Churchly piety puts the emphasis on corporate processes—baptism, submission to the elders and pastors, catechesis in the church's historical confessions ... Today, however, most evangelical churches stress individualistic piety, which emphasizes private devotions and spiritual disciplines, small group fellowship (with little or no elder oversight), personal witness and service, and participation in many broadly evangelical cooperative ventures." Which version of piety is most commonplace in your church? Which of the following suggestions for a balanced "ecclesial revivalism" are most helpful to you?

   • Preach for conversion, yet honor communicant status.

   • Develop a way of examining candidates for membership.

   • Recover catechesis so it is communal, participatory, and physically embodied.

   • Recognize that seekers need a process that is both evangelistic and theologically edifying.

   • Use the baptism and reception of members to instruct and disciple.

   • Use the anticipation of the Lord's Supper as a springboard for a season of preparation focused on covenant renewal.

Chapter 7

CONNECTING PEOPLE TO THE CITY

The gospel does more than connect Christians to one another; it also connects us to those in our cities who do not yet know God and who have needs we can help meet through ministries of justice and mercy. In the West, two sets of ministry concerns—emphasizing word or deed, proclamation or service—have been split off from each other into rival political and denominational factions for nearly a century. "Conservative" ministry stresses the importance of personal morality and approves of calling people to conversion through evangelism and preaching of the gospel; "liberal" ministry stresses social justice and rejects overt calls to convert others. But Jesus calls his disciples to both *gospel messaging* (urging everyone to repent and believe the gospel) and to *gospel neighboring* (sacrificially meeting the needs of those around them, whether they believe or not). The two concerns must always go together. Let's see why.[1]

First, word and deed go together theologically. The resurrection of Jesus shows us that God not only *created* both body and spirit, but that he will also *redeem* both body and spirit. The salvation Jesus will eventually bring in its fullness will include liberation from all of the effects of sin—not only the spiritual effects, but physical and material ones as well. Jesus himself came both preaching the Word *and* healing and feeding. The final kingdom will be one of justice for all. Christians can faithfully proclaim the gospel through both words and deeds of compassion and justice, serving the material needs of people around us even as we call them to faith in Jesus.

In addition to the theological harmony of these concerns, they also go together practically. In some ways, gospel neighboring *is* gospel messaging. Loving deeds of service to someone, regardless of their race or faith, are always an attractive testimony to the truth and motivational power of the gospel. The church's ministry to the poor makes great sense as a corporate witness to the community of Christ's transforming love and as an important "plausibility structure" for the preaching of the gospel.

Biblical Foundations for Ministries of Mercy and Justice

To examine in greater depth the theological foundations for this type of ministry, let's look at three primary biblical concepts: neighbor, service, and justice.

1. Christians are to love their neighbor. It is typical to think of our neighbors as people of the same social class and means (Luke 14:12). The Old Testament, however, called Israel to recognize the immigrant, the single-parent family, and the poor as neighbors, even if they were from another nation or race (Lev 19:34). In Luke 10:25 – 37, Jesus takes this even further. He says that your neighbor is anyone you come into contact with who lacks resources, even someone from a hated race or another religious faith. Our responsibility to neighbors includes love and justice — two things the Bible closely links. When God says, "Love your neighbor as yourself" (Lev 19:18), he also commands us not to defraud, pervert justice, show partiality to the poor or favoritism to the great, or do anything to endanger our neighbor's life (vv. 13 – 17). According to Jesus, God is a God of justice, and anyone who has a relationship with him will be concerned about justice as well (Luke 18:1 – 8).

2. Christians are called to serve. The Greek word *diakoneō* denotes humbly providing for the most basic and simple needs through deeds. The root meaning of the word is "to feed someone by waiting on a table." Luke gives the example of Martha preparing a meal for Jesus (Luke 10:40). A group of women disciples followed Jesus and the apostles and provided food and other physical needs, and this ministry is called *diakonia* (Matt 27:55; Luke 8:3). The work of providing daily necessities for the widows in the early church is also referred to as *diakonia* (Acts 6:1). In the upper room, Jesus asks the question, "Who is greater, the one who is at the table or the one who serves [*diakonōn*]?" (Luke 22:27). This question is remarkable because in the value system of the culture of that day, serving others was considered demeaning work. Against this backdrop, Jesus makes the startling statement that Christian greatness is the polar opposite of the values of the world: "I am among you as one who serves (*diakonōn*)" (Luke 22:27). A *diakonos*! A busboy! This is the Christian pattern of greatness, and it directly follows the pattern of Christ's work. Our acts of service for others are the evidence that God's love is operative in our lives: "If anyone has material possessions and sees a brother or sister in need but has no pity on them, how can the love of God be in that person? Dear children, let us not love with words or speech but with actions and in truth" (1 John 3:17 – 18).

3. Christians are instructed to "do justice" or "live justly." Evangelicals tend to translate this phrase (as in Mic 6:8) as "live righteously" and generalize it to mean a broad understanding of Christian obedience to God's Word or simply a commitment to avoiding certain egregious sins. This understanding simply isn't adequate, especially when we study the term as used in the Old Testament.

So what does the Bible mean by doing justice? Old Testament scholar Bruce Waltke defines justice in this startling way: "The righteous (*ṣaddiq*) are willing to disadvantage themselves to advantage the community; the wicked are willing to disadvantage the community to advantage themselves."[2] Most people think of "wickedness" as disobeying the Ten Commandments, as actively breaking the law by lying or committing adultery. And those things are, of course, wicked! But lying and adultery are best understood as the visible tip of the iceberg of wickedness. Below the surface, less visible but no less wicked, are things like not feeding the poor when we have the power to do so or taking so much income out of the business we own that our employees are paid poorly or shoveling snow from our own driveway without even thinking to do the same for our elderly neighbors. In all these ways we disadvantage others by advantaging ourselves.

With this understanding, we begin to see that justice is an everyday activity; it is not to be pursued only in courts or legislatures. Living justly means living in constant recognition of the claims of community on us; it means disadvantaging ourselves in order to advantage others. This works itself out in every area of life—in our family and sexual relationships, our jobs and vocations, in our use of wealth and possessions, the rights of citizenship, how we pursue our leisure, how we seek and use corporate profits, how we communicate and present ourselves, and how we form and conduct friendships. It means going well beyond what is legally required of us. A CEO who is willing to say, as Job did, that "justice was my robe" (Job 29:14) cannot think only of his shareholders' profit but must also think of the good of his employees and the community in which the business operates. Many things that managers of a bank can legally do are, according to the Bible, unjust. The Old Testament makes it clear that God's justice means to share food, shelter, and other basic resources with those who have smaller amounts (Isa 58:6 – 10).

Note that in the Bible, acts that meet basic human needs are not just called acts of *mercy* (see Luke 10:37), which implies compassion for the undeserving; they are considered acts of *justice*, which implies giving people their due. Why? We do not all start out with equal privileges and assets. For example, inner-city children, through no fault of their own, may grow up in an environment extremely detrimental to learning. People may argue over who is primarily at fault in this situation—the parents, the culture, the government, big business, systemic racism, the list goes on. But no one argues it is the child's fault that they are in this situation! Everyone would recognize that as far as the children are concerned, their plight is part of the deep injustice of our world—one of the effects of the fall—that we are duty bound to help improve.

It's one thing to want to help remedy injustice; it's another thing to go about it wisely. One of the main reasons this is especially difficult is the unbalanced political ideologies and unbiblical reductionisms that reign in our culture today. Many conservatives are motivated to help the poor solely out of a disposition of mercy—a motivation perhaps rooted in a belief that poverty is almost solely a matter of individual irresponsibility. But this attitude often overlooks the fact that the "haves" are in their position to a great degree because of the uneven distribution of opportunities and resources at birth. As Christians, we know that every material blessing we have is a *gift* from God. If we fail to share the material benefits we have been given or are impatient and harsh with the poor, we are not just guilty of a lack of mercy; we are guilty of injustice. On the other hand, many liberals are motivated to help the poor out of a sense of indignation over aborted justice. But this too misses an important truth, namely, that individual responsibility *does* have a great deal to do with helping people escape from the cycle of poverty.

So conservatives may advocate "compassionate, responsibility-based" solutions that can become paternalistic and even patronizing and are blind to many of the sociocultural factors contributing to the problems of poverty. The liberal orientation against "systemic injustice" can lead to anger, rancor, and division. Both views, ironically, become self-righteous. One tends to blame the poor for everything; the other tends to blame the rich for everything. One approach overemphasizes individual responsibility; the other underemphasizes it.

Christians live justly as a response to grace. At first glance, it does not seem logical that Christ's salvation, which is of sheer grace, should move us to do justice. But the Bible tells us it should. In the Old Testament, God tells the Israelites, "The foreigner residing among you must be treated as your native-born. Love them as yourself, for you were foreigners in Egypt. I am the LORD your God" (Lev 19:34). The Israelites had been foreigners and oppressed slaves in Egypt. They did not have the ability to free themselves — God liberated them by his grace and power. Now they are to treat all people who have less power or fewer assets as neighbors, demonstrating love and justice to them. So the theological and motivational basis for doing justice is salvation by grace!

In James 2:14, the writer states that, while we are saved by faith and not works, real faith in Christ will lead us to deeds of service. And then James shows what these deeds look like: "Suppose a brother or sister is without clothes and daily food. If one of you says to them, 'Go in peace; keep warm and well fed,' but does nothing about their physical needs, what good is it? In the same way, faith by itself, if it is not accompanied by action, is dead" (2:15 – 17).

Read in the context of the entire book of James, we see this is the same reasoning that God used in Leviticus 19:34. A desire to help the poor arises from a heart touched by grace, a heart that has surrendered its feelings of superiority toward any particular class of people.

Practical Approaches for Ministries of Mercy and Justice

Once we have answered the question of *why* the church should participate in ministries of mercy and justice, we must still address the question of *how* it will do so. Within this broad question are dozens of practical questions, and as we begin to debate them, it is important to consider different levels of assistance to the poor and to think about the appropriate role of the church in each.

1. Relief. The first level to consider is *relief*—giving direct aid to meet physical, material, and social needs. Common ways of providing relief are such things as temporary shelters for the homeless, food and clothing services for people in need, medical services, and crisis counseling. A form of relief is direct advocacy in which people in need are given active assistance to receive legal aid, find housing, and gain other kinds of support. But relief programs, when not combined with other types of assistance, will invariably create patterns of dependency.

2. Development. A second type of help is necessary at the level of *development*, bringing a person or community to self-sufficiency. In the Old Testament, when a slave's debt was erased and he was released, God directed that his former master send him out with grain, tools, and resources for a new, self-sufficient economic life (Deut 15:13 – 14). Development for an individual can include education, job creation, and training. But development for a neighborhood or community means reinvesting social and financial capital into a social system—housing development and home ownership, as well as other capital investments.

3. Reform. We can call the broadest level of assistance *reform*. Social reform moves beyond the relief of immediate needs and dependency and seeks to change the social conditions and structures that aggravate or cause the dependency. Job declared that he not only clothed the naked but "broke the fangs of the wicked and snatched the victims from their teeth" (Job 29:17). Moses communicated God's stance against legal systems weighted in favor of the rich and influential (Lev 19:15; Deut 24:17) and systems of lending capital that gouged persons of modest means (Exod 22:25 – 27; Lev 19:35 – 37; 25:37). The prophets denounced unfair wages (Jer 22:13) and corrupt business practices (Amos 8:2, 6). Daniel called a pagan government to account for its lack of mercy to the poor (Dan 4:27). As we read the Bible, we realize that Christians should take a stand in their particular communities as they advocate for better police protection, more just and fair banking practices and zoning practices, and better laws.

But even if we agree these are all essential pursuits for Christians (and they are!), we have not yet answered the question of how the institutional church should be involved. For both theological and practical reasons, I believe the local church should concentrate on the first level of assistance (relief) and to some degree the second (development). At the second and third levels, in the domains of community development, social reform, and addressing social structures, I think it is generally best for believers to work through associations and organizations rather than directly through the local church.[3]

Why this distinction? One concern is the allocation of scarce financial resources. Many argue that the second and third levels are too expensive and will take financial resources away from the ministry of the Word. I don't see this as an insurmountable problem, but it is true that development and reform efforts tend to require significant sources of funds beyond what can be provided through the operations of a church. Leadership capacity and focus are other scarce resources. The issues of justice and mercy are so complex that the elders and staff of a church likely do not have the skills or time to deal with them properly.

Another reason relates to independence. Many say (and I agree) that these efforts can require too much political activity and enmeshment and may result in the congregation becoming too allied with particular civil magistrates and political parties in ways that can compromise the witness, independence, and authority of the church. In the end, I have seen that most churches in the United States that are deeply involved in caring for the poor have found it wisest to spin off nonprofit corporations to do community development and reform of social structures rather than seek to do them directly through the local congregation under the oversight of the elders.[4]

With these levels of assistance in mind, let's look at several practical issues of philosophy with respect to this aspect of integrative ministry. Often people with the same basic vision will disagree, so you may have to work hard to come to consensus.

1. Level of priority: How much should we help? This kind of ministry is very expensive. How high a priority should it hold in relationship to other ministries? Should a church wait until it has more people and is better established before doing something in this area? The needs are endless, so how can we know what percentage of the church's energy and money should be devoted to it? Here is a place to start. Deed or diaconal ministry—particularly for people inside the church—is prescribed by the Bible in Acts 6:1 – 7 and many other places. So someone in your church should be set apart to meet material and felt needs through deeds. This should be your commitment, regardless of how extensive the ministry becomes.

2. Defining "the poor": Whom should we help? How do we define *need* so we are sure we are serving those we should be serving? How needy must someone be? What if someone in your church says, "We are helping *him*? Why, he's not so bad off!" Here is a guiding idea. Jonathan Edwards applies the principle "love your neighbor as yourself" to this question. You don't wait until you are absolutely destitute before you do something to change your condition; so then you shouldn't help only the absolutely destitute people around you. Don't be too narrow in your definition of "the poor."

3. Conditional or unrestricted: When, and under what conditions, do we help? What should be required of those we help? Anything? Do you require that the persons come to your church or become part of some ministry? Should you work more with members than nonmembers? A guiding thought is Galatians 6:10: "Let us do good to all people, especially to those who belong to the family of believers." This makes it quite clear that we should give priority to brothers and sisters in our church. But it doesn't mean we shouldn't give help to people who are not members but who are in some relationship to our church—either in the immediate neighborhood or in relationships with believers inside.

4. Relief, development, and reform: In what way do we help? I mentioned that justice ministry can consist of helping individuals through simple relief—but it can also mean taking on unjust social systems. Should the church get into politics or stick with feeding the hungry? Keep in mind our discussion above about relief, development, and reform.

Ultimately, it is impossible to separate word and deed ministry because human beings are integrated wholes—body and soul. It is both natural and necessary that ministers of mercy also minister the Word while they are in the process of meeting human needs, and that communicators of the gospel also show compassion with regard to the material needs of the people they are trying to reach. An integrative ministry means weaving together word and deed ministry as much as possible. When Jesus raised the dead son of the widow of Nain, he spoke words of comfort (Luke 7:13). After he healed the blind man, he returned with a gospel charge (John 9:35 – 38). These go hand in hand. In Acts 2, explosive growth in numbers (v. 41) leads to radical sharing with the needy (vv. 44 – 45). In Acts 4, economic sharing by people inside the church accompanied the preaching of the resurrection outside the church with great power (vv. 32 – 35). The practical actions of Christians on behalf of people in need demonstrated the truth and power of the gospel. The Roman emperor Julian was an enemy of Christianity, but he admitted that believers' generosity to the poor made it highly attractive: "Why do we not observe that it is their [Christians'] benevolence to strangers ... and the pretended holiness of their lives that have done most to increase atheism [Christianity] ... For it is disgraceful that, when no Jew ever has to beg, and the impious Galilaeans support not only their own poor but ours as well, all men see that our people lack aid from us."[5]

DISCUSSION QUESTIONS

1. What does it mean, biblically, to be a *neighbor*, to *serve* others, and to *do justice*? How do our definitions of these terms compare with your own understanding?

2. Discuss the differences between relief, development, and reform. Which of these have you or your church community been involved in? Do you believe the local church should participate in the work of development and reform? Why or why not?

3. Keller writes, "Ultimately, it is impossible to separate word and deed ministry because human beings are integrated wholes—body and soul. It is both natural and necessary that ministers of mercy also minister the Word while they are in the process of meeting human needs, and that communicators of the gospel also show compassion with regard to the material needs of the people they are trying to reach. An integrative ministry means weaving together word and deed ministry as much as possible." How are you and your church seeking to weave together these two aspects of ministry?

Chapter 8

CONNECTING PEOPLE TO THE CULTURE

In the West during the time of Christendom, the church could afford to limit its discipleship and training of believers to prayer, Bible study, and evangelism because most Christians were not facing non-Christian values at work, in their neighborhoods, or at school. They did not need (or did not think they needed) to reflect deeply about a Christian approach to business, art, politics, the use of community resources, or race relations, to name a few examples. In a missional church today, however, believers are surrounded by a radically non-Christian culture. They require much more preparation and education to "think Christianly" about all of life, public and private, and about how to do their work with Christian distinctiveness.

But even this conviction is countercultural. Our Western cultures continue to cherish the Enlightenment "fact-value distinction," namely, that only things that can be proven scientifically are facts, and therefore facts constitute the only legitimate basis for public work and discourse. Conversely, everything religious, transcendent, or subjective belongs in the sphere of values and should therefore be kept private. The implication for persons of faith is that their religious convictions are not to be brought to bear on their work, whether it is banking, acting, teaching, or policy making. In such an increasingly secular and post-Christian culture, it has become normal for believers to seal off their faith beliefs from the way they work in their vocations. The few who resist usually do so by being outspoken about their personal faith rather than by allowing the gospel to shape the way they actually do art, business, government, media, or scholarship. The church plays an essential role in supporting and encouraging individual Christians as they engage the culture, helping them to work with excellence, distinctiveness, and accountability in their professions.

The Gospel Shapes Our Work

Dualism is a philosophy that separates the spiritual/sacred from the rest of life. It originally had roots in Hellenistic thought, which viewed the material world as bad and the spiritual world as good. The Enlightenment's sharp division between the public world of "objective facts" and a private world of "subjective values" and spirituality is a descendant of dualism (as is the false dichotomy we addressed in the previous chapter regarding "conservative" word ministry and "liberal" deed ministry). These divisions continue to shape the way people understand and express their faith, leading to a widespread form of dualism that sees the church and its activities as good and untainted and the secular world as bad and polluting. In this view, the best way to truly serve God is through direct forms of ministry—teaching, evangelizing, and discipling. Christianity is seen as a means of individual spiritual peace and strength, not as a comprehensive interpretation of reality that pervades everything we do. Over the past few generations, this dualistic approach to ministry and life has effectively removed many Christians from places of cultural service and influence.

A Center Church theological vision promotes the centrality of the gospel as the basis for both ministry in the church and engagement with the culture. As we have tried to show, gospel-centered churches examine all that they do in light of the gospel of grace. But this goes beyond confronting legalistic Christianity to include confronting dualistic Christianity. Why? Because the two are actually related! Legalistic Christianity leads to dualistic Christianity. When people fail to grasp the gospel of grace, they tend toward a Pharisaical obsession with ritual purity or cleanness. If we assume we are saved by the purity and rightness of our lives, we are encouraged to stay within the confines of the church, content to be in relationships and situations where we don't have to deal with nonbelievers and their ideas. In addition, the black-and-white mentality of legalism does not allow for the kinds of flexibility and tolerance for uncertainty that are necessary for deep, thoughtful Christian reflection, creativity, and vocation. For example, while the Bible does tell us a great deal about how the church should operate, it doesn't give explicit details about how to run our businesses in a Christian way. To do so requires engaging with the ideas of the world in a thoughtful manner, which is difficult and threatening—and it is easy to revert to dualism.

The opposite of dualism is worldview Christianity. Christianity is more than simply a set of beliefs I hold so I can achieve salvation for my individual soul. It is also a distinct way of understanding and interpreting everything in the world. It brings a distinct perspective on human nature, right and wrong, justice, beauty, purpose, scientific discovery, technology, and work. If I believe the universe was created, entered, and redeemed by a personal, triune, creator God—rather than believing it happened by accident—then I will necessarily have a distinct view on every one of these fundamental issues. And these perspectives will determine how I live my daily life.

The Bible teaches that *all our work matters to God*. The sixteenth-century Protestant Reformers believed that "secular" work is as valuable and God honoring as Christian ministry. When we use our gifts in work—whether by making clothes, building machines or software, practicing law, tilling fields, mending broken bodies, or nurturing children—we are answering God's call to serve the human community. Our work then, whatever it is, matters greatly to God.

It is equally true to say that *God matters to all our work*. That is, we also believe that the gospel shapes the motives, manner, and methods we use in our work. What, then, is the vision for work held by a church that emphasizes the centrality of the gospel, serves the city, engages the culture, and cultivates a missional community? We do not want Christians to privatize their faith away from their work; nor do we want them to express it in terms of a subculture. Rather we want to see Christians growing in maturity, working in their vocations with both excellence and Christian distinctiveness, seasoning and benefiting the culture in which they live.

Churches must help Christians see how the gospel shapes and informs our work in at least four ways:

1. Our faith changes our motivation for work. For professionals and others who are prone to overwork and anxiety, the gospel prevents us from finding our significance and identity in money and success. For working-class people who are prone to captivation to what Paul calls "eyeservice" (Col 3:22 KJV; "their eye is on you," NIV) and drudgery, our faith directs us to "work ... with all [our] heart, as working for the Lord" (Col 3:23).

2. Our faith changes our conception of work. A robust theology of creation—and of God's love and care for it—helps us see that even simple tasks such as making a shoe, filling a tooth, and digging a ditch are ways to serve God and build up human community. Our cultural production rearranges the material world in such a way that honors God and promotes human flourishing. A good theology of work resists the modern world's tendency to value only expertise in the pursuits that command more money and power.

3. Our faith provides high ethics for Christians in the workplace. Many things are technically legal but biblically immoral and unwise and therefore out of bounds for believers. The ethical norms of the Christian life, grounded in the gospel of grace, should always lead believers to function with an extremely high level of integrity in their work.

4. Our faith gives us the basis for reconceiving the very way in which our kind of work is done. Every community works on the basis of a collective map of what is considered most important. If God and his grace are not at the center of a culture, then other things will be substituted as ultimate values. So every vocational field is distorted by idolatry. Christian medical professionals will soon see that some practices make money for them but don't add value to patients' lives. Christians in marketing will discern accepted patterns of communication that distort reality, manipulate emotions, or play to the worst aspects of the human heart. Christians in business will often discern a bias to seek short-term financial profit at the expense of the company's long-term health or to adopt practices that put financial profit ahead of the good of employees, customers, or others in the community. Christians in the arts live and work in a culture in which narcissistic self-expression can become the ultimate end. And in most vocational fields, believers encounter workplaces in which ruthless, competitive behavior is the norm. A Christian worldview provides believers with ways to interpret the philosophies and practices that dominate their field and bring renewal and reform to them.[1]

How the Church Can Help

We must, therefore, reject approaches to work that counsel withdrawal or indifference regarding the culture. Members of such churches are told to either evangelize and disciple through the local church or, at the very least, to send in their tithes so the more committed Christians can please God directly by doing the work of ministry. In these types of churches, there is little to no support or appreciation for the "secular" work of Christians. On the other hand, we must also reject the approach that stresses social justice and cultural involvement but fails to call us to repentance, conversion, and holiness. We want to avoid both simple cultural confrontation and cultural assimilation and instead become an agent for cultural renewal. We want to disciple our people to work in the world out of a Christian worldview.

I believe the church needs to help people work in three specific ways: accountably, distinctively, and excellently.

Working Accountably: Vocation-Specific Spiritual Nurture

There is a need to provide the basic "means of grace"—prayer, mutual/peer ministry and accountability, learning in community, shepherding oversight—that both fits the time patterns and addresses the life issues of those in a particular vocation. This will address two common problems. First, the jobs and careers of urbanized culture increasingly do not fit into the traditional "forty hours with weekends off" pattern. They increasingly require travel, have seasonal cycles, and entail many changes of residence, in addition to long and/or changing weekly hours. As a result, many who are moving up in their careers find it difficult to access the normal venues for spiritual nurture—Sunday services and weekly weeknight small groups. So you will need to devise creative ways of providing this nurture as you reflect on these kinds of questions: Should some groups meet only monthly face-to-face but weekly online? Should some church staff be released to do more frequent one-on-three shepherding and discipleship?

The second dynamic is that each vocation presents many spiritual and moral issues, ethical quandaries, temptations, discouragements, and other questions that particularly confront the Christians in that profession. A good deal of spiritual nurture in the church is very general and only addresses generic or private-world matters. But we spend most of our week in our vocational field, and we need to hear how other Christians have dealt with the same problems we face every day. Some vocations are so demanding that Christians will drop out of them if they fail to receive specific encouragement and support. So Christians in the same profession need to mentor and support each other.[2]

At Redeemer, working accountably takes the form of what we call "vocational fellowships," made up of Christians in the same vocation who band together to minister to one another in the ways mentioned above. Some vocational fellowships consist of periodic gatherings in which people in related professions meet, listen to speakers, and discuss a topic. Others have monthly meetings or weekly small groups. Midsized groups can also be based on vocational commonality rather than on geographic location. For example, you might have a monthly or biweekly meeting of artists. Not only do vocation-specific groups provide accountability and encouragement; they can have an interesting evangelistic edge. Often members of a profession who don't profess to be believers will be attracted toward thoughtful and supportive fellowships of Christians whose work they respect.

Working Distinctively:
Worldview Development and Training

For many of us, it is obvious we are working for the Lord when we directly use our gifts to convey Christian messages. But we don't always know how to work *distinctively* for the Lord while going about less obviously Christian cultural and vocational tasks. It is easy for a singer to feel he is using his gifts for Christ as he sings "Every Valley Shall Be Exalted" from Handel's *Messiah*, but how does the gospel make the rest of his work distinctive? Is he just a singer who happens to be a Christian? Or is he a fully Christian singer whose art is shaped by the gospel every day of the week? How will his work be any different from that of a person with radically different beliefs about human nature, God, and the meaning of life? Will the only difference be that he doesn't sleep with his costars or that he only sings religious music? Is career advancement his real motive for what he does, or is he consciously witnessing to the goodness of creation and the meaningfulness of life by the excellence of his art? Will the skill and commitment of his art always testify—even to the most skeptical people—that this world is not an accident, that it is coherent and beautiful, that we were created for a purpose?

Similarly, it is easy for an MBA to feel she is using her gifts for Christ as she sits on the board of a charitable nonprofit or serves as a trustee for her church. But how does the gospel make the rest of her work distinctive? Will she have the same view of corporate profits as a person with different beliefs about human nature, God, and the meaning of life? Does she act in all her business dealings with the awareness that every human being is made in the image of God—each person so precious that God has given his Son for them?

The question for the church is this: If we believe that Jesus is Lord in every area of life, how do we train our people in the practice of that lordship? In general, this practice has to arise out of intentional learning communities that bring together three different groups of people: (1) older accomplished Christians in a field, (2) younger arriving Christians in a field, and (3) teachers knowledgeable in the Bible, theology, and church history. These three groups work together to ensure that the right questions are being addressed and to forge answers to those questions that are both biblical and practical. And what kinds of questions will these be? At the very least, these groups should ask three things of every vocation:

1. What practices in our field are common grace and can be embraced?
2. What practices are antithetical to the gospel and must be rejected?
3. What practices are neutral and can be adapted and revised?

At Redeemer, working distinctively happens in the vocational groups (described above), as well as in Gotham Fellows—a program for young adults who are less than five years out of university and working in their first jobs. Those who participate in the program have a mentor in their field and invest heavily in theological training, worldview reflection, and communal spiritual formation.

Working Excellently: Mentoring and Cultural Production

In concert with working accountably and distinctively, Christians must support and help one another do their work excellently, with diligence and innovation. In some areas this support can be provided through mentoring relationships. Those who are more experienced and accomplished in their field should be moved by the gospel to make themselves available to those who are new in the faith or the field. In other vocational areas, this could even mean cooperative ventures—starting new companies or nonprofits, executing individual artistic projects, initiating a new journal or periodical, creating an art gallery, or starting a volunteer program. This kind of discipleship takes several forms at Redeemer, but one example is the Entrepreneurship Forum in which the church conducts an annual business plan competition and gives grants to the best plan for a for-profit and nonprofit initiative. Those who present plans must show how the gospel informs the integration of their faith and work.

I place the excellence factor last to remind us that if the first two factors are neglected, the resulting ventures are likely to be poorly conceived. Often we think of "Christian businesses" as those that hire born-again Christians and perhaps have a daily Bible study at the office. It is rare to encounter a business that has thoughtfully worked out its mission and its financial and personnel policies theologically. Many "Christian art" productions are in reality just ways of pulling artists out of the world and into the Christian subculture. In general, cooperation in cultural production should not mean Christians banding together to leave the big, bad world; rather, cooperation involves working together—even with nonbelievers—in order to *serve* the world. This cooperation is not likely to happen until greater numbers of Christians become more willing to embrace a less dualistic understanding of their faith.

● ● ●

As we have seen, Christians make two opposing mistakes in addressing the idols of their vocational field. On the one hand, they may seal off their faith from their work, laboring according to the same values and practices that everyone else uses; on the other hand, they may loudly and clumsily declare their Christian faith to their coworkers, often without showing any grace and wisdom in the way they relate to people on the job. An essential part of the church's integrative ministry is to help believers think through the implications of the gospel for art, business, government, media, entertainment, and scholarship. We have to provide creative ways of delivering spiritual nurture so believers can be *accountable* to other believers and to the faith they profess. We teach that *excellence* in work is a critical means for gaining credibility for our faith; if our work is shoddy, our verbal witness only leads listeners to despise our beliefs. And if Christians live in major cultural centers and do their work in an excellent yet *distinctive* manner, it will ultimately produce a different kind of culture from the one in which we now live.

I am often asked, "Should Christians be involved in shaping culture?" My answer is, "We can't *not* be involved in shaping culture." But I prefer the term *cultural renewal* to *culture shaping* or *cultural transformation*. For a possible model, think about the monks in the Middle Ages, who moved out through pagan Europe, inventing and establishing academies, universities, and hospitals. They transformed local economies and cared for the weak through these new institutions. They didn't set out to take control of a pagan culture. They let the gospel change how they did their work—which meant they worked for others rather than for themselves. Christians today should strive to be a community that lives out this same kind of dynamic, which will bring the same kind of result.

DISCUSSION QUESTIONS

1. In your own ministry context, how have you seen and experienced the effects of dualism? Where have you seen secular institutions retreating from partnership with religious institutions? How has dualism led you to be less integrated in public and in your relationships with others? Where is your church unwittingly retreating from culture and accepting this premise of a private/public dichotomy?

2. If you currently serve in full-time ministry, have you ever worked outside of professional ministry? If so, how does your time in the workforce inform the ways you prepare your congregation for Christ-honoring vocation? If you haven't worked in another vocation, have you ever felt limited in your ability to compellingly argue for biblical ethics and integration at work?

3. This chapter suggests four ways that churches can help Christians see how the gospel informs and shapes their work:

   • Our faith changes our motivation for work.

   • Our faith changes our conception of work.

   • Our faith provides high ethics for Christians in the workplace.

   • Our faith gives us the basis for reconceiving the very way in which our kind of work is done.

Which of these is most meaningful to you right now? How can you begin to teach and disciple believers to reflect on each of these four ways of relating faith to work?

4. Keller writes, "Each vocation presents many spiritual and moral issues, ethical quandaries, temptations, discouragements, and other questions that particularly confront the Christians in that profession. A good deal of spiritual nurture in the church is very general and only addresses generic or private-world matters. But we spend most of our week in our vocational field, and we need to hear how other Christians have dealt with the same problems we face every day." Think about the various vocations represented in your church and community. How can you begin to encourage and nurture believers to work accountably in their profession?

REFLECTIONS ON INTEGRATIVE MINISTRY

*Daniel Montgomery and Mike Cosper, pastors at Sojourn
Community Church in Louisville, Kentucky*

Some of you will remember the shifting landscape of evangelicalism at the turn of the century. At the time, we were twenty-five (Daniel) and nineteen (Mike) years old, preparing to plant Sojourn Community Church in Louisville, Kentucky. The culture of church as we knew it was changing dramatically. Talk of "postmodernism" dominated conversations. Church planting was an experience of being unmoored, for better or worse. We were without oversight, free to shape the life and culture of this new church, Sojourn, as we saw best.

We soon discovered we were not alone in our quest. Many people were asking questions about ecclesiology and postmodernism, questions that would dramatically shape the next decade of North American Christianity. In a few short years, seeker-sensitive ministry—the biggest church trend in the late 1980s and '90s—would all but disappear. The new buzzwords were *emergent*, *organic*, and *holistic*. People were talking about *new Calvinism* and *neo-liturgical*.

As young leaders with little in the way of guidance, we read voraciously, searching for the Holy Grail of ministry. We believed that somewhere out there was a book or a pastor or a strategy that could impart us with a center: a sense of identity or a way of organizing our ministry that made sense of the very real chaos of planting a church. In one way or another, we were attracted to, labeled by, or invited into a dozen different streams.

We encountered each of these voices like a pinball meeting a bumper, spinning and bouncing from one model to the next.

- "Maybe we should just get day jobs and turn Sojourn into a house church network."
- "Or maybe we should do membership like the seventeenth-century Baptists, à la 9Marks."
- "Let's shoot some contemplative videos, like *Nooma*."
- "We definitely need to read *The Reformed Pastor* by Richard Baxter."
- "We also need more incense."
- "Can you turn up my guitar amp?"

Our search led us through many of these streams, and we tried on each of them as the seasons of our church changed. You can see their influence in the evolution of our church's vision statements:

2000: Our vision is to glorify God by enjoying him in community. (Our Piper-ian beginnings.)

2001: To challenge people who are saying no to God to say yes to God in every stage and facet of their lives.

2002: Created for Community. (Here we traded clarity for poetry. This was about the time some of our conservative friends and neighbors began to label us "emergent," though that title never reflected any kind of reality at Sojourn.)

2003: Until Christ Is Formed in You. (This was the beginning of the Dallas Willard era at Sojourn, whom we labeled our patron saint for many years and continue to love and appreciate now.)

2007: To See the Gospel Change Everything, starting with us as individuals and spreading to our church community and outward to the city and the world.

The 2007 statement will sound familiar to those who've read Tim Keller. If it's not directly lifted from him, it's certainly inspired by him.

That shift in 2007 marked what is best described as a wholesale reorganization of our church. By God's grace, we were led to the conviction that the gospel was not merely the entrance point of the Christian life, but the center of it all. A Christian never graduates from the gospel; we grow in and through it.[1] What might sound obvious today was a new revelation for us. For most of our lives, the gospel was about "getting in" with God, and our perpetual struggle with our ministry identity was an endless reckoning with how to articulate what comes next.

In those years and in the years to come, Tim Keller and several others enabled us to see the gospel not just as an entryway but as a rallying point—a place to which both the believer and unbeliever are called back again and again. This led us to begin rethinking how we went about all of our ministries—preaching, worship, counseling, member care, community groups, and mercy ministry. Keller's writings—especially the Redeemer Church Planting Manual on which many of these chapters are based—were our manifesto.[2]

Keller understands that the message of the gospel is complex and multilayered, and it compels us to mission in many different ways. Like many emergent voices, Keller shares a concern for contextualization. Like the new Calvinists, he shares a concern for the centrality of the cross. If you look at the pet causes of a wide variety of Christian traditions—spiritual formation, ministry to the poor, evangelism, and apologetics—you'll find that Keller has at one time or another emphasized all of them, and Redeemer has found ways to give expression to all of them.

In chapter 2 of *Center Church*, Keller puts it this way: "There is an irreducible complexity to the gospel. I do not mean that the gospel can't be *presented* simply and even very briefly ... [Rather] I want to resist the impulse, mainly among conservative evangelicals, toward creating a single, one-size-fits-all gospel presentation that should be used everywhere, that serves as a test of orthodoxy."[3] And his vision for ministry is driven by this understanding of the gospel.

Integrative Ministry as Response to a Complex Gospel

So how does our approach to ministry relate to this "complex" understanding of the gospel? In the same way that Christians tend to latch on to one, and only one, way of communicating the gospel, churches and movements tend to latch on to one, and only one (or two), understandings about what the church is meant to do or be, and they shape their entire ministry around that. Keller reminds us that the gospel itself is what calls us to a greater breadth than any single ministry focus: "Because the gospel is presented to the world not only through word but also through deed and community, we should not choose between teaching and carrying out practical ministry to address people's needs. Because the gospel renews not only individuals but also communities and culture, the church should disciple its people to seek personal conversion, deep Christian community, social justice, and cultural renewal in the city. These ministry areas should not be seen as independent or optional but as interdependent and fully biblical" (p. 103).

Anything less than an integrated, multifaceted ministry fails to accurately depict the complexity of the gospel. Keller writes, "The truth is that if we don't make a strong effort to do *all* of these in some way at once, we won't actually do *any* of them well at all. In other words, Center Church ministry must be *integrative*" (p. 104). Only a diverse and integrated approach can result in Christians who are "doing all the things the Bible tells us that Christians should be doing!" (p. 104).

Keller defines the work of the church primarily in the language of calling. He quotes Edmund Clowney: "The calling of the church to minister directly to God, to the saints, and to the world is one calling" (p. 108). This means that the various ways the church ministers and serves cannot be separated from one another. Keller lists four integrative ways of doing ministry (p. 107): (1) connecting people to God (through evangelism and worship); (2) connecting people to one another (through community and discipleship); (3) connecting people to the city (through mercy and justice); and (4) connecting people to the culture (through the integration of faith and work).

Notice that these are vision-oriented descriptions. Connecting people to God is an answer to the question, "What is the goal of evangelism and worship?" The same is true for the other three categories. Ministries exist for a reason—to move the church forward on its mission.

Integrative Ministry and Ecclesiology

We found it helpful to compare Keller's definition of integrative ministry to the various approaches to ecclesiology outlined by Gregg Allison in his book *Sojourners and Strangers*. Much of what Keller says seems to fit with what Allison defines as "functional ecclesiology," a way of defining the church based on its "activities, roles, or ministries." It's an ecclesiology that is based on what a church *does*. Citing missional church expert Craig Van Gelder, Allison lists six different versions of functional ecclesiology, including seeker-sensitive models and purpose-driven models. The sixth of these seems to match Keller's understanding of how integrative ministry works: "a church for the twenty-first century that emphasizes the development of the church 'as a major anchor of ministry that can specialize in a variety of niche markets.'"[4]

Yet Keller's vision of integrative ministry also has elements of what Allison calls the "teleological approach" to ecclesiology—an approach in which the church is primarily defined by its *telos*, that is, its goal, objective, or vision. The structure of the church is based on what the church is *for*. Here Allison points to Jonathan R. Wilson's definition for the church's *telos*: "life in the kingdom and knowledge of Jesus Christ."[5] The church's functions are not ends in themselves, but means to the greater end. In these chapters, we can see how Keller's vision for integrative ministry has elements of this teleological approach. For example, each ministry (e.g., evangelism and worship) is linked to a larger vision statement (e.g., connecting people to God).

A Third Way: The Ontological Approach to Ecclesiology

While the teleological approach has advantages over the functional approach, Allison argues for a third way altogether—an ontological approach. An ontological approach "seeks to define and discuss the church in terms of its attributes and characteristics. For an example of this approach, we may consider the historical attributes as affirmed by the early church in the Apostle's Creed: 'I believe in one holy, catholic, and apostolic church.' Unity, holiness, catholicity (or universality), and apostolicity were the four specific characteristics affirmed by the earliest Christians in their discussion and confession of the nature of the church. The key is to note that early church ecclesiology had a definite ontological orientation to it."[6]

In other words, we must place a priority on understanding the "identity markers of the church."[7] Allison cites a brilliant question by Simon Chan that puts the urgency of the question into perspective: "Is the church to be seen as an instrument to accomplish God's purpose in creation, or *is the church the expression of God's ultimate purpose itself?*"[8] To put it another way, is the church a means or an end? Do we place a priority on what the church *does* or on who the church *is*? Is the most important question its *actions* or its *essence*? Does the church make itself through action or does Christ make his beloved a new creation? Allison argues that the priority is on the church's essence and identity, which are formed by God's grace and precede both mission and ministry.

The ontological approach appropriately emphasizes the gospel as the catalyst for the church. The gospel transforms a people (the church), and their response to the gospel is the functional ministries of the church. What we do flows from who we are—who the gospel has made us. An ontological understanding of the church places a priority on the work of the gospel, which results in the work of the church.

With this in mind, it seems incongruent with Keller's own articulations of the gospel to define the church in a functional way, as he seems to in these chapters. A functional ecclesiology says "do" and "do in order to be." But where religion (or law) says "do," the gospel says "done."

When we define the church by what it does, we subtly undermine the centrality of the gospel. We define the church, not by the gracious action of God, but by its ability to live up to God's expectations for it.

An ontological ecclesiology starts with the declaration "It is finished." Because the work is done, what remains is not a demand (*to be the church, you must do these things*), but an invitation to be who we are (*because you are the church, you are free to do these things*). The gospel forms the church, and the church lives out the gospel in all of the ways described in the New Testament.

The distinction here may seem too subtle. But it will shape how we approach ministry and understand ourselves as part of the church. It is particularly helpful pastorally. If we define the church functionally, then the ministries of the church tend to be a bar we're perpetually trying to reach. Defined ontologically, the church's ministries are an invitation to live out our identity in Christ.

Ontology and Worship

To make this more concrete, let's examine the way Keller talks about the worship and preaching ministries of the church in chapter 5. Keller's insight here and his ability to navigate the controversies around worship are absolutely brilliant. This chapter is a helpful, clear, and practical guide for pastors who are thinking about worship in their congregations. Keller's descriptions of and prescriptions for evangelistic worship should be required reading for every pastor, worship leader, and worship planner.

Likewise, his admonition to pastors regarding their own cultural preferences expresses something seldom heard: "Far too many ministers create worship services that delight their own hearts but do not connect at all to people who are less theologically and culturally trained. In reply, the ministers maintain that this is 'biblical' or 'rich' worship, that in our culture people just want to be entertained, that we have to raise people up to a worthy level, not lower ourselves to their level, and so on. But quite often the problem is simply that the minister has created a service that inspires *him* and few others" (p. 118).

This chapter is enormously helpful, but here we would highlight our critique. Because Keller only addresses worship as a functional ministry, he misses the opportunity to make the connection between corporate worship and the New Testament reality of "all of life" worship (see, e.g., John 4:1–26; Rom 12:1; Col 3:17). As Harold Best describes it so well, "We do not go to church to worship. But as continuing worshipers, we gather ourselves together to continue our worship, but now in the company of brothers and sisters."[9]

In Best's framework, worship isn't something we turn on and off. All of our lives are marked by "continuous outpouring," a steady stream of praise toward something—whether it is God, self, or some created object. In Christ, that outpouring is gathered up and sanctified. He is—quite literally—our worship leader (Heb 8:1–2), and when we enter into a relationship with him by faith, all of our lives are gathered up and perfected in Christ (Phil 3:9).

So rather than seeing worship as a function (i.e., a duty or calling) that stands outside of ourselves, we need to learn to see it as fluidly connected to this deeper, gospel-formed reality: The gospel has made us (true) worshipers. We were always worshiping before Christ, though the object and quality of our worship was questionable. But in Christ, our whole lives are gathered up and made fragrant. An ontological understanding of the church frames our conversations about worship. What we do flows from who we are.

This distinction between a functional and ontological definition has significant implications for our pastoral practice in leading worship. For starters, the language of "connecting people to God" should be called into question. A worship service, in the light of unceasing worship, doesn't actually connect people to God, unless we're purely speaking in terms of evangelism (which Keller isn't). As Best writes, "The Christian needs to hear but one call to worship and offer only one response."[10] A Christian arrives at a gathering already connected to God but not yet fully oriented to God's world.

This raises the question of *why* the church is admonished to continue meeting (Heb 10:25). While a full answer would fill volumes,[11] we need look no further than the ancient church's principle *lex orandi, lex crendendi*: The law of prayer is the law of belief, or in the vernacular, "So we pray, so we believe." This principle illuminates a reality of worship that is all too easy for us to forget. While most folks are seriously committed to having their theology shape their worship practices, the inverse is also true: what we pray (or sing or declare together in prayers, creeds, and litanies) profoundly shapes our beliefs. This means our gatherings are crucial spaces for the spiritual formation of our congregations.

This is congruent with all that Keller has to say about contextualization and evangelistic worship. In fact, Keller's thoughts on the need for clarity for the sake of outsiders applies equally to insiders. Thinking evangelistically will prevent pastors and worship leaders from using Christianese—stale, boring, uncontextualized language that Christians can process by rote without actually being challenged to think. (It's worth mentioning that there's no better example of this kind of preaching—with fresh language and contextual metaphors—than Tim Keller.)

But the goal of such clarity (in the case of believers) isn't to connect them to God, but rather to edify them, to immerse them in the story of the gospel through word, prayer, bread, and wine in such a way that they are continually reoriented to life in God's kingdom. Worship isn't merely a function—something we do occasionally; it's intrinsic to who we are. The gospel has made us (true) worshipers, and when we gather with the church, we worship in a way that forms and shapes our whole-life worship.

Ontology and Community

To further illustrate this, we take a look at chapter 6. Keller opens the chapter with a line that can be read ontologically: "The gospel creates community" (p. 133). But he doesn't give us a vision for how community is formed and maintained. Instead we're given descriptions of what community does, of its functions. "Community," Keller writes, "is best understood as the way we are to do all that Christ told us to do in the world" (p. 146). He even uses the language of "function" when describing the ministry that happens in community (p. 134).

An ontological definition of community would start with the gospel and describe the effects of the gospel, and ministries would be seen as the fruitful outworking of the gospel. Keller describes the functions of community as witness, character, and behavior, and in this he's right—these are all elements of what community *does*. But we would press further and ask, "How do we form and sustain this kind of community?"

When Paul describes community in the church in his letter to the Colossians, he approaches it ontologically: "Here there is no Gentile or Jew, circumcised or uncircumcised, barbarian, Scythian, slave or free, but Christ is all, and is in all. Therefore, as God's chosen people, holy and dearly loved, clothe yourselves with compassion, kindness, humility, gentleness and patience. Bear with each other and forgive one another if any of you has a grievance against someone. Forgive as the Lord forgave you" (Col 3:11–13).

What the church *does* (loving one another, forgiving, bearing each other's burdens, and so forth) flows from who the church *is*—a new humanity formed and united in Christ. Jesus illustrates this point vividly: "Pointing to his disciples, he said, 'Here are my mother and my brothers. For whoever does the will of my Father in heaven is my brother and sister and mother'" (Matt 12:49–50).

To be sure, this takes nothing away from the helpful way in which Keller talks about community. Our critique is not the content itself, but in the way the content is structured and presented. Is a functional description of community the best way to go about forming community?

Most Christians, at some point, find themselves frustrated with their community. Churches divide into sects and cliques. People are marginalized for socioeconomic, racial, and political reasons. Individuals struggle to feel at home because of their own cultural, psychological, and emotional reasons. As the disciples demonstrated, community can be powerful (e.g., Luke 10:1–24), but it can also be rather pathetic (e.g., Mark 10:35–45).

When divisions arise, our definitions help us to diagnose and address the problem. A functional definition of community points to the community itself and implies, "Try harder." An ontological definition, on the other hand, tells us that something is wrong with our application of the gospel.

Operating with a functional understanding of community, a church might respond to racial divisions by reexamining its strategy for bringing people together and reaching out to people of different races and subcultures, and where they are creating opportunities for dialogue. All of these are good and probably necessary responses, but they may lack the fuel for real change if they aren't connected with the gospel, which tells us we are "one new humanity" in Christ (Eph 2:15).

Community isn't something we do; it is a way of describing the oneness that Jesus prayed for in John 17 and accomplished in his finished work, sending the Spirit to seal his promise and unite us forever. Our churches never have a "community problem." Problems in community stem from problems in our understanding and application of the gospel.

Applying Keller's Vision in Louisville

As we mentioned in our opening paragraphs, Keller's work has profoundly influenced the way we approach ministry at Sojourn Community Church. Keller's balanced definition of the gospel and his integrative vision for ministry were the inspiration for our own philosophy of ministry. But there were a few hindrances to applying his vision at our church. One, hinted at above, was the range of complexity Keller employs to describe the gospel (more on that to come). The second hindrance was the "functional versus ontological" approach to ecclesiology. We've addressed how those concerns affect our worship and community ministries, and in what follows, you'll see how our approach is different in mercy and cultural engagement as well.

Once we became convinced of the centrality of the gospel, we sought to find a way to reorient all of our ministries so they were "gospel-centered." Like Keller, we sought to ask, "What is the gospel?"

Keller answers this question by first noting the gospel's irreducible complexity. He proceeds to provide two methods, three themes, and three aspects of the gospel to frame his answer, while noting that many other themes and aspects exist.

One important thing that can be said about this approach is that it is *biblical*. Keller's approach honors the fact that the Scriptures are a mix of literary genres whose meanings are layered and interconnected. To narrowly define the gospel as only atonement or only a kingdom message or only [fill in the blank] betrays the nature of both the Scriptures and the gospel. Keller has done a fine job of emphasizing the priority of the atoning work of Jesus while retaining the broader implications of the gospel as essential to its meaning and purpose.

Our question is more pastoral in nature: Is this the best way to equip an individual with tools they can use to better understand the gospel, apply it to their lives, and proclaim it with others? To put it another way, is Keller's method reproducible?

To us, what Keller is doing is akin to calculus, and while lots of folks love calculus, neither of us took any math class higher than high school algebra. We believe that Keller's complex gospel approach is important, but there is also wisdom in giving folks a simple but broad framework for the gospel, one that an average church member can hold on to and reproduce, yet also one that provides inroads to all of the gospel's layered depth.

Taking Keller's work as our starting point, we developed a vision for doing ministry that is built on a threefold emphasis: A Whole Gospel for a Whole Church in the Whole World.[12]

Whole Gospel

We wanted to articulate an understanding of the gospel that is both comprehensible and appropriately nuanced. The whole gospel is one gospel with three aspects: God's kingdom, God's cross, and God's grace. By focusing on the kingdom, we're given inroads to talk about the narrative of redemption history. By focusing on the cross, we are able to talk about sin, atonement, and individual salvation. By focusing on God's grace, we're able to talk about the more intimate, relational dynamics of the gospel—God's unconditional love, the doctrine of adoption, etc.

We believe this tri-perspectival understanding of the gospel provides enough simplicity to be memorable and enough depth to provide inroads to talking about the gospel in its many facets, and as we acknowledged in *Faithmapping*, we got this more or less from Keller.

Keller argues that there are three frameworks, or lenses, or aspects to the gospel—three ways to understand the gospel that are equally true and central for the Christian on his or her journey:

1. The gospel of Christ is the historical truth of Jesus, who lived, died, and was resurrected, paying for our sins with his life.

2. The gospel of sonship is about God's radical, transforming, adopting grace. It's about God's accepting us because he accepts Jesus and not because of anything we've done.

3. The gospel of the kingdom is about God's kingdom coming to earth through Jesus and through the church. It's about the renewal of creation, the new-making of all things, a cosmic redemption project that has been inaugurated by Jesus.

The tendency, Keller argues, is to latch on to one or another of these aspects to the exclusion of the others. If we tend to see legalistic moralism as the problem, Keller says, we'll gravitate toward the gospel of sonship "with more emphasis on … emotional freedom." Likewise, if we tend to think that Christians are too relativistic and don't respect God's law, we'll gravitate toward the gospel of Christ, which puts our sins on display in the crucified body of Jesus.[13]

Whole Church

From there, we began to examine how this message might shape our understanding of the church. We asked these questions:

What if, instead of starting with all the external definitions of "church," we started with the internal definitions of the church— that the church is a population formed by the gospel? What if the conversation started there and flowed outward? What if the decisions we made as a church all had to come back to the centrality of that simple and deep message?[14]

Building from this foundation, we talk about what it means to be the church in terms of the church's ontology—its identity in Christ. What the church does in ministry flows from who they are. After investigating the many images and actions of the church in Scripture, we came to emphasize five primary identities. So we talk about how the gospel makes us:

- worshipers—who are glorifying God gathered with his people and scattered throughout all of life
- family—who are united in Christ as a new community
- disciples—who are learning to live their lives as Jesus would were he in their place[15]
- servants—who are servants of God and servants of all
- witnesses—who testify to what they've seen and heard about God's kingdom, cross, and grace[16]

What we do, then, flows from who we are. Ministries, instead of being functions, flow from these identities. Likewise, Christians (and the church) live out these identities in their whole lives. The challenge is not "achieve" but "be who you are; be who Christ has made you."

Whole World

Just as we say, "Be who you are," we say, "Be where you are." We are the church gathered and scattered, and our whole lives are meant to be places where these identities find expression. As we unpack it, there are five dimensions to the world:

- location—where I am with my family
- vocation—where I work
- recreation—where I rest/play
- restoration—where there is need
- multiplication—where the gospel needs to be heard[17]

In his chapters about integrative ministry, Keller describes quite brilliantly how the church engages the city and the culture. We see a lot of crossover between his prescriptions for the city and what we call restoration, as well as culture and vocation. We would also add that multiplication—the evangelistic ministries of the church, whether we're talking about interpersonal evangelism, church planting, or international missions—bleeds through in everything Keller writes here. We would note here too that the spiritual formation that happens in the church forms people for their family lives as well. Likewise, the gospel invites us to a radically countercultural recreation. The church has a dimension of recreation that includes rest, a forgotten virtue of our culture. Because the gospel provides us with a new identity, we're freed from finding our identity in our work, whether it's in the marketplace, the church, the education system, or as a stay-at-home parent. We can recreate and rest.

So to compare side by side:

	KELLER	MONTGOMERY/ COSPER
GOSPEL	"Gospel Calculus" Two methods: systematic, narrative Three major themes: (Home/ Exile, Yahweh/Covenant, and Kingdom) Three aspects: the incarnation and the "upside-down" aspect, the atonement and the "inside-out" aspect, and the resurrection and the "forward-back" aspect	Kingdom Cross Grace
CHURCH	1. Connecting people to God (through evangelism and worship) 2. Connecting people to one another (through community and discipleship)	Worshipers Disciples Family Servants Witnesses
WORLD	3. Connecting people to the city (through mercy and justice) 4. Connecting people to the culture (through the integra-tion of faith and work)	Location Vocation Recreation Restoration Multiplication

This chart is helpful in how it illustrates exactly what Keller means by integrative ministry. For him, the work of the church must extend beyond the ways the church ministers to itself. Integrative ministry means placing mercy ministries and faith and work ministries on an equal platform with church gatherings — both large (in preaching and worship) and small (in community). It's remarkable to consider the implication here. Most would agree you can't faithfully preach the gospel without ministries like preaching and worship, but Keller is also implying that you aren't faithfully preaching the gospel without some engagement with mercy ministry and faith and work ministry. It's a challenge to many ministry models, and it reflects the nuanced and many-layered understanding of the gospel that Keller preaches.

Our model seeks to communicate these same concepts by seeing our identities not only as functions in the church but also as ways we live out our whole lives. We are [fill in an identity], no matter where we are in the world. All of this depends on an ontological understanding of the church to make sense of it.

Conclusion

The task of critiquing Tim Keller makes us feel like Hobbits critiquing Gandalf. Just as he might scold them about how "a wizard is never late," we are quite certain that Dr. Keller is never uncertain of the church's ontology.

So we offer these critiques humbly, desiring that they might illuminate without obscuring the vision you read in Keller's chapters on Integrative Ministry. These chapters have been extremely helpful and important in shaping our own ministry. We feel certain that if you read them carefully, they will be profoundly practical for bringing the gospel to the center of every ministry in your church.

RESPONSE TO DANIEL MONTGOMERY AND MIKE COSPER

Timothy Keller

At Redeemer, we are careful not to privilege one ministry area over others, whether it is worship, outreach, community formation, education and instruction, outreach and evangelism, or mercy and justice. We also work hard to encourage each ministry to infuse and work interdependently with the others. So Redeemer is not particularly known as a "justice" church or an "outreach" church or an "intentional community" church. I am grateful that Daniel Montgomery and Mike Cosper recognize this a few pages into their essay: "If you look at the pet causes of a wide variety of Christian traditions—spiritual formation, ministry to the poor, evangelism, and apologetics—you'll find that ... Redeemer has found ways to give expression to all of them" (p. 171). That is, to me, very high praise and I'm thankful for it.

These chapters on integrative ministry contain a series of case studies on how the ministries of the church can be done integrally. The first, "Connecting People to God," shows how worship and evangelism can cohere. The second, "Connecting People to One Another," demonstrates how fellowship is integral to teaching spiritual formation. "Connecting People to the City" and "Connecting People to the Culture" similarly show how both evangelism and caring for the needy can permeate the whole church and work through and with the other ministries, including discipleship for work and cultural life.

Because these chapters are primarily case studies, I refrained from doing much in the way of biblical-theological grounding. My intention here is not ministry *definition* but ministry *description*. In my final endnote for chapter 4 (p. 278), I set the stage for my approach: "It is important to point out that what follows is not a thoroughgoing theology of worship, community, diaconal ministry, and public discipleship. Nor is it a balanced survey of ministry methods. Rather, it is a set of observations about how each area of ministry interacts with the others."

I'm not sure, however, that I got this point across to my good conversation partners, Daniel and Mike—since they conclude that "much of what Keller says seems to fit with what [Gregg] Allison defines as 'functional ecclesiology'" (p. 173). Allison's book on the doctrine of the church classifies working ecclesiologies in three ways: functional (defining the church by what it *does*, i.e., by its ministries), teleological (defining the church by what it is *for*, i.e., its mission and vision), and ontological (defining the church by what it *is*, i.e., its identifying marks.) Using this schema to evaluate these chapters on integrative ministry, they conclude that I chiefly "define the church in a functional way."

I disagree with Montgomery and Cosper in two ways.

1. The ecclesiological basis for integrative ministry. First, I disagree that I'm defining the church principally in terms of its functions. As I said, these chapters primarily show at a practical level how the various ministries of a church can integrate with each other. Nevertheless, I believe the brief remarks I do make about ecclesiology provide enough information to be able to conclude that the functional ecclesiology label doesn't best fit me or Redeemer.

In chapter 4 (pp. 105–6). I include a section on the biblical metaphors of the church, a crucial resource for constructing a biblical doctrine of the church. The dominant images are the people of God, the kingdom and body of Christ, and the fellowship of the Holy Spirit. There are many others—bride, priesthood, nation, school (disciples), flock, vine, field, temple, and house.

Edmund Clowney, in his books *The Church* and *Living in Christ's Church*, argues that each of the metaphors contributes something crucial to our understanding of what the church *is* and at the same time suggests particular kinds of ministry—something the church *does*. For example, the image of us as the body of Christ does not suggest evangelism in the way that some of the others do. Being the nation of God does not suggest union and community like the image of the fellowship of the Spirit does. If we let one metaphor dominate our imagination and church life—teaching or worship or community relationships or evangelistic proclamation or social justice or something else—over the others, we will diminish our vision of integrative ministry. Because the church is not solely the body or the kingdom or the fellowship or any of the other images, the functions or ministries of the church need to be integral. A full-orbed biblical understanding of what the church *is* will avoid reductionistic approaches to what the church *does*. Here I think I am in agreement with Montgomery and Cosper.

Yet all the church is and does can be described in one phrase. In chapter 10 ("The Church as Organized Organism"), I point to 1 Peter 2:9: "You are a chosen people, a royal priesthood, a holy nation, God's special possession, that you may declare the praises of him who called you out of darkness into his wonderful light." Notice that there are several metaphors used to convey the rich, multifarious character of the church. But there is basically one mission: "to declare the praises."

Clowney is insightful in expounding this verse. He says that all ministries of the church are essentially aspects of this one calling. First, we are to praise God *to God*, and this is called worship. This honors him. Second, we are to praise God *to each other*, and this is called edification, instruction, counseling, and the building of community. This changes *us* (since the only way to change what we are is to change what we love and adore the most). Finally, we are to praise God *to the world*, and this is showing the world his glory with both our words (evangelism) and our deeds (mercy and justice, integration of faith and work). So this one ministry of praising the Lord has many aspects, which we call worship, preaching, community formation, education, evangelism, mercy, and justice. Since they are all only facets of one diamond, they need to be integrated, to interpenetrate one another, and to be dependent on each other.

My first disagreement point is this: Though it is not the main burden of these chapters, I do ground my practical observations in the biblical metaphors for the church and how a balanced ecclesiology leads to balanced and integrated ministry. *Center Church* assumes the rich exposition of the doctrine of the church found in Clowney's books. There is nothing resembling "functional ecclesiology" in the pages of his books.

2. An ecclesiology of both doing and being. My second area of disagreement is broader, and I only can give it a brief mention. At one point, Montgomery and Cosper ask, "Do we place a priority on what the church *does* or on who the church *is*? Is the most important question its *actions* or its *essence*?" (p. 174). The implication is that what the church *is* is more important than what it *does*. Yet, in my mind, this is just as problematic as making the church's actions more important.

As we have seen, 1 Peter 2:9 gives us what the church is and what it does in virtually the same breath. We are the people, nation, and priesthood belonging to and treasured by God and called to praise the one who saved them. Who we are and what we are to do is a seamless whole. God's telling us what we are to do informs who we are; God's description of who we are informs what we do. We can't understand what God wants the church to be without at the same time understanding what he wants the church to do. And vice versa.

I propose an example that helps me highlight both areas of disagreement. Montgomery and Cosper believe that my characterization of worship as "connecting people to God" shows that I am beholden to a "functional ecclesiology." They argue that calling worship "connecting people to God" gives the impression that this is something that has to be achieved through our effort and that it misses the theological truth of the church's identity, that the church is already connected to God in Christ. They suggest that in this functionalist approach I'm being insensitive to the rich theology of worship and missing the biblical teaching that now, in Christ, worship is "all of life," so that when we meet on Sundays, we meet not to connect to God but to edify the saints, immersing them in the Word to reorient them to life in God's kingdom.

In response, first, in *Center Church* the phrase "Connecting People to God" is not intended to be a description of worship. Rather, this is the name for the case study of how evangelism (which has to do, of course, with connecting people to God who have been alienated from him) and worship go together.

Second, as I've said, I don't provide a theology of worship in these pages, but if I were to do so, I wouldn't be able to fully agree with the one that Montgomery and Cosper hold. David Peterson and other authors they cite reason that, since after the coming of Christ all of life is worship, what happens on Sunday is no more "worship" than what happens during the rest of the week. This leaves the Sunday gathering to be a time of instruction and edification.

D. A. Carson, in an introductory essay in *Worship by the Book*, takes on this approach and finds it wanting.[19] Though appreciating the importance of the changes to worship brought about by Jesus' salvation, he concludes that something happens in corporate worship that *does* connect people to God in a way that does not happen otherwise. Yes, we are, ontologically, in Christ, in the presence of God, yet we don't experience his presence in an unvarying way. (The language of the Psalms supports both realities. God always has us by the hand; we always live before God; and yet we can be far from God and need to seek his face.) Corporate worship assumes we are already connected to God in the most fundamental way, and yet we still need to connect to him personally and experientially.

The theology of worship that Montgomery and Cosper are assuming, though largely right, is in my mind a bit reductionistic and could lead to a loss of the sense of the "vertical" in Sunday worship. I don't have the space to go into that here. But I have pointed this out to say that the reason I speak about worship as "connecting to God" is not that I am embracing a functionalist model and have lost sight of the biblical theology of worship. It is that I have a somewhat different theology of worship, one that understands that apart from how we connect to one another in the service, something unique happens in corporate worship in our relationship to God as well.

I'm deeply thankful to Daniel Montgomery and Mike Cosper for the appreciation they express toward Redeemer and me in this essay.

And I'm delighted to learn how much they've been helped over the years. Their critique has caused me to look carefully at not only how I present things but also at what I believe about these matters—and for that, I am grateful. I only hope my explanations of where I think they may have misinterpreted this material will enhance its helpfulness to them and other readers in the future.

Part 3

MOVEMENT DYNAMICS

Chapter 9

MOVEMENTS AND INSTITUTIONS

The missionary enterprise of the nineteenth century offers important insights into the character of effective movements. Early in that century, many of the new churches established by Western missionaries in the non-Western world were locked into unhealthy patterns of dependency. These congregations and denominations had the traditional marks of a true church—the faithful preaching of the Word of God, the right use of the sacraments, and a functioning system of discipline.[1] They held to sound doctrine and included ministers and leaders from the local population, yet they were unable to propagate themselves readily or to support themselves financially. As a result, they remained dependent on Western missionaries and money indefinitely.

An alternate approach to missions—pioneered by John Nevius, Hudson Taylor, Roland Allen, and others—sought to plant churches that were self-sustaining from inception. The goal was establishing congregations that grew naturally, without the artificial "life support" of foreign aid, not only by winning converts effectively within their own cultures but also by attracting and developing new indigenous leaders at such a rate that the churches regularly reproduced themselves. In short, they wanted churches to have a dynamism that made them able to grow from within without needing to be propped up with money and leaders from outside. They wanted these churches to be more than just sound institutions; they wanted them to be vital and dynamic *movements*.

The title of Roland Allen's book, *The Spontaneous Expansion of the Church*, gets at this idea.[2] It evokes the image of spontaneous combustion—combustion without an external ignition source. A church (or group of churches) with movement dynamics generates its own converts, ideas, leaders, and resources from within in order to realize its vision of being the church for its city and culture. Unless the environment is extremely hostile (e.g., heavy persecution, war, economic collapse), the church grows in numbers and in spiritual maturity. In the language of missiologists, such a church is "self-propagating, self-governing, and self-supporting." It will reproduce into other churches that reproduce themselves for the same reasons. The more ideas, leaders, and resources that are pooled and deployed, the more the movement dynamic strengthens and snowballs. As long as the reproducing churches keep a unified vision, the movement can build steam and grow steadily, even exponentially.

Churches with no movement dynamics are like a person on a life support machine. I have seen at least three ways in which churches survive without movement dynamics:

1. Some churches have a denominational structure or a missionary structure that subsidizes the church financially.

2. Some churches have a substantial endowment and a building that serves as a community center for the local population. In this situation, there is no need for outside financial or leadership assistance in the near term, but the church does not produce additional resources or dynamism to sustain growth through conversions and the spiritual growth of its members. It essentially operates as a well-run business. Finances come from a judiciously managed endowment, supplemented by income from rentals, fees, and a few donations. Many churches sustain themselves as institutions in this way.

3. Some churches have a small, overworked core of people within a larger, stagnant structure. While the congregation has no movement dynamism, it is propped up from within. That is, a small handful of people give an inordinate amount of time and money to keep a stagnant or declining church going. These individuals may be spiritually vital Christians themselves who cannot spread this vitality to the rest of the church, or they simply may

be hardworking people with deep roots in the church, which creates a sacrificial loyalty. This solution is temporary. At some point, the few people who are keeping the church alive through their sacrificial giving grow too tired to continue, and in the absence of an ability to reproduce, the church eventually dies.

How Movements and Institutions Contrast

I am not suggesting simplistically that movements are good and institutions are bad—rather, that organizations should have both institutional characteristics and movement dynamics, though there are some tensions and trade-offs in the balance. Institutions promote stable patterns of behavior through rules and policies that change slowly, thereby limiting and shaping people's choices and practices.[3] But this intentional limiting of choices is often a healthy thing. Think for a moment of a grocery store. Customers typically have a good idea of how to check out. They know where to go and where to stand; they know about lines (queues) and about how long to expect to stand in line; and they know what to do when they get to the head of the line. What would it be like if every week the way you pay for your items changed drastically? It would be chaotic. Institutionalization makes it possible for millions of people each day to shop for the things they need in a grocery store. Some of the institutional practices are formal (like how to pay), while some of them are informal (like how long people expect to wait in line). If you try to pay for your food at the grocery store with a bar of gold, it just won't work. If customers have to wait for an hour in line, anger will break out. Why? Because "everyone knows" that an hour is too long to wait (at least in a Western country). The grocery store is obligated (informally) to not make you wait that long. If it violates this bond of trust, you probably won't come back. Your expectations and behaviors have been limited, directed, and shaped by this institution. No one could go into a grocery store and shop efficiently if not for institutionalization.

Hugh Heclo defines institutions this way: "Institutions represent inheritances of valued purposes with attendant rules and moral obligations" stewarded by those with authority.[4] This is an abstract, academic description, but it leads us in a helpful direction. Institutions rely on submission to an established authority that preserves the values and purposes of the past. Institutions are necessary and helpful, providing established, reliable systems and frames for accomplishing what needs to be done. Heclo writes, "To live in a culture that turns its back on institutions is equivalent to trying to live in a physical body without a skeleton or hoping to use a language but not its grammar."[5] Institutions bring order to life and establish many of the conditions for human flourishing and civilized society.

Movements, on the other hand, have more to do with the assertion of individual preference and bringing forth the realities of the future. Here are four key characteristics of a movement: vision, sacrifice, flexibility with unity, and spontaneity.

1. First and foremost, movements are marked by a compelling vision. A vision consists of an attractive, vivid, and clear picture of the future that the movement and its leaders are seeking to bring about. A movement states, "If this is where you want to go, come along with us." This picture of the future is accompanied by a strong set of values or beliefs to which the movement is committed. The content of this vision must be expressed so that others can grasp it readily; it must not be so esoteric or difficult that only a handful of people can articulate it.

The content of a vision must be compellingly expressed so that others can learn it and carry it out in their own community without a great deal of centralized control or assistance. So, for example, the transforming concept of the Alcoholics Anonymous twelve-step group has been compellingly expressed and applied in innumerable books. Because of this, a person with a vision for changing lives through such a group can often simply pick up the literature and get started. They won't need anyone's permission or money, and there are many ways to get excellent training. Or, to use a less sanguine example, we could note that one of the reasons al-Qaeda has been effective is that it disseminates its worldview broadly and clearly. People imbibe it and educate themselves with it, and many form terrorist cells that operate without central control or communication. In some cases, they may go to an al-Qaeda training camp to become more effective, but afterward they are largely trusted to work out their own local strategy. The point of these examples is that AA and al-Qaeda are vital, constantly growing movements rather than centralized institutions. This is the reason for their effectiveness and their ability to grow with relatively modest amounts of capital. The key to the success of the vision is its simplicity and availability, often in the form of content that transmits, expounds, and applies the vision.

By contrast, though institutions almost always have a purpose statement written down somewhere (e.g., schools are there to educate, businesses to produce their product, hospitals to heal the sick), the glue that holds the institution together is really its rules, regulations, and procedures. In a movement, a shared vision is what guides the day-to-day choices; in an institution, it is typically the rules and established patterns.

2. The unifying vision in a movement is so compelling that it leads to a culture of sacrificial commitment and intrinsic rewards. Individuals put the vision ahead of their own interests and comfort. In the early days of any movement, the main actors often work without compensation, constantly living in the threat of bankruptcy. The satisfaction of realized goals is their main reward. Some refer to this as "intrinsic" reward—internal, personal fulfillment that comes from knowing you have been instrumental in bringing about so much good. In an institution, however, every position has highly defined rights and privileges, as well as clear compensation and benefits. The main incentive in an institution is centered around these "extrinsic" rewards. Institutional members certainly know there is a job to do, but their work output is balanced carefully against concrete rewards. There is no more practical index of whether your church has movement dynamics than examining whether you have a culture of sacrifice. If the top leaders of the church are the only ones making all the sacrifices, then you don't have a movement culture.

3. Movements are characterized by a stance of generous flexibility toward other organizations and people outside their own membership rolls. Movements make the *what*—the accomplishment of the vision—a higher value than *how* it gets done and *who* gets it done. The vision encourages sacrifice, and members of a movement are willing to make allies, cooperating with anyone who shares an interest in the vision.

Institutionalized organizations, on the other hand, are more committed to the importance of inherited practices, right procedures, and accredited persons. They often choose to *not* achieve a result—though it may be strongly desired—if they can't get it done in the prescribed way and with the properly accredited parties.

The spirit of flexibility that we find in a movement means there is a great deal of unity—within the movement as well as in relationship to other organizations. Institutions do not typically encourage this type of unity, even internally. They tend to consist of a set of turf-conscious silos, each more concerned for its own welfare than for the good of the whole. Often, institutions lack organizational unity and may even be hostile toward other organizations.

4. Movements spontaneously produce new ideas and leaders and grow from within. Institutions by their very nature are structured for long-term durability and stability and are prone to resist risky new ideas. But movements are willing to take new risks because the members are already making sacrifices to be part of the work. A movement also tends to attract and reward leaders who produce results. Again, the reason is that accomplishing the vision is so important. Institutions, however, because they value stability and durability, tend to reward leadership according to tenure and the accrual of accepted qualifications and credentials.

Summarizing the important differences between movements and institutions in their strongest forms helps us more clearly see the distinctions (see the table on the next page).

As we see these contrasting characteristics, we begin to better understand why movements are spontaneously generative. A movement is able to generate new ideas because it encourages people to brainstorm and is more willing to experiment and try out new ideas. Movements are "flatter"—less hierarchical and siloed than institutions—and therefore new ideas get traction more quickly. Movements also are better able to generate new leaders because they can attract the most ambitious and creative people. Because they are results oriented, they can quickly identify emerging leaders and promote them. Movements grow faster because their testing of new ideas keeps them adapted to the changes in the environment.

INSTITUTION	MOVEMENT
Held together by rules and procedure	Held together by common purpose, vision
A culture of rights and quotas; a balance of responsibilities and rewards	A culture of sacrificial commitment
Emphasis on compensation, "extrinsic" rewards	Emphasis on celebration, "intrinsic" rewards
Changes in policy involve long process, all departments, much resistance and negotiation	Vision comes from charismatic leaders; accepted with loyalty
Decisions made procedurally and slowly	Decisions made relationally and rapidly
Innovations from top down; implemented in department silos	Innovations bubble up from all members; executed by the whole
Feels like a patchwork of turf-conscious mini-agencies or departments	Feels like a unified whole
Values: security, predictability	Values: risk, serendipity
Stable, slow to change	Dynamic, quick to change
Emphasis on tradition, past, and custom; future trends are dreaded and denied	Emphasis on present and future; little emphasis on past
Jobs given to those with accreditation and tenure	Jobs given to those producing best results

How Movements and Institutions Converge

Young church leaders can get excited about movements and speak long and loudly against the blindness and deadness of the institutional church. Indeed, anyone skimming the left-hand column of the table knows that too many churches *are* too institutionalized. David Hurst, a Harvard scholar, nicely sums up how movements become institutions—vision becomes strategy, roles become tasks, teams become structure, networks become organizations, and recognition becomes compensation.[6]

Remember, however, that it is wrong to draw too sharp a line between the two forms, or even to pit them against each other so starkly when we look at actual examples. While there are good reasons for Christian movement literature to be highly critical of institutionalism, the impression often left is that all authority, centralized control, and formal processes are bad for ministry. The reality is far more complex. First, though new churches and ministries work hard at remaining informal, noncodified, and noncentralized, institutionalization is unavoidable. As soon as we make a choice—the creation of a new policy, administrative structure, or consensus of value and belief—and begin carrying it into the future, thus shaping people's routines, expectations, and allowable preferences, we have begun to institutionalize that value or belief.

And some institutionalization is even desirable. As pointed out earlier, a unified vision —held by every member of the movement—is critical to movement dynamics. But this vision cannot change every day, or even every year, or it will create chaos in the movement and retard its growth. Ironically, this means the vision itself requires some codification and control. In other words, maintaining the engine of movement dynamics—a unified vision—necessitates adopting some of the aspects of institutions. The vision becomes, as it were, a "tradition" that the movement guards and passes on.

In addition, we noted that movements rely heavily on the sacrificial commitment of their members, especially when they are just getting started. In this start-up mode, members may max out their credit cards and tap into their savings to get things going. But this way of living is unsustainable. Any vision that is compelling will be a big one, and big visions require long-term effort—an effort that will require, for example, bringing in enough revenue so the founders can pay off their credit cards and eventually have enough to live on and raise their families. In other words, a movement must eventually settle into a sustainable business model that generates enough resources to cover expenses. If it fails to do this, it will end up burning out the best people and failing to progress toward the vision.

A strong, dynamic movement, then, occupies this difficult space in the center—the place of tension and balance between being a freewheeling organism and a disciplined organization. A movement that refuses to take on some organizational characteristics—authority, tradition, unity of belief, and quality control—will fragment and dissipate. Movements that fail to resist the inevitable tendency toward complete institutionalization will end up losing their vitality and effectiveness. The job of the movement leader is to steer the ship safely between these two perils.

DISCUSSION QUESTIONS

1. What would happen if your organization suddenly had to leave its building, was cut off from denominational support structures, was deprived of endowments and bank balances, and experienced the loss of its senior leader? Would there be a resilient institution remaining that could pick itself up, start over by the grace of God, and raise up new leaders from within? If not, which of the three types of stagnant structures (subsidized from without, managed by endowment life support, or propped up by a small overworked core) best describes your congregation or organization?

2. This chapter suggests four key characteristics of a movement: vision, sacrifice, flexibility with unity, and spontaneity. How have you experienced these in your own ministry or church setting? In your experience, how does each of these characteristics contribute to the dynamics of the movement?

3. Review the table contrasting institutions with movements. As you consider your own church, what characteristics of a movement do you see? What characteristics of an institution are present? What can you do to encourage additional movement dynamics in your church?

Chapter 10

THE CHURCH AS AN ORGANIZED ORGANISM

As we clarify the differences between institutions and movements we must acknowledge that churches are and must be institutions.[1] But they must also be movements. As we have seen over the centuries, churches can meet doctrinal and institutional standards and still lack effectiveness in propagating the faith in their society. At this point, it is natural to ask, "Is there biblical warrant for being attentive to this distinction and balance between institution and movement?" I believe there is. The Scriptures envision churches that are both *organism* and *organization*—or, to put it simply, churches that are organized organisms.

The book of Acts describes the life of the church in organic language. Several times we are told that the church or the number of disciples increased, grew, or spread (4:4; 6:1, 7; 9:31; 16:5). We are also told that the Word of God spread, increased, or grew (6:7; 12:24; 19:20). Acts 19:20 speaks of the Word growing in power, as if the Word of God, the gospel of Christ, has a life and power of its own (cf. Rom 1:16 – 17). Paul speaks of the gospel continually "bearing fruit and growing" (Col 1:6).

The church grows, but it does not grow as other human organizations do—as a business, a sports league, a government agency, or even a viral online movement would grow. The church increases in numbers because the Word of God grows when it reaches listeners in the power of the Spirit (cf. Acts 10 – 11). This biblical language suggests there is an organic, self-propagating, dynamic power operating within the church. In Acts, we see it working essentially on its own, with little institutional support or embodiment—without strategic plans or the command and control of managers and other leaders.

And yet, even though this power operates spontaneously, we see that when the Word of God produces a new church, Paul is always careful to appoint elders—leaders with authority—in every town before leaving it (cf. Acts 14:23). We may be inclined to wonder, "How was Paul able to discern so quickly those with leadership ability among the brand-new converts? Wouldn't it have been better to let the new body of believers grow for a couple of years—just meeting together to study and to love and serve each other—before imposing an authority structure on them?" Paul's behavior indicates just how important it was for these dynamic, spontaneously growing churches to have an authority structure as a way of ensuring that members would embody the church's apostolically inherited teaching and purpose.

From the beginning, the church was both an institution and a movement. This dual nature of the church is grounded in the work of the Spirit, and it is the Spirit who makes the church simultaneously a vital *organism* and a structured *organization*.[2] One helpful way of understanding this balance is to look at the way the ministry of Jesus is carried out in the church in a general sense through every believer, as well as through specialized roles—a distinction commonly referred to as the *general* and *special* office.

The General and the Special Office

Jesus Christ has all the powers and functions of ministry in himself. He has a *prophetic* ministry, speaking the truth and applying it to men and women on behalf of God. Jesus was the ultimate prophet, for he revealed most clearly (both in his words and his life) God's character, saving purposes, and will for our lives. Jesus also has a *priestly* ministry. While a prophet is an advocate for God before people, a priest is an advocate for the people before God's presence, ministering with mercy and sympathy. Jesus was the ultimate priest, for he stood in our place and sacrificially bore our burdens and sin, and he now brings us into God's presence. Finally, Jesus has a *kingly* ministry. He is the ultimate king, ordering the life of his people through his revealed law.

The General Office of Believers

Every believer, through the Holy Spirit, is to minister to others in these three ways as well.

1. The Bible refers to every believer as a prophet. In Numbers 11:29, Moses states, "I wish that all the LORD's people were prophets," and in Joel 2:28 – 29, this blessing is predicted for the messianic age. In Acts 2:16 – 21, Peter declares that in the church this prophecy is now fulfilled. Every believer is led by the Holy Spirit to discern the truth (1 John 2:20, 27). Each believer is directed to admonish with the word of Christ (Col 3:16), as well as to instruct (Rom 15:14) and encourage other believers (Heb 3:13). Christians are also called to witness to the truth before their nonbelieving friends and neighbors. In Acts 8:4, all of the Christians "who had been scattered" out of Jerusalem "preached the word wherever they went." In 1 Thessalonians 1:8, Paul states that "the Lord's message rang out" from the new converts all over Macedonia and Achaia. Paul exhorted the Corinthian Christians to imitate him in conducting all aspects of life in such a way that people come to salvation (1 Cor 9:19 – 23; 10:31 – 11:1). In Colossians 4:5 – 6, Paul tells all Christians to answer every nonbeliever with wisdom and grace, and in 1 Peter 3:15, Peter charges all believers to give cogent reasons for their faith to non-Christians. Behind all these exhortations is the assumption that the message of Christ is dwelling richly in every Christian (Col 3:16). It means that every believer must read, ponder, and love the Word of God, be able to interpret it properly, and be skillful in applying it to their own questions and needs and to those of the people around them.

2. The Bible calls every believer a priest— "You are ... a royal priesthood" (1 Pet 2:9). Just as every believer is a prophet, understanding the Word of God now that Jesus has come, so every believer is a priest, having access in the name of Christ, the great High Priest, to the presence of God (Heb 4:14 – 16). Believers, then, have the priestly work of daily offering themselves as a living sacrifice (Rom 12:1 – 2) and of offering the sacrifices of deeds of mercy and adoring worship to God (Heb 13:15 – 16). The priesthood of all believers means not only that all are now active participants in joyful public worship (1 Cor 14:26), but also that they have the priestly calling "to do good and to share with others" (Heb 13:16). As prophets, Christians call neighbors to repent, but as priests they do so with sympathy and loving service to address their needs. This is why Jesus calls us to live such lives of goodness and service that outsiders will glorify God (Matt 5:16).[3]

3. The Bible calls every believer a king. All believers rule and reign with Christ (Eph 2:6) as kings and priests (Rev 1:5 – 6). Although elders and leaders have the responsibility of church governance and discipline, the "kingship of all believers" means that believers have the right and responsibility to discipline one another. Christians are supposed to confess their sins not only to a minister but to one another, and they are called to pray for one another (Jas 5:16). They are not to rely only on the discipline of elders but are to exhort each other so they don't become hardened by their sin (Heb 3:13). It is the responsibility of not only elders and ministers to discern sound doctrine; all believers must rely on the anointing the Spirit gives them to discern truth (1 John 2:20, 27). The kingly general office is one of the reasons that many denominations have historically given the congregation the right to select its own leaders and officers, with the approval of the existing leaders (Acts 6:1 – 6). In other words, the power of governing the church rests in the people. Though pastors and teachers are uniquely called to build up the body into spiritual maturity (Eph 4:11 – 13), every Christian is called to help build up the body into maturity by "speaking the truth in love" to one another (Eph 4:15). The kingship of every believer also means that every believer has the authority to fight and defeat the world, the flesh, and the devil (cf. Eph 6:11 – 18; Jas 4:7; 1 John 2:27; 4:4; 5:4).

All of these facets of ministry are brought together in 1 Peter 2:9. Here we are told that followers of Christ have been made kings and priests — "a royal priesthood" — that we "may declare the praises of him who called you out of darkness," which is the work of a prophet. The Spirit equips every believer to be a prophet who brings the truth, a priest who sympathetically serves, and a king who calls others into accountable love — even if he or she lacks specialized gifts for office or full-time ministry. This Spirit-equipped calling and gifting of every believer to be a prophet, priest, and king has been called the "general office." This understanding of the general office helps prevent the church from becoming a top-down, conservative, innovation-allergic bureaucracy. It helps us understand the church as an energetic grassroots movement that produces life-changing and world-changing ministry—all without dependence on the control and planning of a hierarchy of leaders.

The Special Office of Minister

The Spirit gives every Christian believer spiritual gifts for ministry (1 Cor 12 – 14) so that service to Christ will constantly arise out of the grassroots of the church. Yet the Spirit also gives gifts and creates "special offices"—roles that carry out a ministry within the church—that sometimes entail authority. The very same Spirit who generates the spontaneous, explosive ministry and growth is also the giver of the gifts of apostle, prophet, evangelist, and pastor/teacher (Eph 4:11), as well as of governance (Rom 12:8). To be exercised, these gifts must be publicly recognized by the congregation, which requires some kind of organization. There is no way to exercise the gift of governing (Rom 12:8) unless we have an institutional structure—elections, bylaws, ordination, and standards for accreditation. No one can govern without some level of agreement by the whole church about what powers are given to the governors and how these powers are legitimately exercised. So the growth and flourishing of spontaneous ministry depends on some institutional elements being in place.

The special office represents the way Jesus orders and governs his church by the Spirit. Jesus commissions the leaders of the church by assigning them gifts, and so when we select our church's leaders, we are simply recognizing the calling and gifts of the Lord. The distinctive blueprint for your church—the pattern of ministries God desires it to have—is shaped by the gifts assigned to the leaders and members by Jesus himself. Why are some churches particularly effective in reaching some kinds of people more than others? God has given them a particular pattern of gifts and therefore a particular pattern of ministry.

The special office means that the Spirit chooses some people to be leaders and pacesetters for all aspects of the general office. While all Christians should teach and evangelize, the Spirit calls some to be teachers and evangelists (Eph 4:11). All believers should share what they have with the needy, yet the church calls some leaders to be deacons and lead in the ministry of mercy (Acts 6:1 – 6; 1 Tim 3:8 – 13). All Christians should watch over one another and call one another to account (Gal 6:1 – 2; Heb 3:13), and yet every congregation is to have "elders" (Acts 14:23; Titus 1:5) who will look after the people as shepherds care for their sheep (Acts 20:28 – 31; 1 Pet 5:1 – 4). Believers are to submit to the authority of their leaders (1 Thess 5:12; Heb 13:7, 17). When these leaders exercise their gifts, they are also exercising Christ's ministry.

Churches that are solidly grounded in their historical tradition normally have a strong bias for the importance of the special office. They must actively seek to cultivate a greater appreciation for the dynamic and fluid nature of the general office. One way to do this is through the *commissioning of unordained lay leaders and staff*—men and women working alongside traditional ordained leaders. In this way, churches can honor both the dynamic and organizing work of the Spirit.

The Holy Spirit, then, makes the church both an organism and an organization—a cauldron of spontaneously generated spiritual life and ministry, as well as an ordered, structured community with rules and authority. If God only gave gifts to all believers and did not call anyone into a place of authority, the church would be only an organic, spontaneous movement with virtually no institutional structure. If he only gave gifts to "special officers"—ordained ministers—then the church would be exclusively a top-down, command-and-control institution. But God's Spirit creates both the general and the special office—and so we speak of the *ardor* of the Spirit (creating the movement) and the *order* of the Spirit (creating the institution). This dynamic balance of the Spirit's work is what makes the church (in human terms) sustainable.

We see these dynamics vividly come together in 1 Peter 2:4 – 5, where Peter describes Christians as "living stones" in a new temple. Stones in a building represent a *non*organic metaphor. But Peter tells us that the stones of this temple are alive, and so the temple does, indeed, "grow" (see Eph 2:21). This suggests we should understand the church to be both an organism (which grows naturally) and an organization (which is structured and ordered).

It is vital to recognize the Holy Spirit as the author of both aspects of the nature of the church. Sometimes the ministries that directly produce converts and visibly changed lives (e.g., evangelism, worship, preaching) are seen as more spiritual than ministries of administration and ongoing programs (e.g., governance structures, church discipline, church management, rules of operation, membership assimilation programs, finance, stewardship, building maintenance, and so on). This is an understandable error.[4] Centuries of experience have taught us that it is very difficult to keep order and ardor together. The proponents of order tend to see only the advantages of stable institutions and only the disadvantages of spontaneous movements. They see pride and arrogance in radical new movements and dismiss them as unstable, shortsighted, and self-important. Often they are right, but just as often they are wrong. On the other hand, the proponents of more dynamic, less hierarchical movements tend to see only the disadvantages of institutions. They see self-interest, rigid bureaucracy, and idolatry, and dismiss the institutions as dead or dying. Sometimes they are right, but just as often they, too, are wrong. The church, at its healthiest, is both organized and organic. Because the author of both aspects is the Holy Spirit, they must be able to exist in harmony with one another.

Movement Dynamics in the Local Church

In the previous chapter, we identified four key characteristics of a movement: vision, sacrifice, flexibility with unity, and spontaneity. What does it look like when these characteristics are present in individual churches and ministries? How do we encourage movement dynamics in the local church that are biblically balanced with institutional dynamics?

The Vision and Beliefs Create Oneness

A church with movement dynamics is driven by a clear vision for a particular future reality based on common beliefs. Vision is a set of strong beliefs animating a concrete picture of a future. So, for example, one compelling vision could be to increase the number of evangelical churches in a city tenfold within a generation. (A vision of this magnitude may seem outrageous in the United States, but it is quite possible in Western Europe, for example.) The concrete picture in this case is the tenfold increase, a picture of what the city would look like with an enlarged church in its midst within the span of a generation. This vision is wedded to strong beliefs—the classic evangelical gospel of the revivals and the Reformation.

Contextualization bears heavily on the communication of a church's vision. A compellingly articulated church vision is, in reality, a contextualized way of expressing the biblical teaching about the gospel and the work of the church. For example, a church may say that its vision is to "seek the peace and prosperity of the city" and then spell out clearly what this means. This vision expresses the biblical call to the people of God in Jeremiah 29 and Romans 12. Another church may express its vision as "changing lives with the gospel" and then clearly and attractively describe what this changed life looks like. This vision expresses the biblical call to the church to make disciples with the power of the Word and Spirit. Each of these vision statements, though they emphasize different aspects of the biblical call, will be galvanizing if they are stated in ways that are clear and persuasive to people of a particular culture.

Devotion to God's Kingdom over Self or Tribe Enables Sacrifice

People in a church with movement dynamics put the vision ahead of their own interests and needs. What matters to the members and staff is not their own individual interests, power, and perks, but the fulfillment of the vision. They want to see it realized through them, and this satisfaction is their main compensation. The willingness to sacrifice on the part of workers and members is perhaps the key practical index of whether you have become a movement or have become institutionalized. Members of a church with movement dynamics tend to be more self-motivated and need less direct oversight. They are self-starters.

How does this happen? Selfless devotion is not something that leaders can create—indeed it would be dangerous emotional manipulation to try to bring this about directly. Only leaders who have the vision and devotion can kindle this sacrificial spirit in others. A dynamic Christian movement convinces its people—truthfully—that they are participating in God's redemptive plan in a profoundly important and practical way. Participants say things like, "I've never felt more useful to the Lord and to others." Church meetings in movement-oriented churches feel deeply spiritual. There is much more "majoring in the majors"—the cross, the Spirit, the grace of Jesus. People spend more time in worship and prayer.

Emphasis on Unity Creates Cooperation across Lines

Openness to cooperation is another essential movement dynamic. Because members of the movement are deeply concerned with seeing the vision accomplished, they are willing to work with people who are also materially committed to the vision and share primary beliefs but who differ in preferences, temperaments, and secondary beliefs or are members of other organizations. Because institutions are more focused on protocol and rules than on results and outcomes, their members tend to look askance at groups or people who don't do things in the same way. In the Christian world, this means Christian groups with movement dynamics are more willing to work across denominational and organizational lines to achieve common goals.

Movement-oriented churches think more about reaching the city, while institutionalized churches put emphasis on growing their church's particular expression or denomination. In general, leaders of churches with movement dynamics have a high tolerance for ambiguity and organizational messiness. What matters is that people hear the gospel and are converted and discipled, which results in cooperation with people from outside their own membership and involves learning from them.

As always, balance is crucial. A sectarian, highly institutionalized church or agency may refuse to cooperate with bodies that don't share all its beliefs, including secondary and tertiary ones. We rightly criticize this posture as being antithetical to movements. But so is the opposite posture. It is important to be doctrinally vigilant and willing, when necessary, to respectfully contend for important theological truths when we believe that ministry partners are losing their grasp on those truths. A cowardly refusal to speak the truth in love is neither cooperative nor loving. The critical truths that ministry partners must hold in common should be clearly stated, and if there is movement away from them, there should be straightforward conversation about it. But how do we talk about doctrinal differences in a way that is not unnecessarily destructive to unity?

Spontaneity without Top-Down Command Enables Growth

A church or organization with movement dynamics has spiritual spontaneity; it constantly generates new ideas, leaders, and initiatives within and across itself—not solely from the top or from a command center outside of itself. As we noted, spontaneous combustion means ignition from within, not from outside. A church or organization that is highly institutionalized, however, is structured so that individuals cannot offer ideas and propose projects unless asked or given permission. A church with movement dynamics, however, generates ideas, leaders, and initiatives from the grassroots. Ideas come less from formal strategic meetings and more from off-line conversations among friends. Since the motivation for the work is not so much about compensation and self-interest as about a shared willingness to sacrifice for the infectious vision, such churches naturally create friendships among members and staff. These friendships become mini-engines powering the church, along with the more formal, organized meetings and events.

Another aspect of the spontaneity dynamic is the natural growth in leadership. This doesn't mean a church should not have formal training programs. Rather, it means (1) that the vision of the movement (especially as its content is disseminated) attracts people with leadership potential and (2) that the work of the movement naturally reveals emerging leaders through real-life experience and prepares them for the next level of leadership in the movement. An example is Reformed University Fellowship, a campus ministry of the Presbyterian Church in America. RUF recruits recent college graduates to be campus interns, many of whom go on to become full-time campus staff.[5] Working on college campuses trains workers to be evangelistic, to work with the emerging edge of culture, and to do ministry through fluid, nonformal processes. All of this makes campus ministers who leave the RUF staff more comfortable planting new churches than merely taking positions in established ones. As a result, RUF has created a continual flow of dynamic, fruitful church planters and young laypeople (former Christian university students) who are excellent core-group members for new congregations.

RUF is typical of dynamic movements in that it was not originally founded to produce church planters; the powerful "church planter formation" dynamic happened spontaneously, as the natural fruit of an excellent campus ministry. Most denominations, of course, create institutionalized agencies to recruit and train church planters, but organic leadership development pipelines such as RUF are often more productive. When a denomination experiences these gifts from God, it should recognize them and do what it can to support and enhance the experience without strangling it. Many churches are so institutionalized in their thinking that it makes it difficult to do so.[6]

Creative Tension

Scripture suggests that churches cannot choose between being a movement or an institution; they must be both. And yet in this book we are emphasizing movement dynamics over institutional ones. Why? Because over time, movements inevitably become institutions. Therefore, it is necessary for churches to *intentionally* cultivate the dynamics that characterize a healthy movement.

This process is difficult not only because movement dynamics push against organizational inertia but also because the movement dynamics themselves can be in tension with one another. Consider two movement dynamics we have identified: vision and spontaneity. On one hand, if everyone gets to define the *vision* according to what seems correct in their own eyes (Judg 17:6; 21:25), the movement falls apart. The vision and beliefs are the glue that must be guarded and rearticulated. They can evolve and be sharpened, but usually only gradually and by the top leaders. They must be codified and committed to media, and leaders must subscribe to them in some way. So the need for unity almost always pushes a movement toward structure in this area. The *spontaneity* dynamic, however, means new initiatives and creative ideas—aligned with and in pursuit of the vision—must emerge from everywhere. Making people wait a long time for "orders from headquarters" only suppresses their contributions, and much of the movement energy is lost. This spontaneity dynamic tends to get suppressed as the organization becomes more formal and codified.

The pursuit of unity and spontaneity will inevitably lead to change as the movement grows in size. If a church has four elders, then most decision making will take on a flat, collaborative shape. Elders have a lot of time to discuss issues and come to consensus. But what happens when the church grows and now has a team of twenty elders? The meetings become interminable, and reaching consensus can take months. It is only natural, then, for the church to designate groups of elders that make decisions to be routinely approved by the entire elder board. This looks suspiciously like a committee structure, which many (especially authors of Christian movement literature) believe is an unhealthy form of institutionalization. But from another perspective it can be seen as a form of trust, motivated by a desire to avoid controlling everything from the center. So delegation can be more of a movement dynamic than a sign of institutionalization.

How difficult it is to maintain this dynamic balance! Churches, laypersons, and ministers regularly have bad experiences in imbalanced churches and in response flee to the opposite extreme—an equally unbalanced form of ministry. When a lay-driven ministry goes off the rails, its victims tend to move toward a much more authoritarian, tightly controlled ministry. Meanwhile, refugees from "top-down" churches often rush to the opposite kind of church. Each kind of imbalance chokes the *movement-ness* of the church.

On the surface, the description of the church as a movement seems far more attractive than the description that focuses on the institutional aspects of a church and its ministry. In movements, the structure clearly serves the cause, whereas in institutions, the cause tends to serve the structure. And ultimately, this is how it should be. Some church or ministry structures are directly biblical (and therefore nonnegotiable), but most are humanly made (and therefore negotiable). The Bible instructs churches to have elders, for example, but it says virtually nothing about how this team is to be organized. A key to navigating the creative tension of Scripture is to avoid allowing humanly made structures to become idols — relative, finite things elevated to the status of unquestioned divine authority.

For a movement to stay a movement, then, it needs to achieve and maintain balance as an "organized organism." On the continuum below, a movement-driven church would need to have its X toward the right. Since churches always migrate toward institutionalism, they often must be brought back toward a movement dynamic.

Institution   **Movement**

——————————————————————————————————X———————————

A practical key to maintaining an organized organism is experiencing a season of renewal in the church or organization that parallels the way an individual person is spiritually renewed. There must be times for what the Bible calls "covenant renewal." Israel was brought into its original covenant relationship with God at Mount Sinai in Exodus 19 – 20, and the nation was formed as God's people and called to live in a particular way in the world. Whenever Israel faced a major new chapter in their journey, however, they were led through a season of covenant renewal — in Joshua 24, before they entered the promised land; in 1 Samuel 12, before they received a king; and in Nehemiah 8 – 9, as they returned from the Babylonian exile. These times of covenant renewal always had three parts: (1) the people returned to biblical texts in order to remember the things God had called them to do and be; (2) they looked forward to the next chapter, to the new challenges facing them; and (3) they rededicated their lives and resources to God for the next stage of the journey. This renewal must happen frequently in any church for it to remain an organized organism. It also prepares the church to be an active and generous participant in the movement dynamics in its city.

DISCUSSION QUESTIONS

1. Describe the difference between the *general* office and the *special* office. What are the three aspects of ministry that belong to every believer as part of the general office? What are some of the functions and roles given to the special office? How does the distinction between these two help you to better strike the balance between the church as a vital organism and a structured organization?

2. Keller writes, "The willingness to sacrifice on the part of workers and members is perhaps the key practical index of whether you have a movement or have become institutionalized." Take a moment to check the temperature of your volunteer culture. Look at the faces in your church directory and ask how aggressively they are sacrificing. Is the answer indicative of a movement or have you become institutionalized? How might this relate to the vision of your church, or the lack of vision?

3. Keller writes, "Churches, laypersons, and ministers regularly have bad experiences in imbalanced churches and in response flee to the opposite extreme." Are there any conflicts or dysfunctions in your church that you now understand better in light of this statement?

Chapter 11

CHURCH PLANTING AS A MOVEMENT DYNAMIC

A church that is an organized organism will exhibit movement dynamics not only *inside* itself but also *beyond* itself. So it will naturally be involved in church planting. Church planting is mentioned in many places throughout the New Testament. For example, Paul refers to his work of planting and watering churches with Apollos (1 Cor 3:6 – 7). But the primary place in Scripture to learn about church planting is the book of Acts. All orthodox Christians agree that prescriptive statements of the Bible are normative for us, but the descriptive histories of the Old and New Testaments contain both good and bad examples. Are we always certain which is which? The safest approach, I suggest, is to take the church planting practices of Paul in Acts very seriously while recognizing that it does not give us a fixed rule book for church planting in all times, places, and contexts. It is best to look for general principles rather than rules or detailed practices.[1]

Natural Church Planting

In Acts, planting churches is not a traumatic or unnatural event. It is woven into the warp and woof of ministry, and so it happens steadily and normally. Paul never evangelizes and disciples without also planting a church. For decades, expositors have looked to Acts to make lists of the basic elements of ministry: Bible teaching, evangelism, fellowship, discipleship, and worship. I have always found it odd that right there in Acts, along with everything else the church is doing, is church planting—yet this element of ministry is consistently ignored! I believe

216

there is a dubious, tacit cessationism at work. Almost unconsciously, readers of the book of Acts have said, "Yes, but that was for then. We don't need to do that now." I believe this conclusion misses a key aspect of a healthy church, namely, that church planting must be natural and customary, not traumatic and episodic.

The normal ministry of Paul had three phases that are easily seen in Acts 14. First is *evangelism*. Acts 14:21 states that "[Paul and Barnabas] preached the gospel," but it does not use the common word for "preaching." Instead, a more comprehensive word is used: they *euangelizō*-ed or "gospeled" the city. This Greek word connotes a great deal more than simply preaching sermons. The book of Acts describes Paul in the act of spreading the gospel through preaching in synagogue services, sharing in small group Bible studies, speaking out in marketplaces, leading discussions in rented halls, and simply talking with people one-on-one.

In the second phase of Paul's ministry, we see a clear incorporation into *community*. Immediately after "gospeling" the city, Paul goes to the converts to strengthen and encourage them (Acts 14:22). These two verbs (*epistērizō* and *parakaleō*) are also used together in Acts 9:31 and 15:32. John Stott refers to these verbs as an "almost technical" term for building up new believers.[2] So how did Paul do this? He taught them "the faith" (Acts 14:22)—a definite body of beliefs and theology. But also he "congregated" them. New believers do not simply go on living their lives as they were, but they are brought into a community that assembles regularly.

Finally, in the third phase, we find *leadership development*. In each place Paul visited, he chose elders, a plurality of leaders out of the converts, who then took on the task of teaching and shepherding the people in the faith. In other words, Paul routinely organized his converts into *churches* in their own right—more than just loosely knit fellowships directly under his leadership. These churches had their own leadership and structure. When Paul began meeting with them, they were called "disciples" (Acts 14:22), but when he left them, they were known as "churches" (see Acts 14:23). To put it simply, the multiplication of churches is as natural in the book of Acts as the multiplication of individual converts.

As Tim Chester points out in his essay "Church Planting: A Theological Perspective," we find two basic avenues for launching churches in Acts.[3] In Paul and his companions, we see an example of the first avenue: *pioneer church planting.* Though the Antioch church sent Paul out, and he was accountable to them for his doctrine and behavior (Acts 13:1 – 3), his work in every city was by definition a pioneering work. Paul did groundbreaking evangelism in each place he visited, without the cooperation of other churches.

The other form is *churches planting other churches.* This more implicit example is present in the New Testament, but we have to avoid screening it out by thinking anachronistically about the word *church* when we see it in the text. The churches Paul planted (in fact all of the Christian churches for almost two hundred years) were *household* churches. For example, Lydia's conversion immediately became a bridge to the conversion of her household, making her home the first church in Philippi. By Acts 16:40, Paul and Silas were going to Lydia's home to meet the brethren. The same thing happens in Acts 18 with the household of Crispus. What did this mean? It meant that the church at Philippi, Corinth, and everywhere else could only grow naturally by multiplying new assemblies or house churches. Though Paul wrote to the "church" (singular) at Corinth, it is obvious by the end of the book that he was addressing a number of household churches—Chloe, Stephanus, et al. Because in the early church the household church was the basic building block of the movement, church planting was built into the church's very nature. You could only grow churches by multiplying new household-based assemblies of Christians who met under elders.

Today as well, these two basic approaches are still the main avenues for church planting (see table).

PIONEERING CHURCH PLANTING	CHURCH-LED CHURCH PLANTING
Ministers/leaders are often self-initiators	Church leaders are selected by church body, but a church can also call and send
No core members; pioneer gets all core members through networking and evangelism	Members come from (1) pooling cell groups and (2) hiving off distant families
Money from (1) mission agency, (2) raising of personal support from friends and churches, (3) tent-making/self-employment, or (4) two or all of the above	Money from (1) core group pledge, (2) gift/subsidy from mother church, (3) outside grants from distant churches or individuals, or (4) two or all of the above
Mentor is a distant pastor or leader, seen infrequently; or reading-only mentor (dead or distant)	Regular meetings with nearby mentor; often peer supervision possible
Model is often innovative, forging new models or imitating distant ones	Model is similar to mother church, though never identical

Making Church Planting Natural

A natural church planting mind-set means church leaders will think of church planting as just one of the things the church does along with everything else. Church planting should not be like building a building—one big traumatic event followed by a deep collective sigh of relief that it's done. Paul was continually engaged in evangelism, discipleship, *and* church planting. In fact, I believe church planting is actually a fifth "ministry front" that works alongside the four aspects of integrative ministry outlined in part 2. There we said that every church should connect people to God (worship and evangelism), to one another (discipleship and community), to the needs of the city (justice and mercy), and to the culture (integrating faith and work). But the fifth ministry front is the multiplication of a church into new churches with the other four ministry fronts. So church planting should be as much an ongoing, natural part of your ministry as worship, evangelism, fellowship, education, and service.

A natural church planting mind-set can be described in terms of three key mind-set shifts. The hard truth is that if you and your team can't make these mind-set shifts, it is highly unlikely that your church can plant churches naturally and effectively.

1. You must be willing to give away resources and lose control of your money, members, and leaders. I hesitate to use the cliché, but it's true in this case: Paul "empowered" these new leaders. He gave them ownership, and in doing so, he surrendered a lot of control. Many churches cannot bear the thought of losing key leaders, money-giving families, or even just friends. Ministers are also afraid of giving away some of their glory. If your ministry adds people who are assimilated into your church and incorporated into Bible studies and new ministries in your church, it swells your numbers, and you gain both control and glory. But if you organize new people into new churches, you lose money, members, numbers, leaders, and control. Yet this is exactly what Paul did! An additional issue is that when we let go, we lose direct control but can't avoid responsibility for the problems that arise. It's a bit like being the parent of an adult child. We are not allowed to directly tell them what to do, but if a problem arises, we are expected to help clean it up.

An evangelical church in our area occupied a small, historic building. They had filled one hundred seats to maximum capacity for four years in a row but had resisted church planting, fearing it would result in the loss of money and people. Eventually, they sent fifty people to a new town to form a new church. Just two years later, nearly 350 people were coming to the daughter church. Meanwhile, the mother church once again filled its seats—in about three weeks! Soon they were kicking themselves, realizing that over the course of this time, they could have planted another three churches with nearly a thousand people in the church family, all able to do missions, youth ministry, and many other initiatives together. They realized they needed to make the transition to a natural church planting mind-set.

2. You must be willing to give up some control of the shape of the ministry itself. Doing so is especially scary for those of us who care deeply about the preservation of biblical truth. But it's a simple fact that the new church will not look just like the original. It will develop its own voice and emphases. On the one hand, you must take pains to be sure that the difference is not too great, or else fellowship and cooperation will be strained. We must not forget that the book of Acts speaks of "the faith." There is *one body of true doctrine* at the heart of Christianity. On the other hand, if you insist that the new church must be a clone, you reveal that you are not willing to admit the reality of contextualization in the biblical sense of adapting and incarnating. Different generations and cultures *will* produce a different kind of church. This does not undermine the soundness of the mother church; it testifies to it.

As noted above, Paul appointed elders in each church, giving them a certain amount of independence. He was able to do this because the natural church planting mind-set is not as much a matter of trusting new leaders as it is a matter of trusting God. Paul does not call the new churches to fend for themselves or leave them to the care of others. Rather, he "committed them to the Lord" (Acts 14:23). Paul's heart and character were such that he did not need to keep control; he had faith that God would continue the work he had started in the church. A natural church planting mind-set requires a high level of spiritual maturity and trust in God's providence.

3. You must be willing to care for the kingdom even more than for your tribe. We see this demonstrated in the way Paul speaks of Apollos, who is affirmed even though he is not Paul's disciple (Acts 18:24 – 28). Paul refers to him in the warmest terms (1 Cor 3:6; 4:6; 16:12), even though Apollos's disciples evidently considered themselves a particular party, distinct from Paul's (1 Cor 1:12; 3:4). We also see this in the way Paul willingly takes his hands off the new churches he plants (see Acts 16:40: "Then they left."). Paul is concerned not about his or his party's power (even then, different apostles had their followers and emphases) but about the kingdom as a whole.

A new church in the community usually leads existing churches to face this issue of kingdom-mindedness. New churches typically draw most of their new members from the ranks of the unchurched, but they will also attract some people from existing churches. When we lose two or three families to a church that is bringing in a hundred new people who weren't going to any other church before, we have a choice! We must ask ourselves, "Are we going to celebrate the new people the kingdom has gained through this new church, or are we going to bemoan and resent the families we lost to it?" In other words, our attitude to new church development is a test of whether our mind-set is geared to our own institutional turf or to the overall health and prosperity of the kingdom of God in the city. Any church that bemoans its own small losses instead of rejoicing in the larger gains of the kingdom is betraying its narrow interests. Yet the benefits of new church planting to older congregations can be great, even if that benefit is not initially obvious.[4]

We began with a warning that we must be careful not to read the book of Acts as a strict rule book for church planting. Yet our secular, urbanized, global world today is strikingly like the Greco-Roman world in certain ways. For the first time in fifteen hundred years, there are multiple, vital, religious faith communities and options (including true paganism) in every society. Traditional, secular, and pagan worldviews and communities are living side by side. Once again, cities are the influential cultural centers, just as they were in the Greco-Roman world. During the Pax Romana, cities became furiously multiethnic and globally connected. Since we are living in an Acts-like world again rather than the earlier context of Christendom, church planting will *necessarily* be as central a strategy for reaching our world as it was for reaching previous generations.

Ultimately, though, we don't look to Paul to teach us about church planting, but to Jesus himself. Jesus is the ultimate church planter. He builds his church (Matt 16:18), and he does so effectively, because hell itself will not prevail against it. He raises up leaders and gives them the keys to the kingdom (Matt 16:19). He establishes his converts on the word of the confessing apostle, Peter—that is, on the word of God (Matt 16:18). When we plant the church, we participate in God's work, for if we have any success at all, it is because "God has been making it grow." Thus, "neither the one who plants nor the one who waters is anything, but only God, who makes things grow" (1 Cor 3:6 – 7).

Answering Objections

There is a common objection to reading the book of Acts the way we suggest here: "That was then! Now, at least in North America and Europe, we have churches all over the place. We don't need to start new churches; we should strengthen and fill our existing churches before we do that." Let me give several answers to this common objection.

Fully Evangelistic Churches

The way to evangelize a city is not through evangelism programs but through fully evangelistic churches.

Evangelism programs aim at getting people to make a decision to follow Christ. Experience, however, shows us that many of these "decisions" disappear and never result in changed lives. Why? Many decisions are not true spiritual conversions; they are only the beginning of a journey of seeking God. (I must add that some decisions definitely mark the moment of new birth, but this differs from person to person.) Many people come to full faith through a process of mini-decisions. Only a person who is hearing the gospel in the context of an ongoing worshiping and shepherding community can be sure of finally coming home into vital, saving faith. Evangelism programs, grafted onto a church that is unable to embrace and support inquirers and doubters, cannot do the job. What the city needs is not more evangelism programs but far more wholly evangelistic churches.

Growing the Number of Churches in the City

The way to grow the number of Christians in a city is not mainly through church renewal but through church planting.

When stagnant churches go through a renewal phase and begin to grow, it is typically through transfer growth from other churches. Strong programs attract believers who are suffering under poor preaching, poor discipleship offerings, or other signs of unhealthy discipleship elsewhere. But even older renewed churches cannot integrate unchurched persons like a new congregation can. Studies confirm that the average new church gains one-third to two-thirds of its new members from the ranks of people who are not attending any worshiping body, while churches over ten to fifteen years of age gain 80 to 90 percent of new members by transfer from other congregations.[5] The average new congregation, then, will bring new people into the life of the body of Christ at six to eight times the rate of an older congregation of the same size. Why is this so?

As a congregation ages, powerful internal institutional pressures lead it to allocate most of its resources and energy toward the concerns of its members and constituents rather than toward those outside its walls. This is natural—and to a great degree desirable. Older congregations have a stability and steadiness that many people (especially long-term residents) thrive on and need. They also have the trust of the local community. Older congregations are inevitably more influenced by the people groups that have been in the neighborhood for a long time. They do not contain (or typically open their leadership ranks to) the members of the growing people groups in the area—new ethnic groups, new generations. As a result, many people can only be reached by churches with deeper roots in the community and with the trappings of stability and respectability.

Nevertheless, these same dynamics explain why most congregations thirty to forty years old or older are experiencing numerical decline. Older congregations of necessity must focus on the needs and sensibilities of the churched and the long-term residents, even at the expense of any appeal to the unchurched or newer people groups. New congregations, by contrast, have no organizational traditions they must honor or oppose. In general, they are forced to focus on the needs of their *non*members simply to get off the ground. There are no members with many years or decades of tenure, and so new Christians and newer members are able to get their voices heard in ways that would not happen in an older congregation. This is generally why new churches do a far better job of outreach.

Thus, the only way to significantly increase the number of Christians in a city is by significantly increasing the number of new churches. Here's a thought experiment that illustrates this point. Imagine Cities A, B, and C are the same size, and each has one hundred churches. In City A, all the churches are more than twenty years old, and so the overall number of active Christian churchgoers in this town will be shrinking, even if four or five of the churches catch a wave and grow in attendance. The most likely reason is that they are pulling Christians from the other churches. Most churches in City A will be declining, and the renewed churches will likely simply be retaining Christians, not reaching the unchurched. Overall, the number of Christians in town is shrinking steadily.

In City B, let's say ten of the hundred churches are less than ten years old. Roughly one new church is being planted per year—a mere 1 percent. These churches will likely be bringing in three to five times more unchurched people (proportionately) than the rest, and some of the renewed older congregations will also be winning new people to Christ. But it is likely that the growth experienced here will merely offset the normal declines of most of the older churches. Thus, the number of active Christian churchgoers in City B will be staying the same or perhaps slowly declining.

Finally, in City C, twenty-five of the hundred churches are less than ten years old. In other words, new congregations are being planted at 2 to 3 percent the rate of the existing total per year. In this city, the overall number of active Christian churchgoers will be on a path to grow 50 percent in a generation.

Renewing Existing Churches

The way to renew the existing churches of a city is by planting new ones.

In any discussion on new church development, these questions often arise: What about all the existing churches in the city? Shouldn't we be working to strengthen and renew *them*? The answer is that planting a lot of new churches *is* one of the best ways to renew existing churches.

1. New churches bring new ideas to the whole body. They have freedom to be innovative, and so they become the "Research and

Development" department for the whole body in the city. Often older congregations are too timid to try a particular approach, convinced it "could never work here." But when the new church in town succeeds with a new approach, other churches take notice and muster the courage to try it themselves.

2. New churches raise up new, creative Christian leaders for the city. Older congregations attract leaders who support tradition, have tenure, appreciate routine, and have kinship ties. New congregations, on the other hand, attract a higher percentage of venturesome people who value creativity, risk, and innovation. Older churches often box out people with strong leadership skills who aren't comfortable working in traditional settings. New churches thus attract and harness many people in the city whose gifts wouldn't otherwise be used in the body's ministry.

3. New churches challenge other churches to self-examination. Sometimes it is only in contrast with a new church that older churches can finally define their own vision, specialties, and identity. Often the growth experienced in a new congregation brings about humility and repentance for defeatist and pessimistic attitudes.

Indeed, it is also often the case that a daughter church does so well that the mother church is renewed though its influence, resources, excitement, and vision. Though some pain may be involved in seeing good friends and gifted leaders go away to form a new church, the mother church often experiences a surge of self-esteem and an eventual influx of new enthusiastic leaders and members. Some of the new leaders, ministries, additional members, and income "wash back" into the mother church in various ways and strengthen and renew it.

4. New churches can be an evangelistic feeder system for a whole community. The new church often produces many converts who end up in older churches for a variety of reasons. Sometimes the new church is exciting and outward looking but is also unstable or immature in its leadership. Some converts cannot stand the tumultuous changes that regularly happen in the new church, and so they move to an existing church. Sometimes the new church reaches a person for Christ, but the new convert quickly discovers that he or she doesn't fit the socioeconomic makeup of the new congregation and gravitates to an established congregation where the customs and culture feel more familiar. In general, the new churches of a city produce new people not only for themselves but also for the older church bodies.

To summarize: Vigorous church planting is one of the best ways to *renew* the existing churches of a city, as well as the best single way to *grow* the whole body of Christ in a city.

Addressing Diversity

The way to reach the sheer diversity of the city is through new churches.

New churches are the single best way to reach (1) new generations, (2) new residents, and (3) new people groups. *Young adults* have always been disproportionately located in newer congregations. Long-established congregations develop traditions (such as time of worship, length of service, emotional responsiveness, sermon topics, leadership styles, emotional atmosphere, and dozens of other tiny customs and mores) that reflect the sensibilities of longtime leaders who have the influence and resources to control the church life. These sensibilities often do not reach the younger generations.

In addition, *new residents* are typically better reached by new churches. In older congregations, it may require years of tenure in the city before a person is allowed into a place of influence, but in a new church, new residents tend to have equal power with longtime area residents.

Finally, *new sociocultural groups* in a community are generally better reached by new congregations. For example, if white-collar commuters move into an area where the older residents were farmers, a new church will probably be more receptive to the multiple needs of the new residents, while older churches will continue to be oriented to the original social group. And a new church that is intentionally multiethnic from the start will best reach new racial groups in a community. For example, if an all-Anglo neighborhood becomes 33 percent Hispanic, a new, deliberately biracial church will be far more likely to create "cultural space" for newcomers than will an older church in town. Brand-new immigrant groups can normally only be reached by churches ministering in their own languages. If we wait until a new group is sufficiently assimilated into American culture to come to our church, we will wait for years without reaching out to them. Remember that a new congregation for a new people group can often be planted *within* the overall structure of an existing church—perhaps through a new Sunday service at another time or a new network of house churches connected to a larger existing congregation. Though it may technically not be a new independent congregation, it serves the same function.

You see, church planting is not only for frontier regions or pagan societies that we are trying to help to *become* Christian. Churched societies will have to maintain vigorous, extensive church planting simply to *stay* Christian. One church, no matter how big, will never be able to serve the needs of such a diverse city. Only a movement of hundreds of churches, small and large, can penetrate literally every neighborhood and people group in the city.

Self-Sustaining Ministry

The way to establish ministries that become self-supporting and expand the base for all other ministries in a city is through new churches.

A city needs many ministries—youth work, Christian schools, missions to new groups, and so on. All of them are charities that need to be supported from outside of their own resources. They will require funding from Christian givers indefinitely. A new church, however, only requires outside start-up funding at its inception. Within a few years, it becomes the *source* of Christian giving to other ministries, not its *target*. Because new churches bring in large numbers of nonchurched people, church planting is by far the fastest way to grow the number of new givers in the kingdom work in a city. New church development helps all the other numerous ministries in a city thrive and grow. These ministries need a constant stream of new volunteers, workers, and givers to keep them going, and new churches are the headwaters of this stream.

How Many Churches Does the City Need? Far More Than You Think.

So how many churches does your city need? The reality is that churches are institutions. Some of them endure because they are continually revitalized, but all of them lose some flexibility; many of them stagnate for long periods between revitalizations, and a certain percentage die every year. We have seen, then, that it requires at least modest church planting in a city just to keep the body of Christ from steadily declining, and aggressive church planting is needed to grow the whole body—meaning ten to twenty relatively new churches in relation to every hundred existing churches.

There is a problem with answering the question in this way, however. The goal should not be to conserve Christianity's "market share" in a given area; it should be to serve, reach, and influence the entire city. How will this be done? Studies and anecdotal evidence indicate that if there is one church per ten thousand residents, approximately 1 percent of the population will be churchgoers. If this ratio goes to one church per one thousand residents, some 15 to 20 percent of the city's population goes to church. If the number goes to one per five hundred residents, the number may approach 40 percent or more. The relationship of the number of churches to churchgoing people is exponential, not linear.[6] We should not, then, simply aim to maintain the church's traditional place in a city or society. We long to see Christianity grow exponentially in conversions, churches, and influence in our city. While it requires many kinds of ministries to achieve this outcome, aggressive church planting is the trigger for them all.

The Stages of Church Planting

In the final section of this chapter, I offer practical advice about how to approach the church planting journey. What are the stages in the process of preparing to launch a new church? You must learn, love, link, and then launch.

Learn

First, it is necessary to learn as much as you can about the people in the community where you feel called to plant. Seek to know the people you will serve and the culture they live in as effectively as you know the gospel. Create a profile of their interior life. What are their greatest hopes, strengths, aspirations, and pleasures? What are their weaknesses, fears, idols, and prejudices? Begin with personal interviews and make use of relevant periodicals and sociological research.[7] You will also want to develop a "contextual life" profile. Which people groups live in your community? Which groups are declining, and which are growing? Use demographic studies to discern the economic groupings in your area, the arranging of social structures, and the power relations evident among people, as well as the education and psychological groupings of people.[8]

You will also want to create a profile of the common worldview of the people in your area. What aspects of truth do they have some grasp of (through common grace)? What aspects do they deny or miss? What symbols or myths function deeply? Where are tensions or pressure points in view? What is the people group's narrative and identity? Who do they see themselves to be — where are they from and where are they going? Understanding the common worldview of the people will help you develop the raw material for apologetics.

You will want to ask questions about the process of contextualization:

1. What are the "defeater beliefs" that make Christianity implausible?
2. What are the tension/pressure points in their defeater beliefs (i.e., where do they fail their own criteria)?
3. What are the "A doctrines" (biblical beliefs similar to what they already accept as true)? What are the "B doctrines" (biblical truths they reject but that are in line with "A" doctrines)?

Finally, you will want to create a profile of the various religious institutions in the area that are involved with the people you seek to reach. How are the religious bodies and churches within this people group doing? How are they organized? What ministry models seem most effective? Successful church planting begins with learning as much as you can about the people you wish to reach with the gospel message.

Love

The second stage of the church planting process is continuing to grow in your love for God through learning to maintain a healthy spirituality. It is necessary to be actively engaged in healthy spiritual disciplines, maintaining balance as you implement your strategy for evangelism and mission. Apply the gospel to yourself regularly and grow through the tearing down of your idols. Begin to share the gospel and spiritually direct people in your neighborhood and community. Model the gospel through community service and in your family life. Pray through the gospel as you bring your requests to God, and begin to experience the gospel in deep community as you develop friendships.

Link

The third stage in the process is to link as you build your emerging insights into a contextualized strategy for reaching people with the message of the gospel. The goal of this stage is to develop a strategy to serve the particular needs of the people (embodying the gospel) while also challenging the flaws, fears, and hopes of the people (communicating the gospel). Think carefully about how to go about effectively linking the gospel to the heart. How will you incorporate Christ's story into the people's story? Consider the viability of communication modes for the culture: Are they rational, intuitive, or concrete-relational? Consider how you will make your points at each stage of the communication process. Begin with the familiar and point to the culture's strengths, proceed to challenge and destabilize around the points of weakness, and then offer comfort with the gospel.

Embodying the gospel involves discerning how best to link the gospel to the community beyond direct communications. How will you work for the common good of the neighborhood? What will make the people in your neighborhood be glad you are there? Connect with individuals and leaders in the community and begin to meet the perceived needs of the community. Be sure to show the people there what *they* would look like as Christians. Strive to have your leadership structure, infra-community structure, and music incarnate the gospel in that culture.

Launch

Finally, you are ready to launch your church. Begin by developing action steps and goals that can be used as benchmarks to track your progress. In your planning, always be sensitive to God's sovereignty. What matters is not so much the final detailed plan itself as the actual process of planning. Reality will always alter your plan, but the planning process will equip you to deal with surprises and new realities in a way that is informed by and consistent with your model and vision. Your specific action steps and plans should include these basics:

- goals for funding and how to reach them
- goals for concrete ministries/programs and how to reach them
- goals for leadership development and how to reach them

When it comes time to finally launch your church plant, there are generally two approaches you can take—the top-down or the bottom-up approach. Each has strengths and weaknesses, depending on the context and the gifts of the planter. Consider the approach that is best in your situation, and brainstorm ways to employ the best of both approaches in your launch strategy.

The top-down approach typically begins with a formal worship celebration (congregational singing, teaching). This works well for daughter plants where a substantial group from a mother church is present, as well as with a church planter who has strong onstage speaking gifts. If left unbalanced, this approach carries within it the temptation to skip the *learn* and *link* stages and simply focus on reproducing the mother church.

In the bottom-up approach, the church planter lives in the community and begins with some evangelistic ministry. He sees some conversions and organizes people into either midsize parish groups (fifteen to sixty people) or small groups (four to ten people). After growing into several small groups or two to three midsize groups, the church launches a Sunday worship time. This approach works best with church planters who have good interpersonal, empowering, and evangelistic gifts. If left unbalanced, this approach can make it difficult to attract people who want to "see something happening." Often the church planter feels significant financial pressure because the congregation may not be producing much income to support the work of ministry.

●　●　●

New church planting is the best way to increase the number of believers in a city, and one of the best ways to renew the whole body of Christ. The evidence for this statement is strong—biblically, sociologically, and historically. Nothing else has the *consistent* impact of dynamic, extensive church planting. This is not, however, to demote all the other things we must be doing—church renewal, theological education, justice and mercy, cultural engagement, and many other kinds of ministry and mission. To show how all these things fit together—and how sectors of the whole body of Christ in a city can begin to exhibit movement dynamics—we turn to our final chapter.

DISCUSSION QUESTIONS

1. This chapter asserts that in a healthy church, "church planting must be natural and regular, not traumatic and episodic." To make church planting a more natural aspect of ministry, begin by honestly considering three questions:

   - *Resources*—Are you able and willing to give away resources and lose control of your money, members, and leaders?
   - *Control*—Are you ready to give up some control of the shape of the ministry itself?

- *Fear*—Are you more concerned about the kingdom or the opinions of your own tribe?

Which of these three areas presents your current ministry team with the greatest barrier to planting a new church? If you are preparing to plant a church, how can you build these considerations into the life of your church from the very beginning?

2. How would you answer the objection that "we don't need to start new churches; we should strengthen and fill our existing churches before we do that." Do you find this chapter's answers to this objection compelling? Why or why not?

3. Keller writes, "The only way to significantly increase the number of Christians in a city is by significantly increasing the number of new churches." What insights do you draw from the comparison of cities A, B, and C in this chapter? When you consider the kingdom math involved, are you convicted? Is your city more like A, B, or C?

4. Review the profiles described in the "Learn" church planting stage (interior life, contextual life, common worldview with defeater beliefs and "A" and "B" doctrines, area religious institutions). What can you learn from this process? Regardless of whether or not you are currently involved in church planting, how might creating these profiles help you apply what you are learning in new ways?

Chapter 12

THE CITY AND THE GOSPEL ECOSYSTEM

How can a city's churches become unified enough to be a movement of the gospel, even a movement of movements? They need to be part of a citywide movement of churches and ministries that exist in a supportive, mutually stimulating relationship. The assumption behind this idea is that no one kind of church—no one church model or theological tradition—can reach an entire city. Reaching a city requires a willingness to work with other churches, even churches that hold to different beliefs and practices—a view sometimes called "catholicity."

Many evangelicals have been conditioned to cringe at the "holy catholic church" phrase in the Apostles' Creed. The Greek word *katholikos* is not used to describe the church in the New Testament, but it certainly expresses a biblical teaching that, as Edmund Clowney put it, "the church as a whole is more than the local church."[1] In Acts, the various local gatherings of believers are constantly called *the* church in a city or region: "Then the church throughout Judea, Galilee and Samaria enjoyed a time of peace and was strengthened. Living in the fear of the Lord and encouraged by the Holy Spirit, it increased in numbers" (Acts 9:31; see 11:22; 15:3). In Acts 1:8, the task of healing the long-standing breach of the northern and southern kingdoms is given, and the summary statements at 6:7; 12:24; 19:20; and 28:31 demonstrate the "peace" described in 9:31. All of this communicates that it is the restored kingdom alluded to in 1:6 that marches into Rome. It is the unified people of God whom the Spirit uses to reach the far ends of the earth (1:8; cf. Isa 8:9; 44:6; 48:20; 62:11) with the gospel—even Rome! In other words, unity is not simply the work of the Spirit but the very instrument through which the Spirit works. This is why it is vital to maintain the unity of the Spirit (Eph 4:3; Phil 2:1 – 4).

Catholicity-denying *sectarianism* results in unnecessary division. If two churches differ in their beliefs and practices of baptism and the Lord's Supper, then two different churches they will have to be—but it doesn't mean they can't cooperate in other ways. To be estranged in ministry from other true believers who are members of the "wrong" denomination is to fail to welcome those whom Christ himself has welcomed. A movement needs the dynamic of cooperation that encourages people of different temperaments and perspectives to come together around their common vision and goals. In fact, part of what we see in the dynamism of a movement is people who "knock heads" and then come up with creative new initiatives because they *share a vision* and yet are very different in terms of denominations, temperaments, and personalities. If this bias for cooperation is absent in a city, the movement dynamic typically stalls or erodes.

Catholicity-denying *racism* reflects a lack of cultural flexibility and gospel humility. Embracing people of different races and cultures requires each cultural group within the church to flex as it serves the others. Cultural differences will range from the small (punctuality, for instance) to the great (music's form and words or the illustrations and applications of the preaching of the Word).

Catholicity and nonsectarianism are important for an additional reason. Unlike the Christendom era that fostered a sense of Christian distinctives among Christian groups, it is much more illuminating and helpful today for churches to define themselves in contrast to the values of the non-Christian culture. As noted earlier, if we bash and criticize other kinds of churches, we play into the common opinion that all Christians are intolerant. If we are not united, the world writes us off, and perhaps, in light of Jesus' high priestly prayer in John 17:23 ("[May] they be brought to complete unity. Then the world will know that you sent me"), they have a right to do so! While we must continue to align ourselves in denominations that share our theological distinctives, at the local level our bias should be in the direction of cooperation with other congregations.

Because of this belief, Redeemer Presbyterian Church has for a number of years given money and resources to churches of other denominations that are planting churches. We have helped to start Pentecostal churches, Baptist churches, and Anglican churches, as well as Presbyterian churches. For our efforts we have received sharp criticism and a lot of amazed stares. We believe this is one clear way to practice the kind of catholicity that turns a city of balkanized Christian churches and denominations into a movement.

Church Models and Movements

There is no single way of doing church that employs the right biblical or even the right cultural model. What the Bible tells the church to do—witness, serve the needy, preach the Word, disciple people, worship—is so rich and multifaceted that no church will ever do all of them equally well, simply because no single church has all the spiritual gifts in equal proportions. While no church should stop trying to do everything that God calls it to do, no one church will fulfill these roles perfectly. So the city as a whole needs all kinds of churches. Recognizing the reality of multiple church models humbles us—we see we can't be all things to all people—and also encourages us to reach out and cooperate with other churches.

In our discussion of the need for balanced ministry fronts in chapter 4, we looked at the five models of church proposed by Avery Dulles: "the church as institution" (which we might call *doctrine driven*); "the church as mystical communion" (*worship driven*); "the church as sacrament" (*community driven*); "the church as herald" (*evangelism driven*); and "the church as servant" (*justice driven*). In a later edition of his book, Dulles offers a model called "the church as community of disciples" in which he envisions a church that combines all the elements in proper balance.[2] Naturally, I concur that all good churches include these five elements and emphases to some degree. This is why the healthy example of each model emphasizes its main element(s) while also giving some weight to the emphases of other models. An unhealthy version of each model emphasizes one or two of these aspects and virtually ignores the others. Above all, a church's gift mix and context will dictate what it will do best in certain ministries and at certain seasons in its life.

Not only is it important to enlarge your vision to see the necessity of all models in a city movement; it is vital to identify the features of the church model where you presently serve. Many problems arise if we minister as though we are in one particular model when we are really in another. When I was in college and seminary, I participated in fairly healthy churches that were closest to the doctrine-driven model. They stressed excellent public teaching and preaching and intense Bible study. After seminary, the first church I served was in a small, blue-collar factory town in the South. At that time, almost none of its members had attended college, and most of the older members had not finished high school. It had been a church of 100 to 150 people for thirty years and was relatively unhealthy. Although I had a strong notion of the difference between unhealthy/stagnant and healthy/renewed, I had no concept of different church models. I had only seen healthy churches within the framework of one particular church model worked out only in college towns filled with professors and students. My vision for this church's renewal was great Bible exposition, seminars and classes on Christian subjects, and intense small group Bible studies.

Over the years, I came to discover that this was a congregation filled with diaconal gifts ("priestly" gifts, not "prophetic" gifts of teaching, knowledge, and evangelism). It was fundamentally a community-driven model. Grasping this was a slow and frustrating process. As I look back, my emphases did help the church because they contributed to balancing its community model with better (but never excellent) teaching, education, and evangelism. Eventually, I stopped trying to force things and began to accept more of what the church actually was. I was very slow and stubborn, but in the end I gave in before anyone lost too much patience with me. A key to this process was staying at the church for nine years.

Years after I left this church, the congregation hosted a reception for Kathy and me on the twenty-fifth anniversary of my ordination. At one point in the festivities, a number of people shared one thing they remembered hearing me say during my ministry among them. It struck me afterward that not one person quoted my words from a sermon! Every single person shared something I had said during one-on-one pastoral care. This experience vividly illustrates the difference in church models. In New York City, people let me pastor them because they appreciate my preaching. In Hopewell, Virginia, people let me preach to them because they appreciated my pastoring. In a community-driven model, the pastoring sets up the preaching; it earns you the right to preach. In the doctrine-driven model of Redeemer in New York, the preaching sets up the pastoring and even the leading. People will let you into their lives and follow you if you demonstrate your expertise in communication.

Why is understanding church models essential in enabling a city's churches to work together in unity? Without this understanding, *there will be no catholicity in your city*. Unless you accept the fact that there is not one exclusively biblical church model, you will not see the need for strong fellowship and connections to other denominations and networks, which usually embody different emphases and strengths than the ones that characterize your model. What's more, *there also will be no catholicity in your church, denomination, or movement*. Without an acceptance of multiple biblical church models, your own movement and network may plant cookie-cutter churches in neighborhoods where that model is inappropriate or may employ leaders whose gifts don't fit it. Your own movement would risk becoming too homogeneous, reaching only one kind of neighborhood or one kind of person, and fail to reflect the God-ordained diversity of humanity in your church. As much as we want to believe that most people will want to become *our* particular kind of Christian, it is not true. The city will not be won unless many different denominations become dynamic mini-movements.

Gospel City Movements and Gospel Ecosystems

We have seen the prerequisites for churches and ministers to contribute to gospel city movements—including an understanding and appreciation of various church models and a spirit of catholicity that is nevertheless doctrinally robust and sensitive. But what exactly is a gospel movement in a city?

When a church or a church network begins to grow rapidly in a city, it is only natural for the people within the ministry to feel that God is making a difference in that place. Often, however, what is really going on is "Christian reconfiguration." When churches grow, they typically do so by drawing believers out of less vital churches. This can be a good thing if the Christians in these growing churches are being better discipled and if their gifts are being effectively deployed. Nevertheless, if this is the key dynamic, then the overall body of Christ in the city is not growing; it is simply reconfiguring. Reaching an entire city, then, takes more than having some effective churches in it, or even having a burst of revival energy and new converts. *Changing a city with the gospel takes a movement.*

When a gospel city movement occurs, the whole body of Christ grows faster than the population so that the percentage of Christians in the city rises. We call this a *movement* because it consists of an energy that extends across multiple denominations and networks. It does not reside in a single church or set of leaders or in any particular command center, and its forward motion does not depend on any one organization. It is organic and self-propagating, the result of a set of forces that interact, support, sustain, and stimulate one another. We can also call it a *gospel ecosystem*. Just as a biological ecosystem is made of interdependent organisms, systems, and natural forces, a gospel ecosystem is made of interdependent organizations, individuals, ideas, and spiritual and human forces. When all the elements of an ecosystem are in place and in balance, the entire system produces health and growth as a whole and for the elements themselves.[3]

Can we produce a gospel city movement? No. A movement is the result of two broad sets of factors. Once again I'll refer to the metaphor of gardening (see 1 Cor 3:6 – 8). A garden flourishes because of the skill and diligence of the gardener *and* the condition of the soil and the weather. The first set of factors — gardening — is the way we humanly contribute to the movement. This encompasses a self-sustaining, naturally growing set of ministries and networks, which we will look at in more detail below.

But the second set of factors in a movement — the conditions — belongs completely to God. He can open individual hearts ("soil") to the Word ("seed") in any numbers he sovereignly chooses. And he can also open a culture to the gospel as a whole ("weather"). How does God do this? Sometimes he brings about a crisis of belief within the dominant culture. Two of the great Christian movements — the early church of the second and third centuries and the church in China in the twentieth and twenty-first centuries — were stimulated by crises of confidence within their societies. The belief in the gods of Rome — and belief in orthodox Marxism in China — began falling apart as plausible worldviews. There was broad disaffection toward the older "faiths" among the population at large. This combination of cultural crisis and popular disillusionment with old ways of belief can supercharge a Christian movement and lift it to greater heights than it can reach in a culture that is indifferent (rather than hostile) to Christians. There can also be catastrophes that lead people of a culture to look to spiritual resources, as when the Japanese domination of Korea after 1905 became a context for the large number of conversions to Christianity that began around that time.

In short, we cannot produce a gospel movement without the providential work of the Holy Spirit. A movement is an ecosystem that is empowered and blessed by God's Spirit.[4]

What is the ecosystem that the Holy Spirit uses to produce a gospel city movement? I picture it as three concentric rings.

First Ring — Contextualized Theological Vision

At the very core of the ecosystem is a way of communicating and embodying the gospel that is contextualized to the city's culture and is fruitful in converting and discipling its people, a shared commitment to communicating the gospel to a particular place in a particular time. Churches that catalyze gospel movements in cities do not all share the same worship style, come from the same denomination, or reach the same demographic. They do, however, generally share much of the same basic "DNA": they are gospel-centered, attentive to their culture, balanced, missional/evangelistic, growing, and self-replicating. In short, they have a relative consensus on a Center Church theological vision — a

A GOSPEL ECOSYSTEM FOR A CITY

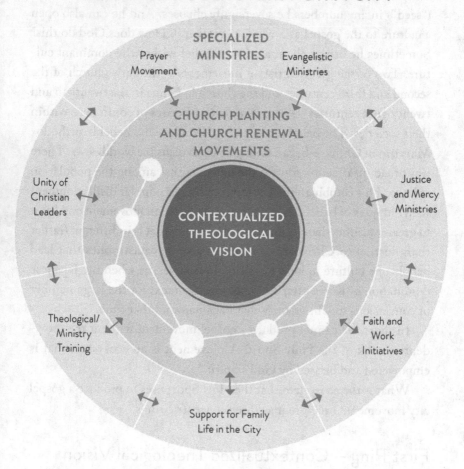

SPECIALIZED MINISTRIES

Prayer Movement

Evangelistic Ministries

CHURCH PLANTING AND CHURCH RENEWAL MOVEMENTS

Unity of Christian Leaders

Justice and Mercy Ministries

CONTEXTUALIZED THEOLOGICAL VISION

Theological/ Ministry Training

Faith and Work Initiatives

Support for Family Life in the City

set of biblically grounded, contextual strategic stances and emphases that help bring sound doctrine to bear on the people who live in this particular cultural moment.

Second Ring — Church Planting and Church Renewal Movements

The second layer is a number of church multiplication movements producing a set of new and growing churches, each using the effective means of ministry within their different denominations and traditions.

Many look at cities and see a number of existing churches, often occupying buildings that are nearly empty. It is natural to think, "The first thing we need to do is to renew the existing churches with the gospel." But as we saw in the previous chapter, the establishment of new churches in a city is a key to renewing the older churches. New churches introduce new ideas and win the unchurched and non-Christians to Christ at a generally higher rate than older churches. They provide spiritual oxygen to the communities and networks of Christians who do the heavy lifting over decades of time to reach and renew cities. They provide the primary venue for discipleship and the multiplication of believers, as well as serve as the indigenous financial engine for the ministry initiatives.

Third Ring — Specialized Ministries

Based in the churches, yet also stimulating and sustaining the churches, this third ring consists of a complex set of specialty ministries, institutions, networks, and relationships. There are at least seven types of elements in this third ring.

1. A prayer movement uniting churches across traditions in visionary intercession for the city. The history of revivals shows the vital importance of corporate, prevailing, visionary intercessory prayer for the city and the body of Christ. Praying for your city is a biblical directive (Jer 29:4 – 7). Coming together in prayer is something a wide variety of believers can do. It doesn't require a lot of negotiation and theological parsing to pray. Prayer brings people together. And this very activity is catalytic for creating friendships and relationships across denominational and organizational boundaries. Partnerships with Christians who are similar to and yet different from you stimulates growth and innovation.

2. A number of specialized evangelistic ministries, reaching particular groups (businesspeople, mothers, ethnicities, and the like). Of particular importance are effective campus and youth ministries. Many of the city church's future members and leaders are best found in the city's colleges and schools. While students who graduate from colleges in university towns must leave the area to get jobs, graduates of urban universities do not. Students won to Christ and given a vision for living in the city can remain in the churches they joined during their school years and become emerging leaders in the urban body of Christ. Winning the youth of a city wins city natives who understand the culture well.

3. An array of justice and mercy ministries, addressing every possible social problem and neighborhood. As the evangelicals provided leadership in the 1830s, we need today an urban "benevolent empire" of Christians banding together in various nonprofits and other voluntary organizations to address the needs of the city. Christians of the city must become renowned for their care for their neighbors, for this is one of the key ways that Jesus will become renowned.

4. Faith and work initiatives and fellowships in which Christians from across the city gather with others in the same profession. Networks of Christians in business, the media, the arts, government, and the academy should come together to help each other work with accountability, excellence, and Christian distinctiveness.

5. Institutions that support family life in the city, especially schools and counseling services. Significant communities that inhabit cities — such as Jewish and Catholic populations — have long known the importance of having their own schools, recreational and cultural centers, and agencies that provide services to help people stay and raise their children in the city.

6. Systems for attracting, developing, and training urban church and ministry leaders. The act of training usually entails good theological education, but a dynamic city leadership system will include additional components such as well-developed internship programs and connections to campus ministries.

7. An unusual unity of Christian city leaders. Church and movement leaders, heads of institutions, business leaders, academics, and others must know one another and provide vision and direction for the whole city. They must be more concerned about reaching the whole city and growing the whole body of Christ than about increasing their own tribe and kingdom.

When all of these ecosystem elements are strong and in place, they stimulate and increase one another and the movement becomes self-sustaining. How this happens, and what can happen as a result, is our final subject.

Tipping Points That Lead to Change

Isolated events or individual entities crystallize into a growing, self-sustaining movement when they reach a *tipping point*, a moment when the movement dynamics for change become unstoppable. A tipping point is a sociological term — "the moment of critical mass, the threshold, the boiling point."[5] For example, neighborhoods stay largely the same if new types of residents (richer, poorer, or otherwise culturally different from the rest) comprise less than 5 percent of the population. When the number of new residents reaches somewhere between 5 and 25 percent (depending on the culture), the whole neighborhood shifts and undergoes rapid and significant change.

An *ecosystem tipping point* is reached in a city when the ecosystem elements are largely in place and many churches have the vitality, leaders, and mind-set to plant other churches within five to six years of their own beginnings. If God blesses, at this point the movement has begun to be self-sustaining. Enough new believers, leaders, congregations, and ministries are being naturally produced for the movement to grow without any single center of control. The body of Christ in the city largely funds itself, produces its own leaders, and conducts its own training. A sufficient number of dynamic leaders is emerging. The number of Christians and churches doubles every seven to ten years.

The next threshold of the movement's advance is a *citywide tipping point*. This occurs when the number of gospel-shaped Christians in a city becomes so large that Christian influence on the civic and social life of the city — and on the very culture — is recognizable and acknowledged. In New York City, minority groups — whether of the ethnic, cultural, or lifestyle variety — can have a palpable effect on the way life is lived when their numbers reach at least 5 to 10 percent *and* when the members are active in public life. I have heard it said that when the number of prison inmates following Christ reaches 10 percent, the very culture and corporate life of the prison changes. There is no scientific way to precisely determine a city's tipping point—the point at which the gospel begins to have a visible impact on the city life and culture. In New York City, we pray for and work toward the time when 10 percent of the center city population is involved in a gospel-centered church. In Manhattan, this would amount to about 100,000 people.

Today, in a place like Manhattan, the vast majority of residents do not know an orthodox Christian believer (or at least one who has made their spiritual identity known). As a result, it is very easy for them to believe negative stereotypes. Evangelical Christians (as a stereotype) are as strange and off-putting to urban residents as gay people used to be to most Americans. As a result, Christianity isn't even a plausible option as a way to live for most center city dwellers. But imagine what would happen if a place like Manhattan contained so many believers that most New Yorkers would actually know a Christian they respected. The strong attitudinal barriers that block many urban residents from the message of Christianity would come down. Tens of thousands of souls could be redeemed.

How likely is it that an urban gospel movement could grow so strong that it reaches a citywide tipping point? We know this can happen through God's grace. The history books give us examples. We see how the exponential growth of Christianity changed the Roman world in the first three centuries AD and how it changed pagan northern Europe from AD 500 to 1500. We have stories of how the evangelical awakenings in the eighteenth century changed British society in the nineteenth. But we don't yet know what it would look like for one of the great culture-forming global cities of our world today to become 10 percent (or more) gospel-believing Christian in its core, with believers playing key roles in the arts, sciences, the academy, and business, while at the same time using their power, wealth, and influence for the good of those on the margins of society.

Every city in the world needs Jesus Christ. But our cities do not merely need a few more churches and ministries here and there; they need gospel city movements that lead to citywide tipping points. So urban ministers enthusiastically and passionately give their lives to these goals, even though they may not see their consummation in their own lifetimes. As we wait with confident expectation and faithful patience, we keep pursuing our vision to see our cities loved and reached for the glory of Christ.

DISCUSSION QUESTIONS

1. Keller writes, "Reaching a city requires a willingness to work with other churches, even churches that hold to different beliefs and practices—a view sometimes called 'catholicity.'" How have you partnered with other congregations that have historical traditions or theological distinctives different from your own? What led you to partner together?

2. Take some time to envision what the gospel ecosystem looks like— and might look like—in your community. Which elements are strongest and weakest? How can you move beyond ministerial alliances you have made in the past? Which key leaders, congregations, and organizations would need to be on board?

REFLECTIONS ON MOVEMENT DYNAMICS

Alan Hirsch, founding director of the Forge Mission Training Network and founder of 100Movementss

Tim Keller is one of the truly outstanding missionary statesmen in our time, a man who has not only significantly contributed to the renewal of the church but has actually managed to lead a church (in New York, no less) that has evolved under his leadership to be a burgeoning worldwide church planting movement. By his own admission, the key to his ministry is the drive to recalibrate God's people around the centrality of the gospel and then to form a movement organized to deliver it.

I heartily agree. Throughout my own ministry and writing, I have tried to penetrate deeply into the dynamic phenomenon of missional (apostolic) movements.[1] I have come to believe that the future viability of Christianity in Western contexts is bound up with rediscovering the world-transforming power of apostolic movements as a way of being church. The fate of each and every church is affected by this—*one way or another.*

Movements "R" Us

Perhaps the first thing that ought to be said is that movement is essentially a mind-set, a paradigm, rather than an alternative model. As such, movement thinking involves a distinct way of understanding what the New Testament calls *ekklēsia*—and what we call church. This way of thinking more closely reflects the original mind-set of the early church precisely because they were a movement. All New Testament ecclesiology is inherently movemental.

Yet throughout the ages, Christians have read the Bible somewhat anachronistically in this regard, reading later, more formal, institutional ecclesiologies back into the New Testament. We all read the Bible with a particular lens, and in this case, the lens that blurs our vision is the formal structure of church that followed the emergence of Christendom. But apostolic movements, as we see them unfolding in the New Testament church, tend to run contrary to the prevailing ways we think about church and mission. Most apostolic movements today have either an explicit or implicit critique of the church organizations from which they have emerged (or are expelled from). I mention this because we should never underestimate how deeply this institutional mind-set is embedded in our churches and how it unconsciously dominates most thinking about the church. If you were to ask non-Christians today about church, many would likely say the church is primarily a religion run in a building organized by a professional guild called the clergy.

New movements typically identify how the institution is deficient in some way, and they highlight new ways of being church that need to be developed to further the spread of the gospel message. These movements emerge from those parts of the church that are on the edge — those that are most committed to getting the message out in a meaningful way. Because of this, movements tend to be creative, energetic, generative, and adventurous manifestations of the kingdom of God. They are things to be celebrated and cultivated, as Keller advises, because they bring a much-needed answer to the pressing questions that face the church. In addition, they are often the catalyst for the church to extend its intended impact to reach the culture.

"It's the Things People Know That Ain't So"

In his book *Zen and the Art of Motorcycle Maintenance*, Robert Pirsig writes, "If a factory is torn down but the rationality which produced it is left standing, then that rationality will simply produce another factory.

If a revolution destroys a systematic government, but the systematic patterns of thought that produced that government are left intact, then those patterns will repeat themselves ... There's so much talk about the system. And so little understanding."[2]

In the West, where the landscape is dominated by institutional, existing churches, a paradigm shift is needed. Unless we can undergo a mind-set conversion, it is unlikely that the movements we develop will survive. Paradigms are painfully irritating things to see, but once we do get them, they are just about impossible to "unsee." To truly extend the logic and impact of the New Testament message (the gospel), we will need to see the New Testament church in its original design as the primary means of delivering the gospel. In other words, to become a movement, we need to first think like a movement.

How do we precipitate this paradigm change? Here are several suggestions:

1. Feel the challenge/call at the heart level. All of this must begin in the heart. Leaders must work to cultivate holy discontent, creating a sense of urgency by defining the problem and calling people to live into the answer. In doing this, a leader will activate the latent potential that is embedded into the church. Movement, or the possibility of movement, is latent in all of God's people because that's how God has made us! We need to awaken our ancient-future imagination and use it.

2. Change the metaphor, change the game. We must move from the metaphors that are oriented around stability and control to ones that correspond to a more fluid understanding of the church (e.g., body, living temple, pilgrims, seeds, trees, and the like). Along with movement leader Dave Ferguson, we suggest:

> The reason why metaphors are powerful descriptors is that they filter and define reality in a simple fashion (for example, "Richard is a lion," "the brain is a computer," or "organizations are machines"). Even simple words like *amoeba, beehive, fort,* and *cookie cutter* provide clues as to how people see and experience paradigms in relationship to organizations. For instance, if I said that such-and-such church was an elephant, what images come to mind? What if I had used

the term *starfish*? Each metaphor will convey different information about reproductive capacities, mobility, strength, wisdom, personality, courage, and so on. Identifying the metaphors thus offers significant clues about where to focus the efforts at shifting the paradigm.[3]

Let me use a metaphor to make this point. Deb and I live in the city of Los Angeles. We have been there for seven years now and have lived in three different neighborhoods. For much of that time, LA did not make sense to me as a city or a community. You never seem to *arrive* in LA. The city has a population of approximately seventeen million people, yet it has no real center or any clear boundaries, for that matter. There is no unifying aesthetic, and each region disowns the other one, vying to be "the real LA." Almost no one thinks that downtown *is* actually LA, except perhaps the downtowners themselves.

While I was puzzling over this last year, it dawned on me that I was using the wrong metaphor to understand this community. I was trying to see LA as a city, but to be honest, it does not make sense as a city. Instead I began to see LA as a country (with forty-five different cities). Suddenly I "saw" LA. I understood LA when I recognized it as a small country. After all, it has the same population as my native Australia. What a difference this small shift makes in how I think about my city.

Now apply this to the church. When I tell you that the church is an "institution," how does that affect your thinking and understanding about the church? And how does it differ from what you see when I tell you that the church is a "missional movement"? The metaphors we use affect the way we think and what we experience. Change the metaphor, and you change the way you see and experience church.

3. Tell a different story. Austrian philosopher Ivan Illich is credited with saying, "Neither revolution nor reformation can ultimately change a society, rather you must tell a new powerful tale, one so persuasive that it sweeps away the old myths and becomes the preferred story, one so inclusive that it gathers all the bits of our past and our present into a coherent whole, one that even shines some light into the future so that we can take the next step ... If you want to change a society, then you have to tell an alternative story."[4]

I am convinced he is right. People and societies have always understood themselves by constructing stories that explain why things are the way they are. These defining stories (or controlling narratives) tell us who we are and how we got here. They offer an account of what's been going on before we came on the scene. A story addresses the significant questions of life: *Who am I? Where am I going? Who is going with me?* Like every story, these narratives carry information about the defining incident, the conflict that exists, the challenges we must face, or the problems the organization (or individual) must overcome. The precipitating cause provides the theme around which the entire story unfolds.

Consider the stories the Nazis used when they came to power—how they made sense of the German story. Or what about the story told by Steve Jobs, the driving story behind everything he did to design and create Apple? What about the toxic narrative that jihadists tell themselves to justify the things they do? For good or ill, stories help us orient ourselves in our current situation and provide meaning for our actions—for good or for bad.

Consider the story we read in the Gospels. How does that story shape us? Listen to the tale Luke relates in Acts. We are in this story; we are chapter 29 of the book of Acts. Through a personal encounter with Jesus, we are now invited to leave our old lives behind and enter into Jesus' story (see 2 Cor 5:17).

If you change the underlying story about the church, you begin to change the church. Are we, as a community, defined by the story Jesus tells us about the "good life" (to live for the King, to love others, to serve)? Or are we held together by the prevailing cultural scripts that tell us what constitutes "the good life" (education, wealth, suburban living, consumption, and the like)? What about the national narratives that define our sense of racial and ethnic identities (African American, Anglo-Saxon, Jew, and so forth)? These stories will inevitably define us if we are not shaped by the story of God. The story of the church is the narrative of the unfolding kingdom of God and includes God's call to us to live in covenant relationship with him through Jesus our Lord. How well we know and embrace this story fundamentally influences how we see the church and understand its function. So consider: What is the story that holds *your* church together?

4. Experience liminality. Liminality is a sense of anomaly, marginality, and disorientation — even danger. Experiencing liminality is necessary if we wish to develop a sense of urgency and change the story. From liminality, we find the creative imagination to discover the new metaphors we need to sustain the church in its mission. As Keller reminds us, certain conditions of liminality are necessary to help us recover a more vigorous expression of the church.[5]

Another way to say this is that *movements are felt as much as they are understood.* They have a certain atmosphere. They exude a culture, and people sense the resulting "vibe." These vibes cannot be objectively passed along and studied. They must be caught and experienced, and we "catch the vision" by allowing ourselves to participate in the unfolding story of the church as a transformative gospel movement. For Tim Keller and the folks at Redeemer, the liminal challenge is to be a gospel-centered church existing in the space of New York City. For you and your church, it may mean simply crossing the street to engage with your neighbors.

We change paradigms by creating urgency in conditions of liminality. These lead to the generation of new and dynamic metaphors. We change the language, tell a new story, and begin to transform the guiding template that lies at the core of the organization. If we fail to do this, our efforts at transitioning to a movement will be short-lived.

None of this comes easily, of course, but you *can* do it. Social psychologists tell us there are four stages in progressing from incompetence to competence in any major learning:

1. *Unconscious incompetence.* People in this stage are simply not aware of the issue at hand; they are incompetent, and they don't even know it. At this stage, the leader's task is to raise awareness so the learning process can begin. At the very least, this involves *selling the problem* before suggesting possible solutions and ways forward. Why? Because we know that the vast majority of people have to first experience some level of frustration in their

actions or a significant disruption in their lives (individually or corporately) before they will change. At this stage, holy discontent accompanied by an imaginative search for answers will move people toward the changes necessary to get them participating fully in God's mission. If you've picked up this book, chances are you've moved beyond this stage.

2. *Conscious incompetence.* Here the learner becomes aware of the issue and begins to "see it," but at the same time they become aware of their own relative incompetence in adequately "doing it." So the learner has to decisively push beyond the pressure from their prevailing understandings (which feel very comfortable and natural) and learn to live with significant discomfort and anomaly. This stage involves significant amounts of *unlearning*—even repentance, where necessary—in order to move on. Clearly, practicing the new ideas will feel unnatural at this point. It is critical not to simply retreat to what we know. Courage, vision, and determination are important.

3. *Conscious competence.* This phase happens when people understand the basic dynamics of the new paradigm but still need to concentrate in order to operate well; it is *not yet* second nature or automatic. Like a new driver, navigating the road takes concentration and practice, but the natural reflexes will come. The slogan "Practice makes perfect" may well apply here, until the final phase eventually comes.

4. *Unconscious competence.* Here the paradigm becomes instinctual; it is hard to see reality any other way. Those at this stage are true insiders of the paradigm and are now competent to teach others about what they themselves have learned and integrated.

The lesson here is this: To become "movemental," leaders must make a choice and then stick at it. None of what you do will feel "natural" at first. Yet eventually, that will change. As the paradigm shifts and the culture changes, you'll begin to "feel" this is the way it has always been.

Do you remember learning to drive a manual transmission car? How awkward it was at first, then how natural it felt? Or think about playing tennis (or developing any skill, for that matter). I suspect that the millennial generation and those who follow may better understand this way of thinking than preceding generations because they are familiar with the more fluid, adaptive, polycentric, amorphous, networked, meme-driven world that exists in the twenty-first century. For older leaders, welcome the contributions of these younger leaders and take them seriously.

Missional Ministry for Missional Movement

Movements are made up of people — lots of people. And these people find their place in knowing what the movement stands for. They are the real "believers," willing to sacrifice much to see the movement deliver its message.

To Organize or Not to Organize — That Is the Question

All we have discussed inevitably raises questions about how to best organize, about stability, adaptability, and leadership. I believe that Keller's emphasis on developing "institutions" that will help a movement last beyond the initial phases is vital here. I prefer to use the word *structure* rather than *institution* because I believe structures are always defined by and are subservient to the mission, and not the other way around. Institutions, as Keller points out, have a way of attaining a life of their own. This is especially true in churches where inherited traditions can gain a significance they were never intended to have.

The *forms* of the church ought to remain inherently adaptive. When we institutionalize a form, it easily becomes sacramentalized, placed beyond the pale of human critique. Church organizations, in particular, are notoriously hard to change because they put a Bible verse behind everything they do. This can be theologically and missionally disastrous because people tend to grow attached to the forms, even after they have become obsolete. They hold on to things that once worked but no longer do, to things that were once productive and no longer are.[6] Again, this is a particular danger for religious or faith-based organizations when biblical authority is (con)fused with the institutional structure.

The truth is that all living systems, whether your body or the local church, need a structure and some form of organization. *Ekklēsia* (re)conceived as movement is not devoid of structure or organization. It's just that the organization will tend to be different from what we have grown accustomed to seeing.[7] The general rule in movements is that we structure just as much as is necessary to adequately empower and train every agent/agency in the movement so it can do its job. We seek to decentralize power and function as far as possible, pushing it outward to accomplish the mission. We teach direct accountability to Jesus and his cause and loosen up on control. If people are properly empowered and are living as responsible disciples of Jesus, they need more permission and less regulation if they are to do what Jesus wants to do through them.

In addition, we should seek to develop a deeper unity in Jesus and his cause—a unity that exists in dynamic tension with real diversity. The challenge here is to marry a solid core with a changing/adaptive periphery—what Dee Hock calls chaordic structure.[8] Keller gives evidence throughout his chapters on movement dynamics that he realizes movements may be scary, as well as a little messier than what we are used to. Here I very much affirm Keller's suggestion that we emphasize the movemental aspects of the organization to keep the organization moving forward. We must resist the tendency, innate to every organization, to slow down and lose momentum.

Leadership and Ministry Issues

All of this leads to questions about the structure of leadership in the church. Here is where I am admittedly more radical than Keller in my suggestions. Let me start by saying I believe the traditionally conceived forms of ministry cannot move us beyond the current impasse because they have led to the structures that currently exist—and they continue to sustain them. Albert Einstein's dictum is correct as we apply it to the church: We cannot solve the problems of the church by using the same kind of thinking we used when we created those problems in the first place. In other words, we must thoroughly reconceive how we understand and practice ministry and leadership if we wish to truly be a movement.

Tim Keller understands this. He recognizes that the prevailing understanding of the orders of ministry (those we call the pastor and teacher) is insufficient for producing the kind of movement that is needed. Keller suggests we adopt a tripartite view of ministry instead (prophet, priest, and king; see pp. 203–6). While this is a definite advance over the limitations of the pastor-teacher model, I would point out that this is a later deduction drawn from the ministry of Jesus. It feels somewhat forced when applied directly to the ministry of believers.

I suggest an alternative, one that is explicit in Scripture and provides the typology of ministry that is needed to initiate, develop, and sustain movements—the Ephesians 4:1–16 model for leadership, commonly referred to by the acronym APEST (apostle, prophet, evangelist, shepherd, teacher).

The purpose of my reflections does not allow me to present a full argument for this model, but I mention it now because I believe it is vital if we hope to activate movemental forms of church today. I would start by referring readers to the text in Ephesians, to read it and set aside the prevailing Christendom scripts we've inherited about this passage. We must deliberately try to read what is being said here through the lens of movemental ministry. If we do this, I believe we will begin to see ministry in a whole new light.[9]

The first thing to bear in mind is that Paul—undoubtedly the outstanding practitioner of apostolic ministry in the New Testament—is giving us his best thinking about the nature and function of the church. Right here, at the heart of his letter (Eph 4), is his delineation of the essential ministry of the church. It's written with a "constitutional" weight. Paul presents us with the logic of the church's ministry.

- In verses 1–6, Paul calls us to realize our fundamental unity in the one God.

- In verses 7–11, he says that APEST *has been given* (aorist indicative=constitutional) to the church.
- In verses 12–16, he goes on to say *why* APEST is given. The answer? So that we might be built up, reach unity, become mature, and so forth.

He could not be clearer in what he says here. We cannot be the kind of mature, fully functional church envisioned in verses 12–16 without APEST, *without the full ministry model* that includes apostles, prophets, evangelists, shepherds, and teachers. The traditional Christendom argument does significant violence to the logic and grammar of the text. The phrase "has been given" in verse 7 relates to *all* APEST ministries. How, then, do we end up with our current ministry model of shepherd-teachers and ignore the rest? Why should we expect the outcomes promised in verses 12–16 if we are only operating with two-fifths of the full ministry of the church?

We need to recognize the full movemental power in having all APEST ministries. Let me give you a brief functional definition of each:

- *Apostolic* is the quintessentially missional (*apostellō* = sent = *missio*) ministry. As the name implies, the movement is outward toward the fringes. It involves the healthy extension of Christianity onto new ground. The apostolic person tends to be an innovator, a designer, a builder—someone who will likely have cross-cultural or intra-cultural impact. Important for any movement, the apostolic ensures the integrity and health of the movement across geography and time.
- *Prophetic* ministry involves a strong God-orientation. Prophets are essentially the guardians of the covenant relationship between God and his people. They feel what God feels and speak on his behalf. They call the church to faithfulness, obedience, and at times practice a necessary iconoclasm.
- *Evangelistic* ministry is the ministry of good news. He or she is an infectious person, the sharer of the gospel message. Essentially they *recruit* to the organizational cause. Because

they reach outside the walls of the church, a grasp of cultural relevance is important.

- *Shepherding* ministry is the ministry of care—of healing, reconciliation, discipleship, wholeness, and community. With high EQ (emotional intelligence) and empathy, these people create the necessary social glue for movements to hold together over the long term.
- *Teaching* connects the dots that others cannot easily see. The teacher essentially transfers ideas meaningfully. They foster understanding in depth and impart wisdom for godly life. They guard the worldview and the content of the faith. They are the philosophers who create the intellectual trust of the church.

With these descriptions in mind, let's look at the inherent balance in the system given in Ephesians. APEST has two sides that are necessary for movement. There is the more generative, non–status quo, ministry of the APEs. And on the other side we find the more operative ministries of the STs. The truth is that both of these dimensions are needed. The APE is by nature generative of new forms, more inherently movement oriented. The ST develops sustainability for the movement, akin to a human resources department. Why shouldn't we have them all? And even more important, how can we expect to be a transformative movement if we only have a limited understanding of our mission and ministry? The lack of a full APEST ministry model has led to a serious reduction in our understanding of leadership and ministry and has damaged our ability to mature.

Let me add one final thought. This is what I believe seals the deal—what Americans call "the kicker." Keller rightly asserts that "Jesus Christ has all the powers and functions of ministry in himself" (p. 203). This is precisely the image that Paul wants to convey in Ephesians 4 when he talks about the ascension and Christ's gifting of his church. Let me show you how the principle of Christ's innate ministry is reflected through the lens of the APEST model (instead of the tripartite model). Ponder these questions:

- Is Jesus an apostle? The answer is, yes, of course—he *is* "the sent one" (variation of the root word *apostellō*). He founds the movement and keeps it together, and he is actually called "our apostle" in Hebrews 3:1. He is the archetypal apostle. Check!
- Is Jesus a prophet? Yes, undoubtedly. A major element of his ministry is to call people to repent and render allegiance and faithfulness to God. Check!
- Is Jesus an evangelist? Yes, in fact he *is* the good news, and he came to seek and to save the lost, to give eternal life, and so forth. Check!
- Is he a shepherd? Yes, definitely—he is the Good Shepherd. He creates and sustains the new covenant community. Check!
- Is he a teacher? No brainer—of course. Rabbi? Check!

This is not stretching it at all. We can legitimately say that Jesus is the perfect embodiment of APEST. In light of Ephesians 4, we can say it is the ministry of Christ (as archetypal and embodied APEST) that is expressed through the body of Christ, and this ministry should have a fivefold form among his people. This is *not* merely charismatic, Spirit-empowerment in view here; it is the very ministry of Christ in and through his people. I believe this understanding changes the game. Our understanding of the functions of the body of Christ are at stake here—referred to by some as the marks or characteristics of a church.

Here is the one-billion-dollar question: How can we expect to extend the impact of Jesus' ministry if we only do it in two forms and not in the full five envisioned in Scripture? If Jesus is *the* original and originating APEST, how can the body of Christ truly embody his ministry in just shepherding and teaching forms? The clear answer from Ephesians 4:1–16 is that it cannot, and herein lies the reason for many of the dysfunctions in today's church. At the same time, we find here one of the major keys to unlocking the dormant movemental potential of the church.

Today's Apostolic Movements

Let me conclude with a few general statements about apostolic movements and their importance for us today.

1. Jesus has given the church everything it needs to get the job done. I believe we are coded for world transformation. This is what Jesus intended for us (see Matt 16), and the gospel implies it—that our ultimate goal is cosmic transformation (see Eph 1; Col 1). We can't take this out even if we wanted to because Jesus put it in there. In this sense, the church is its own answer. We need to learn to attend to how God designed us to be. This means the paradigm shift is as much a theological discernment process as a practical and missiological one.

2. Every believer carries within them the potential for world transformation—a truth made clear as we observe how God uses ordinary people in movements (e.g., in the New Testament, in the early church, among the Celts, in Methodism, in the Chinese underground movements, and the like). How else can we explain the fact that uneducated Chinese peasants are changing the world? Consider this: In every seed is the potential for a tree, and in every tree the potential for a forest, but all of this is contained in the initial seed. In every spark there is a potential for a flame, and in every flame is the potential for conflagration, but all of this is potentially contained in the originating spark.

So it is with each believer among God's people. All of the potential for movement is already present in God's people; our job is to bring it out. One underground church in China puts it this way: "Every believer is a church planter; every church is a church-planting church." Folks, this ought to change the way we see God's people—men and women, poor and rich, young and old, white and black.

3. Movements only succeed to the degree that they legitimize and activate the ministry of all of God's people. Each person can be an "ordinary hero." I would go as far as to say that the agency of all believers is the secret weapon that God brings out in times of movemental breakthrough. Everyone gets to play! In one of my books, I suggest that movements need the organized, distinctly ecclesial aspects associated with viral church planting, but they also need to activate the agency of all believers in every sphere and domain of society.[10] When these two aspects come together at the right time and under the right spiritual conditions, we have the possibility for real movements to develop. It can be illustrated in this way:

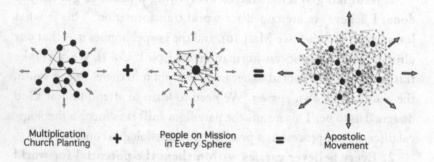

Multiplication
Church Planting
+
People on Mission
in Every Sphere
=
Apostolic
Movement

The diminishment of the agency of all believers and the corresponding professionalization and clericalization of ministry have led to a loss of movement dynamic and an increased control in the church as an institution. In China, the clergy had to be forcibly removed for the church to recover its dormant potentials and transition into hyperbolic growth and impact. Clericalism seems to be a huge blocker to movemental dynamics, as was true for early Methodism and Pentecostalism as well. When will we learn from the lessons of the past?

4. Movements are essentially DNA-based organizations. Like all living systems, organizations replicate and maintain their integrity based on the internal coding present in every part of the organization. Each living cell has the coding for the whole body.

Organizations are only movements to the degree that they do this. Just follow the logic of DNA. If you get the core practices and ideas right and embed them deeply into every possible part of the system, you can step back, pray like mad, and let go. As you do this, remember to practice high accountability and low control.

To use another metaphor, movements are more like starfish than they are spiders. You can kill a spider by taking its head off. Spiders have a centralized control center. On the other hand, when a starfish is cut up, it will produce more starfish. Each part carries the potential for the whole.

5. While all five APEST ministries have a role that is vital and nonnegotiable, the apostolic in particular is the key to an apostolic movement—the kind we see on the pages of the New Testament. This is not an emphasis of importance or priority; it is one of purpose and design. By nature and calling, the apostolic person (the sent one) follows the innate impulses of his or her sentness and pushes the system to the edges in order to establish Christianity onto new ground. They engage in church planting, not just personal evangelism. They incessantly network and seek to maintain core unity within the context of increasing geographic and cultural diversity. The result is a burgeoning movement, the likes of which Tim Keller brilliantly espouses in these chapters and lives out through the Redeemer City to City movement worldwide.

The pattern is clear: Remove apostolic influences, and you won't get apostolic movement. They are inextricably related. The wonderful irony is that though Keller admits to being something of a cessationist regarding his theology of Ephesians 4,[11] he remains one of the best examples of today's apostolic leaders. He demonstrates exactly why we need this kind of ministry in our time.

A ship in harbor is safe, but that is not what ships are built for.

John A. Shedd, "Salt from My Attic"

RESPONSE TO ALAN HIRSCH

Timothy Keller

Alan Hirsch has been a thought leader in the missional church movement for decades, and I'm delighted to have his insights on Movement Dynamics enriching our discussion. Movements are held together more by common vision than by rules and procedures. Their members are sacrificially committed to their causes rather than being in them for the benefits. Movements value risk, innovation, and change rather than safety, tradition, and stability. Movements tend to be "bottom up" and participatory rather than top-down, command-and-control organizations. Hirsch's essay warmly affirms the importance and character of movements, yet does so with significant supplemental insights. I'd like to recap and comment on some that I think enhance the *Center Church* content. He does, however, push back against the material in one area that I will respond to at the end of this essay.

Movements from the Edge

How can a movement mind-set in the Christian church be cultivated? I was intrigued by Hirsch's statement that "movements emerge from those parts of the church that are on the edge." By that he means, I think, the parts of the church that are in a place of insecurity.

Churches that have experienced sharp declines and are facing extinction are "on the edge" and may be open to radical innovation. They also may simply hold on to the past and die, but I have often seen churches at their point of insecurity finally embrace movement dynamics, consistent with Hirsch's insight. I would also argue that church plants are almost all, by definition, "on the edge," because brand-new churches are not secure. They have to serve and reach people to survive. They have no laurels to rest on, no building to make them feel like they have arrived. New churches almost always exhibit more in the way of movement dynamics because of their insecurity.

I can go further. There are basically two kinds of church plants—those with core groups going out from existing congregations with financial and leadership support, and "pioneer" church plants, which essentially start from scratch, without a core group of Christians. We usually see more innovation and vigorous movement dynamics in pioneer churches, because they are more insecure.

This means we should also expect movement dynamics and innovation from churches among the less well-established and "respectable" circles and neighborhoods—churches on the edges of society. This can certainly be seen in how the churches in affluent and powerful areas of North America and Europe are much more institutionalized and stagnant, while churches among the grassroots in Africa, Latin America, and Asia are dynamic. There the classic traits of fast-growing movements are in evidence.

Movements and "Liminality"

A related insight is that movement dynamics are enhanced by an experience of "liminality." Here's Hirsch's important passage on this:

> Liminality is a sense of anomaly, marginality, and disorientation—even danger. Experiencing liminality is necessary if we wish to develop a sense of urgency and change the story. From liminality, we find the creative imagination to discover the new metaphors we need to sustain the church in its mission. Certain conditions of liminality are necessary to help us recover a more vigorous expression of the church (p. 253).

Hirsch immediately applies this idea to Redeemer. Most observers would look at our church, with more than five thousand in attendance, a growing budget and staff, and even a building, and assume we feel very much established and secure. That is not true—Hirsch is right. "For … Redeemer the liminal challenge is to be a gospel-centered church in the space of New York City." Many evangelical Christian doctrines and beliefs are anathema to the NYC powers that be, and their power is very great. Even though we love our city and have an abundance of longtime New Yorkers and have adapted in many ways to the culture, we are still radically different and (we know) "offensive" to our neighbors in a number of regards. We always have a sense of "anomaly and vulnerability" to some degree. And Hirsch is right that this is definitely a factor that vitalizes and empowers movement dynamics in our case.

I can also apply this principle to what has happened to Christianity in North America in the hundred years since the split between fundamentalism and modernism. The mainline churches that were captured by modernism kept the buildings, universities, endowment funds, and all the trappings of the establishment. They remained at the center—literally so. Their churches were on Main Street or on the center square of the town. Evangelicals and Pentecostals were pushed out to the edge—literally so. Their churches were on the outskirts of town or were meeting in rented facilities. Their members were not taken from the leading classes of the town or of the great urban centers. They had to start their own schools and organizations from scratch. They also planted new churches at a rate vastly outstripping the rate of mainline church planting.

Yet all the innovation and energy lay with the evangelicals, who developed remarkable ministries (InterVarsity, Campus Crusade [Cru], and Navigators, just to name three) to convert university students and then new seminaries (Fuller, Gordon-Conwell, Trinity) that moved the numerous converts into church leadership. (I was part of that dynamic in the 1970s.) By the end of the twentieth century, the mainline churches were in sharp decline, with evangelical churches (and seminaries) outpacing the far better funded mainline institutions.

Many observers have seen marks of institutionalization and decline in U.S. evangelicalism for a couple of decades. But I'll make a brief, bold statement, using Hirsch's idea. The recent revolutionary changes in our North American culture's sexual and moral standards may constitute a new forcing of orthodox Christians away from the center to the edges. As was the case one hundred years ago, there will be attrition. Many people will not want to follow their churches "outside the gates" of respectability and cultural acceptability. But the new experience of liminality will create a renewal of our movement dynamics and an explosion of innovation. Also remember that in the non-Western world, Christianity is young but extraordinarily vital, and our brothers and sisters there will be a source of new ideas and resources for the Western church, once our liminal status makes us more open to them. Lots of help may be on the way.

Movements and Leadership

When it comes to the structure of leadership in the church, Hirsch says, "Here I am admittedly more radical than Keller in my suggestions." At this point, he gives perhaps his signature message about the structure of church ministry along the lines of Ephesians 4:11–16. He calls this outline of biblical church leadership APEST—apostles, prophets, evangelists, shepherds, and teachers. Here in a nutshell, and elsewhere at length, he argues that every one of these functions is necessary for a vital Christian church, and that every one of these leadership roles is constitutive, not optional—given to us by God.

With a grin that I can see in my mind's eye, Hirsch ends by writing, "The wonderful irony is that though Keller admits to being something of a cessationist regarding his theology of Ephesians 4, he remains one of the best examples of today's apostolic leaders" (p. 263). That is extremely kind. And he is referring to the fact that I do follow the more traditional reading of Ephesians 4. I don't see these as five abiding, distinct roles given to the church.

But before you read me as rejecting Hirsch's insights, consider this. His concern is that the current model—that all ministry roles and leadership power reside in the ordained minister/pastor—is neither biblical nor able to promote renewal and movement dynamics. I think he's right. And here's one reason my thinking has moved in that direction. Over the past couple of years, I have been reading heavily in John Calvin's works. To my surprise, I found that in his varied writings, he speaks about a varied, multi-role Christian ministry that has similarities to Alan Hirsch's outline. In fact, though he doesn't list them all in any one place, he acknowledges four kinds of ministers. Deacons were caregivers; elders were managers and overseers; teachers or "doctors" were experts in the Bible and instruction (and were not necessarily preachers); and preachers spoke the Word and administered the sacraments.

In most of Calvin's lists, these are the only four kinds of "ministers," yet at one place in his *Institutes* (4.4.2; cf. 4.4.4), he wrote that it made sense for an elder, pastor, or teacher in a particular region to also be designated a bishop. Calvin is quick to deny that bishops should have the power to ordain and excommunicate on their own, as the office had evolved in the Catholic Church. Rather, bishops must remain "subject to the assembly of [their] brethren."[16] Nevertheless, it was almost as if Calvin, while believing that the apostolic office had ceased, nevertheless saw that some had unusual gifts of leadership that should be recognized.

Now this is not identical to Hirsch's APEST structure, but, honestly, it is not too far off. What I am saying is that it is possible to not believe in the continuation of biblical apostles and prophets and still recognize the need for a variegated ministry leadership structure much like the one Hirsch has seen to be so fruitful. This bears more discussion from those of us working in more traditional church denominations.

I thank Alan Hirsch for his encouraging, enriching essay and for his great love for the church of Jesus Christ.

ABBREVIATIONS

Bible Books

Gen.	Genesis	Joel	Joel
Exod.	Exodus	Amos	Amos
Lev	Leviticus	Obad.	Obadiah
Num	Numbers	Jonah	Jonah
Deut	Deuteronomy	Mic.	Micah
Josh.	Joshua	Nah.	Nahum
Judg	Judges	Hab	Habakkuk
Ruth	Ruth	Zeph.	Zephaniah
1–2 Sam.	1–2 Samuel	Hag.	Haggai
1–2 Kgs	1–2 Kings	Zech	Zechariah
1–2 Chr	1–2 Chronicles	Mal.	Malachi
Ezra	Ezra	Matt	Matthew
Neh.	Nehemiah	Mark.	Mark
Esth	Esther	Luke	Luke
Job	Job	John	John
Ps/Pss	Psalm/Psalms	Acts	Acts
Prov	Proverbs	Rom	Romans
Eccl	Ecclesiastes	1–2 Cor	1–2 Corinthians
Song	Song of Songs	Gal	Galatians
Isa.	Isaiah	Eph.	Ephesians
Jer	Jeremiah	Phil.	Philippians
Lam	Lamentations	Col	Colossians
Ezek	Ezekiel	1–2 Thess	1–2 Thessalonians
Dan	Daniel	1–2 Tim.	1–2 Timothy
Hos.	Hosea	Titus	Titus

Phlm........Philemon
Heb.........Hebrews
Jas..........James
1–2 Pet ....1–2 Peter

1–2–3 John 1–2–3 John
Jude.........Jude
Rev.........Revelation

General

cf. .... *confer*, compare
ch(s)........chapter(s)
ed(s)........editor(s), edited by, edition
e.g. .... *exempli gratia*, for example
esp.........especially
et al. .... *et alii*, and others
ff. ....and the following ones
ibid. .... *ibidem*, in the same place

idem ....that which was mentioned before, same, as in same author
i.e..........*id est*, that is
n. ....note
p(p). ....page(s)
rev. ....revised
trans........translator, translated by
v(v).........verse(s)

NOTES

Series Introduction

1. Richard Lints, *The Fabric of Theology: A Prolegomenon to Evangelical Theology* (Grand Rapids: Eerdmans, 1993), 9.

2. Ibid., 82.

3. Ibid., 315.

4. Ibid., 316–17.

5. These three areas correspond roughly to Richard Lints's four theological vision factors in this way: (1) *Gospel* flows from how you read the Bible; (2) *City* flows from your reflections on culture; and (3) *Movement* flows from your understanding of tradition. Meanwhile, the fourth factor—your view of human rationality—influences your understanding of all three. It has an impact on how you evangelize non-Christians, how much common grace you see in a culture, and how institutional (or anti-institutional) you are in your thinking about ministry structure.

6. It can be argued that the Gospel axis is not like the other two. In the other two axes, the desired position is a midpoint, a balance between extremes. However, Sinclair Ferguson (in his lectures on the Marrow Controversy) and others have argued that the gospel is not at all a balance between two opposites but an entirely different thing. In fact, it can also be argued that legalism and antinomianism are not opposites but essentially the same thing— self-salvation—opposed to the gospel. So please note that putting the gospel between these two extremes is simply a visual shorthand.

Chapter 1: The Search for the Missional Church

1. Darrell L. Guder, ed., *Missional Church: A Vision for the Sending of the Church in North America* (Grand Rapids: Eerdmans, 1998).

2. Lesslie Newbigin, *The Open Secret: An Introduction to the Theology of Mission*, rev. ed. (Grand Rapids: Eerdmans, 1995), 18.

3. David Bosch, *Transforming Mission: Paradigm Shifts in Theology of Mission* (Maryknoll, NY: Orbis, 1991), 389–90 (the quotes in this paragraph are from these pages).

4. Newbigin, *Open Secret*, 18.

5. Harvey Cox, *The Secular City* (New York: Macmillan, 1965), 255.

6. Newbigin, *Open Secret*, 18.

7. Ibid., 121 – 23.

8. In *The Open Secret*, Newbigin writes of "the paganism that was showing its power in the heart of old Christendom" (p. 8).

9. *The Open Secret* (Grand Rapids: Eerdmans, 1978); *Foolishness to the Greeks* (Grand Rapids: Eerdmans, 1986); *The Gospel in a Pluralist Society* (Grand Rapids: Eerdmans, 1991).

10. Lesslie Newbigin, "Ecumenical Amnesia," in *International Bulletin of Missionary Research* 18, no. 1 (January 1994): 4 – 5, www.newbigin.net/assets/pdf/93reit.pdf (accessed February 15, 2012).

11. Ibid.

12. Newbigin's phrase "judgment and redemption for all who will accept it" could be interpreted to mean that all people who accept it receive both conviction of sin (judgment) and the acceptance of grace.

13. David Bosch, *Believing in the Future: Toward a Missiology of Western Culture* (Valley Forge, PA: Trinity Press International, 1995), 33.

14. Ibid., 33 – 35.

15. Ibid., 47 – 53.

16. Ibid., 56 – 57.

17. Ibid., 55 – 62. Bosch lists many of these ingredients briefly at the end of the book. He includes addressing ecological issues and listening carefully and respectfully to the theological insights and personal experiences of the churches of the Third World.

18. David Bosch criticized not only the practices of both the liberal and the conservative churches but also their doctrine, particularly their view of Scripture, as being shaped by modernity. For example, in *Transforming Mission* (p. 342), he wrote, "The subject-object dichotomy [of the Enlightenment] meant that, in admittedly very opposite ways, the Bible and, in fact, the Christian faith as such, became objectified. Liberals sovereignly placed themselves above the biblical text, extracting ethical codes from it, while fundamentalists tended to turn the Bible into a fetish and apply it mechanically to every context, particularly as regards the 'Great Commission.'"

19. The book is a compendium of essays from different authors and so does not speak always with one voice. While Newbigin himself was able to mix Transformationist measures with Counterculturalist measures in his agenda for cultural engagement, many of the contributors to *Missional Church* fell more into one camp or the other. For a good discussion of the book and its message and the differences among the authors, see Craig Van Gelder and Dwight J. Zscheile, *The Missional Church in Perspective: Mapping Trends and Shaping the Conversation* (Grand Rapids: Baker, 2011).

20. Van Gelder and Zscheile call this group "'Discovering' Missional," who "tend to utilize missional language to promote a more traditional understanding of mission" (p. 71), i.e., those who consider "mission" to be primarily an

expanding of the church rather than joining with God to renew the creation. (The label is a bit patronizing, since the authors depict them as still discovering the concept but not really understanding it.) They cite Frank Page, *The Nehemiah Factor* (Birmingham, AL: New Hope, 2008), and Rick Rusaw and Eric Swanson, *The Externally Focused Church* (Loveland, CO: Group, 2004) as examples of this group (see lists of authors on pp. 72 – 74).

21. The seminal text for this approach is Michael Frost and Alan Hirsch, *The Shaping of Things to Come: Innovation and Mission for the 21st-Century Church* (Grand Rapids: Baker, 2004). See also the books and website of David Fitch of Reclaiming the Mission (www.reclaimingthemission.com). I also recommend the books of Tim Chester and Steve Timmis; see esp. *Everyday Church: Mission by Being Good Neighbours* (Nottingham, UK: Inter-Varsity, 2011).

22. Van Gelder and Zscheile list Jim Belcher of Deep Church, Dan Kimball, and me, among others (p. 87). I would include Ed Stetzer here as well.

23. Alan J. Roxburgh and M. Scott Boren, *Introducing the Missional Church: What It Is, Why It Matters, and How to Become One* (Grand Rapids: Baker, 2009), 93. Van Gelder and Zscheile (*Missional Church in Perspective*) state that a missional theology calls the church to "reciprocity, mutuality, and vulnerability" (p. 133); because the Trinity is seen as a nonhierarchical, mutual community of persons, the missional church must have a reciprocal, open, and dynamic relationship to the world (p. 110).

24. For one of many places where this horizontal reworking of sin and redemption is carried out, see N. T. Wright, *Evil and the Justice of God* (Downers Grove, IL: InterVarsity, 2006). Wright states, "Evil is the force of anti-creation, anti-life, the force which opposes and seeks to deface and destroy God's good world of space, time, and matter, and above all God's image-bearing human creatures ... [But] it is true, as the Gospel writers have been trying to tell us, that evil at all levels and of all sorts had done its worst and that Jesus ... supremely on the cross had dealt with it, taken its full force, exhausted it" (p. 89).

25. See Wright, *Evil and the Justice of God*. "The New Testament writers report ... the remarkable sign of evil doing its worst and being exhausted. When Jesus suffered, he did not curse, and when he was reviled, he did not revile in return" (pp. 88 – 89). "The death of Jesus is seen ... as the means whereby evil is ... defeated and its power is exhausted" (p. 136).

26. Van Gelder (*Missional Church in Perspective*), who puts himself in this category, criticizes thinkers who don't embrace the implications in the *missio Dei* of what he calls "the social Trinity." He argues that putting the emphasis on the fact that God is a community of mutual love who is redeeming all of creation will keep us from seeing "individual Christians as the focus of God's redemptive work" and will strengthen "the communal nature of the church as well as the corporate nature of discipleship"(p. 84).

27. Despite the fact that Brian McLaren and others in the Emergent network adopted the term, Alan Roxburgh and Scott Boren (*Introducing the Missional*

Church, 47 – 62) show that the emerging church and the missional church are not the same thing. Indeed, as I will argue, it is possible to properly use the term *missional* without buying into the mainline/ecumenical definition of the *missio Dei*.

Much of the work of the mainline-oriented missional church thinkers (represented by the "reciprocal and communal" group) seems to have Karl Barth's shadow behind much of it. Barth reworks the doctrine of election so that (in his view) all people are elect in Christ, even those who do not believe, so that all human beings are essentially *simul justus et peccator*. There is much controversy over how Barth's view works itself out in ministry practice, but many who accept it deem it inappropriate to view non-Christians as being under the wrath of God and in need of personal reconciliation. It is not hard to see how this would move the focus of a church's ministry from calling individuals to conversion to building community and healing society.

28. Conservative evangelicals in particular should bear in mind that the theology of Lesslie Newbigin and David Bosch, while not evangelical, may still be appreciated as a reaction and critique of the thoroughly secular theology of many of the churches that make up the World Council of Churches.

29. Roxburgh and Boren, *Introducing the Missional Church*, 59.

30. See John R. W. Stott, "The Living God Is a Missionary God," in *You Can Tell the World*, ed. James E. Berney (Downers Grove, IL: InterVarsity, 1979), 3 – 9 (first presented at the 1976 Urbana Student Missions Convention).

31. See more on this subject in part 2 ("Integrative Ministry"), as well as a full treatment in chapter 3 ("Equipping People for Missional Living").

32. Those who lean toward a conservative theology may say (as I would) that while the mission of the church qua church (the institutional church) is to evangelize and make disciples, individual Christians must be well-known for their sacrificial service to the poor and common good if a society is going to give the gospel a hearing.

Chapter 2: Centering the Missional Church

1. Michael Wolff, "The Party Line," *New York* (February 26, 2001), http://nymag.com/nymetro/news/media/columns/medialife/4407/index1.html (accessed February 17, 2012).

2. See chapter 5 for an extended discussion of evangelistic worship.

3. See part 3 in *Center Church* ("Gospel Contextualization") for an extended discussion of what a contextualized gospel message looks like.

4. A number of good theological and practical objections can be raised to habitually using the word *incarnational* to describe ministry. However, for our purposes here, we will accept the practice and the main definition given because the term is widely used in missional church discussions.

5. Alan Roxburgh and M. Scott Boren (*Introducing the Missional Church: What It Is, Why It Matters, and How to Become One* [Grand Rapids: Baker, 2009],

69) define an "attractional" church this way: "One of the ways the basic story of the gospel has been compromised is that it has become all about us and how God is supposed to meet our needs, and we have created attractional churches that are about how God does just that."

6. David Fitch, "What Is Missional? Can a Mega-Church Be Missional?" www.reclaimingthemission.com/blog/153 (accessed February 17, 2012).

7. Ibid.

8. Michael Frost and Alan Hirsch, *The Shaping of Things to Come: Innovation and Mission for the 21st-Century Church* (Grand Rapids: Baker, 2004), 211.

9. See ibid., 210 – 24.

10. Roxburgh and Boren, *Introducing the Missional Church*, 21.

11. For example, Darrell Guder (*Missional Church* [Grand Rapids: Eerdmans, 1998]) reasons that if God's purpose in mission is to "restore and heal creation" (p. 4), then the idea of salvation means bringing the reign of God to bear on communities and organizations. He writes, "For a bank, it might mean granting loans in formerly redlined neighborhoods. For a public school, it might mean instituting peer mediation training among students" (p. 136).

12. Dieter Zander, "Abducted by an Alien Gospel," www.baskettcase.com/blog/2006/11/01/abducted-by-an-alien-gospel/ (accessed February 17, 2012).

13. D. A. Carson, "Three Books on the Bible: A Critical Review" (April 2006), www.reformation21.org/shelf-life/three-books-on-the-bible-a-critical-review.php (accessed February 17, 2012).

14. See Timothy Keller, *Generous Justice: How God's Grace Makes Us Just* (New York: Dutton, 2010), esp. 92 – 108.

15. While Luther expounds on this concept in many places, the two seminal works are "To the Christian Nobility of the German Nation" and "The Babylonian Captivity of the Church." These two are joined to "The Freedom of a Christian" in Martin Luther, *Three Treatises* (Minneapolis: Fortress, 1970). For an early modern evangelical effort to recapture the importance of lay ministry, see John R. W. Stott, *One People* (Downers Grove, IL: InterVarsity, 1968).

16. For a case that every lay Christian is to minister the Word — that is, evangelize and disciple from the Bible — see Colin Marshall and Tony Payne, *The Trellis and the Vine: The Ministry Mind-Shift That Changes Everything* (Kingsford, Australia: Matthias Media, 2009), 41 – 60. For resources containing ideas on how to release laypeople to deepen relationships in their neighborhood to do service and witness, see Mike Breen and Alex Absalom, *Launching Missional Communities: A Field Guide*, and Tim Chester and Steve Timmis, *Everyday Church: Mission by Being Good Neighbours* (Nottingham, UK: Inter-Varsity, 2011). For a brief overview of how to help people integrate their faith and work, see part 2 ("Integrative Ministry") in this volume, and Timothy Keller, *Every Good Endeavor: Connecting Your Work to God's Work* (New York: Dutton, 2012).

17. Dietrich Bonhoeffer (*Life Together* [New York: Harper & Row, 1954], 23) writes, "All we can say, therefore, is: the community of Christians springs solely

from the biblical and Reformation message of the justification of man through grace alone; this alone is the basis of the longing of Christians for one another."

18. See section on "Missional Evangelism through Mini-Decisions" in the next chapter.

19. See section on "Believers with Relational Integrity" in the next chapter.

20. See part 3 ("Movement Dynamics").

Chapter 3: Equipping People for Missional Living

1. Ryan Bolger, "Marks of a Missional Church," http://thebolgblog.typepad.com/thebolgblog/2006/01/marks_of_a_miss.html (accessed February 17, 2012).

2. John R. W. Stott, *Motives and Methods in Evangelism* (Leicester, UK: Inter-Varsity, 1962), 14.

3. Michael Green, *Evangelism in the Early Church*, rev. ed. (Grand Rapids: Eerdmans, 2003), 243, quoting Adolf von Harnack.

4. Ibid.

5. Ibid., 244.

6. Ibid., 315.

7. Ibid., 318–38.

8. Ibid., 339.

9. Many of these examples are adapted from the ones found in Colin Marshall and Tony Payne, *The Trellis and the Vine: The Ministry Mind-Shift That Changes Everything* (Kingsford, Australia: Matthias Media, 2009), 54–56. I've added some new examples and contextualized the ones found in the book.

10. Francis Schaeffer, *2 Contents, 2 Realities* (Downers Grove, IL: InterVarsity, 1975), 31–32.

11. For several good ideas on engagement, see Tim Chester and Steve Timmis, *Everyday Church: Mission by Being Good Neighbours* (Nottingham, UK: Inter-Varsity, 2011), ch. 4 ("Everyday Mission").

12. See Christian Smith, *Souls in Transition: The Religious and Spiritual Lives of Emerging Adults* (New York: Oxford University Press, 2009), 209.

13. Alan Kreider, "'They Alone Know the Right Way to Live': The Early Church and Evangelism," in *Ancient Faith for the Church's Future*, ed. Mark Husbands and Jeffrey P. Greenman (Downers Grove, IL: InterVarsity, 2008), 169–70.

14. Two other must-read books about the early Christians and their witness through lay ministry are Green, *Evangelism in the Early Church*, and Rodney Stark, *The Rise of Christianity* (New York: HarperCollins, 1990).

15. For excellent, easily remembered outlines to give to laypeople for informal pastoral care and evangelism, see Chester and Timmis, *Everyday Church*, ch. 3 ("Everyday Pastoral Care") and ch. 5 ("Everyday Evangelism").

16. See David Stroud, *Planting Churches, Changing Communities* (Milton Keynes, UK: Authentic Media, 2009), 172.

17. For practical suggestions on how to do this, see Marshall and Payne, *The Trellis and the Vine*, ch. 9 ("Multiplying Gospel Growth through Training Coworkers").

18. For a comprehensive treatment and list of evangelistic venues, see Michael Green, *Evangelism through the Local Church* (Nashville: Nelson, 1992). Though dated, it is the most complete guide to the subject of its title.

19. See Timothy Keller, *The Reason for God Study Guide and DVD: Conversations on Faith and Life* (Grand Rapids: Zondervan, 2010).

20. See Timothy Keller, *Jesus the King* (New York: Riverhead, 2013).

Reflections on Missional Community

1. In the sidebar (p. 254, *Center Church*), Keller reproduces Newbigin's short list of ingredients for a missionary encounter with Western culture: (1) a new apologetic (that takes on the so-called neutrality of secular reason), (2) the teaching of the kingdom of God (that God wants not only to save souls but heal the whole creation), (3) earning the right to be heard through willingness to serve others sacrificially, (4) equipping the laity to bring the implications of their faith into their public calling and so transform culture, (5) a countercultural church community, (6) a unified church that shows the world an overcoming of denominational divisions, (7) a global church in which the older Western churches listen to the non-Western churches, (8) courage.

2. See further Tim Chester, *Good News to the Poor: Sharing the Gospel Through Social Involvement* (2004; repr., Wheaton, IL: Crossway, 2013).

3. See Engstrom's posts in the "Practices of Healthy Missional Communities" section at www.toddengstrom.com/resources.

4. See Engstrom's posts in the "The Four Stages of Missional Community Formation" section at toddengstrom.com/resources.

Chapter 4: The Balance of Ministry Fronts

1. Edmund P. Clowney, "Interpreting the Biblical Models of the Church: A Hermeneutical Deepening of Ecclesiology," in *Biblical Interpretation and the Church*, ed. D. A. Carson (Nashville: Nelson, 1985), 64–109.

2. Avery Dulles, *Models of the Church* (Garden City, NY: Image, 1978). I speak more extensively about church models and Dulles's book in the section on "Church Models and Movements" in chapter 12.

3. Edmund P. Clowney, *Living in Christ's Church* (Philadelphia: Great Commission, 1986), 140.

4. I make the case for this distinction in *Generous Justice: How God's Grace Makes Us Just* (New York: Dutton, 2010, ch. 6).

5. It is important to point out that what follows is not a thoroughgoing theology of worship, community, diaconal ministry, and public discipleship. Nor is it a balanced survey of ministry methods. Rather, it is a set of observations about how each area of ministry interacts with the others. Of course, each of these ministry areas or "fronts" deserves a book-length treatment, which I either have done (e.g., *Generous Justice*), am doing (e.g., *Every Good Endeavor*), or hope to do.

Chapter 5: Connecting People to God

1. See "Reformed Worship in the Global City," in *Worship by the Book*, ed. D. A. Carson (Grand Rapids: Zondervan, 2002), 193 – 239.

2. A good, though dated, volume outlining these approaches is Paul Basden, ed., *Exploring the Worship Spectrum: Six Views* (Grand Rapids: Zondervan, 2004).

3. For a good, brief description of the regulative principle of worship, see R. Michael Allen, *Reformed Theology* (Edinburgh: T&T Clark, 2010), 116 – 21.

4. Scots Confession, www.creeds.net/Scots/c20.htm (accessed February 21, 2012). The Confession goes on to say, "For as ceremonies which men have devised are but temporal, so they may, and ought to be, changed."

5. For a critique of contemporary Christian worship as practiced by many megachurches, see D. H. Williams, "Contemporary Music: The Cultural Medium and the Christian Message," *Christianity Today* 55, no. 6 (June 2011): 46, www.christianitytoday.com/ct/2011/june/culturalmedium.html (accessed February 21, 2012). Williams follows many others in charging that contemporary worship aims directly at the emotions rather than shaping the mind and habits, and that it has been shaped by "consumerist culture ... creating a mall-like environment marked by splashiness and simplistic messages." An overlapping but somewhat different critique of evangelical worship is offered by James K. A. Smith, *Desiring the Kingdom: Worship, Worldview, and Cultural Formation* (Grand Rapids: Baker, 2009). Smith is targeting nonliturgical, sermon-oriented worship, which he sees as too oriented to reason and the mind and does not shape the "habits of the heart" as does liturgical worship.

6. Allen, *Reformed Theology*, 133 – 34.

7. Historical traditions of worship are based on centuries of wisdom and experience, and to rely on one prevents us from having to "reinvent the wheel" every week.

8. John Calvin, *Institutes of the Christian Religion*, ed. John T. McNeill (Philadelphia: Westminster, 1960), 2:1208.

9. See Paul Barnett, *1 Corinthians: Holiness and Hope of a Rescued people* (Fearn, Ross-shire, UK: Christian Focus, 2000); F. F. Bruce, *1 and 2 Corinthians* (Grand Rapids: Eerdmans, 1971); Gordon D. Fee, *The First Epistle to the Corinthians* (Grand Rapids: Eerdmans, 1987); Leon Morris, *1 Corinthians* (Downers Grove, IL: InterVarsity, 2008); Anthony C. Thiselton, *The First Epistle to the Corinthians* (Grand Rapids: Eerdmans, 2000).

10. I believe he is saying that tongues only make nonbelievers feel "alien" and judged — but that this kind of judgment does not lead to conversion.

11. "Fencing of the table" refers to instructing those in the worship service that only believers who are committed to forsaking their sins should partake of the Lord's Supper.

Chapter 6: Connecting People to One Another

1. C. S. Lewis, *The Four Loves* (New York: Harcourt Brace Jovanovich, 1960), 92 – 93.

2. I am acutely aware that many readers will not share the same view of baptism and the Lord's Supper I am assuming here by using the word *sacraments* instead of *ordinances*. In general, those who name them "ordinances" believe they are signs and symbols representing the benefits of salvation, while those who describe them as "sacraments" believe that at some level or another they are also "seals" that bring something of the grace signified. Despite these long-standing differences on an important subject, I believe readers across the ecclesiastical spectrum can accept virtually all of what I am saying in this section about the importance of churchly piety.

3. John Coffey, "Lloyd-Jones and the Protestant Past," in *Engaging with Martyn Lloyd-Jones: The Life and Legacy of "the Doctor,"* ed. Andrew Atherstone and David Ceri Jones (Nottingham, UK: Inter-Varsity, 2011), 318. Coffey argues convincingly that, despite the negative results of revivalism, its critics often overplay their hand. Instead of seeing revivalism as a completely novel development, he points out its continuity with elements within the Reformation and Puritanism and critics' tendency to overlook the great achievements of revivalism (see p. 319). For a good but more negative assessment of revivalism, see R. Michael Allen, *Reformed Theology* (Edinburgh: T&T Clark, 2010), 88 – 94.

4. Nevin, a proponent of what has been called "high church Calvinism," was a student at Princeton under Alexander and Hodge. He appreciated the confessional, ecclesial emphasis but felt it was inconsistent to put such an equal emphasis on conversion and experience. He believed it was subjectivizing Christianity to tell members or baptized children that they should be sure they were converted. For a profile highly sympathetic to Nevin, see D. G. Hart, *John Williamson Nevin: High Church Calvinist* (Phillipsburg, NJ: P&R, 2005).

5. See Archibald Alexander, *Thoughts on Religious Experience* (Edinburgh: Banner of Truth, 1967), esp. 59 – 78; Charles Hodge, *The Way of Life* (Edinburgh: Banner of Truth, 1959).

6. See Alexander, *Thoughts on Religious Experience*, 13 – 35.

7. J. I. Packer and Gary A. Parrett, *Grounded in the Gospel: Building Believers the Old-Fashioned Way* (Grand Rapids: Baker, 2010).

8. Dietrich Bonhoeffer, *Life Together: The Classic Exploration of Christian in Community* (New York: Harper & Row, 1954), 22 – 23.

Chapter 7: Connecting People to the City

1. I have written two books on this subject — *Ministries of Mercy: The Call of the Jericho Road*, 2nd ed. (Phillipsburg, NJ: P&R, 1991), and *Generous Justice: How God's Grace Makes Us Just* (New York: Dutton, 2010). For that reason, this chapter will only sketch out a few basic ideas and principles.

2. Bruce Waltke, *The Book of Proverbs: Chapters 1 – 15* (Grand Rapids: Eerdmans, 2004), 97; see idem, "Righteousness in Proverbs," *Westminster Theological Journal* 70 (2008): 207 – 24.

3. We must be careful not to dogmatically draw lines here. Different social and cultural conditions can affect how directly the church is involved in addressing issues of justice. Looking back, we now applaud the Anglo churches that preached against and worked against the evils of African slavery in America. So too, the African-American church, under the extreme conditions of slavery and near-slavery, bravely took on all three levels of ministry to the poor, and their work continues to this day.

4. See Keller, *Generous Justice*, ch. 6.

5. Julian (the Apostate), *The Works of the Emperor Julian* (Loeb Classical Library; New York: G. P. Putnam's Sons, 1923), 69, 71.

Chapter 8: Connecting People to the Culture

1. For a full-length treatment of the particular ways in which a gospel-centered worldview applies to work, see Timothy Keller, *Every Good Endeavor: Connecting Your Work to God's Work* (New York: Dutton, 2012).

2. Of course, we must strike a balance here. In some ways it would be as wrong to segregate Christians by vocation as it would be by race. Suspicion among members of certain professions can be raised, and it is liberating and healthy to build friendships across these kinds of barriers. Some people will not want or need spiritual nurture that is vocation specific. But many others will not otherwise be given the care they need to handle the temptations and quandaries that are unique to their vocation—and so they will abandon either their careers or their beliefs.

Reflections on Integrative Ministry

1. We describe this journey in more detail in *Faithmapping: A Gospel Atlas for Your Spiritual Journey* (Wheaton, IL: Crossway, 2013).

2. Keller's writings in *Center Church* seem to be a direct descendant of that Church Planting Manual.

3. Timothy Keller, *Center Church* (Grand Rapids: Zondervan, 2012), 39.

4. Gregg R. Allison, *Sojourners and Strangers: The Doctrine of the Church* (Wheaton, IL: Crossway, 2012), 50.

5. Ibid., 51.

6. Ibid., 51.

7. Ibid., 53.

8. Ibid., 52, emphasis added.

9. Harold Best, *Unceasing Worship: Biblical Perspectives on Worship and the Arts* (Downers Grove, IL: InterVarsity, 2003), 47.

10. Ibid., 47.

11. See, e.g., Harold Best's *Unceasing Worship* or David Peterson's *Engaging with God: A Biblical Theology of Worship* (Downers Grove, IL: InterVarsity, 2002).

12. For much more detail, see our book *Faithmapping*, which we were tempted to title "Keller for Dummies."

13. Montgomery and Cosper, *Faithmapping*, 21.

14. Ibid., 102.

15. Tip of the old hat to Dallas Willard for this definition.

16. See Montgomery and Cosper, *Faithmapping*, 105–92.

17. Ibid., 202–15.

Response to Daniel Montgomery and Mike Cosper

1. D. A. Carson, ed., *Worship by the Book* (Grand Rapids: Zondervan, 2002), 11–63.

Chapter 9: Movements and Institutions

1. For a simple description of the marks of a genuine church as discerned by the Protestant Reformers, see J. I. Packer, "Word and Sacrament: How a Genuine Church Is Identified," in *Concise Theology* (Wheaton, IL: Tyndale House, 2001), 204–6. Reformed churches have always named these three marks (Word, sacrament, discipline), though others have argued that church discipline is necessarily involved in a right use of the sacraments, and therefore, they reason, there are properly only two marks of a true church. Whether we break these into two, three, or four line items is not critical as long as all the functions and purposes are recognized. The true church communicates sound biblical doctrine through its teachers and also incorporates people through baptism and the Lord's Supper into a visible covenant community in which its leaders provide wise spiritual oversight.

2. The first to recognize the dependency of the non-Western churches were the British Anglican Henry Venn and the American Congregationalist Rufus Anderson, both of whom urged a model called "indigenization" in which Western missionaries were expected to preach and pastor new churches and eventually raise up indigenous, national leaders and hand the churches over to them. Later, the British Anglican Roland Allen and the American Presbyterian John Nevius urged that this process be started further back and argued that Western missionaries should never act as church planters and sole pastors of non-Western churches. Instead, new converts should be trained and helped to establish churches themselves. Roland Allen wrote *Missionary Methods: St. Paul's or Ours?* (London: Robert Scott, 1912) and *The Spontaneous Expansion of the Church, and the Causes Which Hinder It* (London: World Dominion Press, 1927), while Nevius wrote *The Planting and Development of Missionary Churches* (New York: Foreign Mission Library, 1899).

3. Hugh Heclo's great little book *On Thinking Institutionally* (Boulder, CO:

Paradigm, 2008) lays out the diverse definitions that scholars have given to the idea of institutions.

4. Heclo, *On Thinking Institutionally*, 38.

5. Ibid.

6. David K. Hurst, *Crisis and Renewal: Meeting the Challenge of Organizational Change* (Cambridge, MA: Harvard Business School Press, 2002).

Chapter 10: The Church as an Organized Organism

1. See Edmund P. Clowney, "Perspectives on the Church," in *Living in Christ's Church* (Philadelphia: Great Commission, 1986); idem, "Doctrine of the Church" (unpublished course syllabus); Lon L. Fuller, "Two Principles of Human Association," in *Voluntary Associations*, ed. J. Roland Pennock and John W. Chapman (New York: Atherton, 1969); Lyle Schaller, "Tribes, Movements, and Organizations," in *Getting Things Done* (Nashville: Abingdon, 1986); idem, *Activating the Passive Church* (Nashville: Abingdon, 1981).

2. See Edmund P. Clowney, *The Church* (Downers Grove, IL: InterVarsity, 1995), esp. 199 – 214; see also idem, *Living in Christ's Church*, 111 – 12.

3. See the important essay by Alan Kreider, "'They Alone Know the Right Way to Live': The Early Church and Evangelism," in *Ancient Faith for the Church's Future*, ed. Mark Husbands and Jeffrey Greenman (Downers Grove, IL: InterVarsity, 2008), 169 – 86.

4. Books such as *The Trellis and the Vine* by Tony Payne and Colin Marshall (Kingsford, Australia: Matthias Media, 2009) give the strong impression that institutional forms and structures are, at best, a necessary evil and that management and governing gifts are not really involved in our carrying out the work of the Spirit or our building up the church. On the other hand, many of the critics of revival and broad evangelicalism who call for a greater emphasis on the ordained ministry and the institutional church can make the opposite mistake.

5. RUF produces church planters and missionaries for the PCA, along with Campus Outreach, which is a nondenominational campus ministry with strong ties to the denomination.

6. Most effective leadership pipelines grow organically out of movements rather than institutions. I once learned about a denomination outside the United States that had an evangelical wing. For a number of years, this evangelical wing had leadership "nurseries" in the college ministries of prominent, vital congregations in two or three university towns. College students were drawn to these ministries in great number, and many were inspired to reproduce the community and ministry of the Word they experienced. Dozens of young people from these churches went into the preaching ministry because they experienced movement dynamics there. However, when those churches installed new pastors who weren't as interested or successful in college ministry, the pipelines dried up, and the whole evangelical cause in that country suffered.

Chapter 11: Church Planting as a Movement Dynamic

1. The general rule when discerning which practices of Scripture to apply today is that "the purpose of God in Scripture should be sought in its didactic rather than its descriptive parts." (John Stott, *Baptism and Fullness: The Work of the Holy Spirit Today*, 3rd ed. [Downers Grove, IL: InterVarsity, 2006], 21). The cardinal rule of biblical interpretation is that the meaning of the text of the Scripture is determined by the author's intent, i.e., what the biblical writer was intending to say. This is why in the didactic parts of the Bible—where prophetic and apostolic writers directly address how God's people should live—it is easier to discern authorial intent than in the historical narratives, where many things are described as having happened but may not be exemplary or serve as a model of behavior for all times.

Christians have argued for centuries about the "normativity" of the book of Acts—mainly over issues of church government and the operations of the Holy Spirit. But Acts is focused on missions, evangelism, and church planting. I believe we can learn much from the material for our own ministries, but since it is written in narrative form, we must be careful not to apply too rigidly the things we learn. See, e.g., David Peterson's remark that the patterns of the laying on of hands and tongues speaking "are not to be regarded as normative for ongoing Christian experience" (*The Acts of the Apostles* [Grand Rapids: Eerdmans, 2009], 532).

2. John R. W. Stott, *The Message of Acts* (Downers Grove, IL: InterVarsity, 1994), 234.

3. Tim Chester, "Church Planting: A Theological Perspective," in *Multiplying Churches: Reaching Today's Communities through Church Planting*, ed. Stephen Timmis (Fearn, Ross-shire, UK: Christian Focus, 2000), 23 – 46.

4. In Redeemer's early days, we were joined by people who came from other congregations in the city. But as we've gotten bigger and older, we have often seen our own members go off to newer and younger congregations where they felt their gifts could be well utilized. They go with our blessing. Older churches are always tempted to resent the loss of members to newer churches, but if we care about reaching the whole city for Christ, we must be glad that we trained people in our congregation who then opt to become involved in new mission opportunities.

5. See Donald McGavran and George G. Hunter III, eds., *Church Growth: Strategies That Work* (Nashville: Abingdon, 1980), 100; see also C. Kirk Hadaway, *New Churches and Church Growth in the Southern Baptist Convention* (Nashville: Broadman, 1987); Ed Stetzer, *Planting Missional Churches: Planting a Church That's Biblically Sound and Reaching People in Culture* (Nashville: Broadman and Holman, 2006). Stetzer writes, "Churches under three years of age win an average of ten people to Christ per year for every hundred members … Churches over fifteen years of age win an average of three people per every hundred members" (p. 8).

6. These numbers are taken from a study—conducted by the Values Research Institute of New York and commissioned by Redeemer City to City—that looked at church attendance and church growth in New York City over the past several decades. These figures, while inexact, should be taken seriously as general patterns. The figures basically align with churchgoing and church-per-capita figures in the parts of the United States that are far more religious and traditional than New York City. We have not done research in other countries.

7. Two useful resources for guiding this process are James P. Spradley, *The Ethnographic Interview* (New York: Harcourt, Brace, Jovanovich, 1979), and Edward Dayton, *Planning Strategies for World Evangelism* (Monrovia, CA: MARC, 1974).

8. A helpful resource is Craig Ellison, "Addressing Felt Needs of Urban Dwellers," in *Planning and Growing Urban Churches*, ed. Harvie Conn (Grand Rapids: Baker, 1997), 94 – 110.

Chapter 12: The City and the Gospel Ecosystem

1. Edmund Clowney, *The Church* (Downers Grove, IL: InterVarsity, 1995), 79.

2. This chapter ("The Church: Community of Disciples") was not in the original 1978 edition; see Avery Dulles, *Models of the Church*, expanded ed. (New York: Image, 2002), 195 – 218.

3. Likening a gospel city movement to a biological ecosystem is an analogy, of course, and no analogy illumines the concept at every point. Biological ecosystems consist in some part of stronger animals eating weaker ones. No one should think this means stronger churches should eat weaker ones! Actually, a city in which some churches grow only by drawing members out of other churches is the very opposite of the kind of evangelistic gospel city movement we are seeking. The image of the ecosystem conveys how different organisms are interdependent, how the flourishing of one group helps the other groups flourish.

4. Thanks to Dr. Mark Reynolds for his valuable insights that enhance this section.

5. Malcolm Gladwell, *The Tipping Point: How Little Things Can Make A Big Difference* (New York: Little, Brown, 2000), 12.

Reflections on Movement Dynamics

1. See, e.g., *The Forgotten Ways: Reactivating the Missional Church* (Grand Rapids: Brazos, 2006); *On the Verge: A Journey into the Apostolic Future of the Church* (Grand Rapids: Zondervan, 2011); *The Permanent Revolution: Apostolic Imagination and Practice in the 21st Century Church* (San Francisco: Jossey-Bass, 2013).

2. Robert Pirsig, *Zen and the Art of Motorcycle Maintenance: An Inquiry into Values* (New York: Morrow, 1974), 98.

3. Alan Hirsch and Dave Ferguson, *On the Verge: A Journey into the Apostolic Future of the Church* (Grand Rapids: Zondervan, 2011), 89. Bill Easum

(*Leadership on the Other Side* [Nashville: Abingdon, 2000], 39) writes, "Churches wanting to break free from the quagmire of their dysfunctional systems and climb out of their downward death spiral must learn to feel, think, and act differently than they do now. The times in which we live require us to change our Life Metaphors, something akin to rewiring the human brain."

4. Quoted in Scott Nelson, *Mission: Living for the Purposes of God* (Downers Grove, IL: InterVarsity, 2013), 39.

5. See Michael Frost and Alan Hirsch, *The Faith of Leap: Embracing a Theology of Risk, Adventure, and Courage* (Grand Rapids: Baker, 2012).

6. See Peter F. Drucker, Frances Hesselbein, and Joan Snyder Kuhl, *Peter Drucker's Five Most Important Questions: Enduring Wisdom for Today's Leaders* (New York: Wiley, 2015), 51.

7. See chapter 7 in my *The Forgotten Ways* for an elaboration of movemental organization; see also Hirsch and Ferguson, *On the Verge*, part 2.

8. See Dee Hock, *Birth of the Chaordic Age* (San Francisco: Berrett-Koehler, 1999), and the more recent edition, *One from Many: VISA and the Rise of Chaordic Organization* (San Francisco: Berrett-Koehler, 2005). The challenge Hock gives to every organization is to marry a solid core with a changing periphery; see Hirsch and Ferguson, *On the Verge*, 45–46, 285–86, and my *The Permanent Revolution*, 218–20, for an application of this to movement thinking.

9. I cannot emphasize this strongly enough. I believe this is a cornerstone text with huge implications for the church and her mission. To go deeper, read my *The Permanent Revolution* (devoted to this topic) and *The Forgotten Ways* (ch. 6), which gives the systemic basis for why movements need APEST. Other excellent books on this topic are Neil Cole, *Primal Fire: Reigniting the Church with the Five Gifts of Jesus* (San Francisco: Jossey-Bass, 2014), and J. R. Woodward, *Creating a Missional Culture: Equipping the Church for the Sake of the World* (Downers Grove, IL: InterVarsity, 2013).

10. Hirsch and Ferguson, *On the Verge*, 74.

11. Timothy Keller, *Center Church* (Grand Rapids: Zondervan, 2012), 347.

Response to Alan Hirch

1. John Calvin, *Institutes of the Christian Religion*, ed. John T. McNeill (Philadelphia: Westminster, 1960), 2:1070.

ABOUT THE
CONTRIBUTORS

Tim Chester is a pastor with Grace Church Boroughbridge, North Yorkshire, and a tutor with the Acts 29 Oak Hill Academy. He has a PhD in theology and has been an adjunct lecturer in missiology and Reformed spirituality. He is the author of more than thirty books. He and his wife have two daughters.

Mike Cosper is the pastor of worship and arts at Sojourn Community Church, the author of *Rhythms of Grace,* and the coauthor of *Faithmapping* (with Daniel Montgomery). Mike has produced several albums of original music for Sojourn, as well as *Songs for the Book of Luke* for The Gospel Coalition. He and his wife, Sarah, have two daughters, and live in Louisville, Kentucky.

Daniel Montgomery is founding pastor of Sojourn Community Church, a multisite congregation with three campuses in Louisville, Kentucky, and one in New Albany, Indiana. Daniel serves Sojourn as pastor of teaching, leadership, and church planting. In 2011, he cofounded the Sojourn Network to multiply churches in North America and beyond. He is the coauthor of *PROOF* and *Faithmapping.*

Alan Hirsch is one of the key thought leaders in the global missional conversation. He is the founder of 100Movements, the Forge Mission Training Network, and Future Travelers and is a multi-award–winning author of numerous books on the aspects of movemental Christianity, including *The Forgotten Ways* and *The Permanent Revolution* (www .alanhirsch.org).

Shaped by the Gospel

Doing Balanced, Gospel-Centered Ministry in Your City

Timothy Keller, Author; Michael Horton, Dane Ortlund, Contributors

It is easy to assume that if we understand the gospel and preach it faithfully, our ministry will necessarily be shaped by it—but this is not true. Many churches claim to be gospel-centered but do not have a ministry that is shaped by, centered on, and empowered through the gospel. The implications of the gospel have not yet worked their way into the fabric of how that church does ministry.

Gospel-centered ministry is more theologically driven than program driven. To pursue it, we must spend time reflecting on the essence, the truths, and the very patterns of the gospel itself. The gospel is neither religion nor irreligion, but something else entirely—a third way of relating to God through grace. In *Shaped by the Gospel*, bestselling author and pastor Timothy Keller addresses several current discussion and conflicts about the nature of the gospel and shows how faithful preaching of the gospel leads to individual and corporate renewal.

This new edition contains the first section of *Center Church* in an easy-to-read format with new reflections and additional essays from Timothy Keller and several other contributors.

Loving the City

Doing Balanced, Gospel-Centered Ministry in Your City

Timothy Keller, with new contributions by Daniel Strange, Gabriel Salguero, and Andy Crouch

In *Loving the City*, bestselling author and pastor Timothy Keller looks at the biblical foundations for contextualizing the gospel as we communicate to the culture in a way that is both respectful and challenging. He articulates the key characteristics of a city vision, showing how the city develops as a theme throughout Scripture, from its anti-God origins to its strategic importance for mission to its culmination and redemption in glory.

Loving the City contains the second section of *Center Church* in an easy-to-read format with new essays from several other contributors and Tim Keller's responses to the essays.

◨◧ REDEEMER
CITY to CITY

Any reader of *Center Church* might be interested to know that Timothy Keller founded an organization called Redeemer City to City.

Redeemer City to City carries out the ministry principles you've read about in this book around the world. Coaching and training urban church planters and starting gospel movements in global cities are at the core of CTC's mission.

If you'd like to know more about Redeemer City to City's work, write to us at hello@redeemercitytocity.com.

May Jesus Christ be known in cities.